# The Game Animator's Guide to Maya®

### Michael McKinley

Wiley Publishing, Inc.

Acquisitions Editor: WILLEM KNIBBE
Development Editor: HEATHER O'CONNOR
Technical Editor: KEITH REICHER
Production Editor: DARIA MEOLI
Copy Editor: LINDA RECKTENWALD
Production Manager: TIM TATE
Vice President and Executive Group Publisher: RICHARD SWADLEY
Vice President and Executive Publisher: JOSEPH B. WIKERT
Vice President and Publisher: DANIEL BRODNITZ
Permissions Editor: SHANNON WALTERS
Media Development Specialist: KATE JENKINS
Book Designer: FRANZ BAUMHACKL
Compositor: CHRIS GILLESPIE, HAPPENSTANCE TYPE-O-RAMA
Proofreader: JENNIFER LARSEN, WORD ONE
Indexer: TED LAUX
Cover Designer: RYAN SNEED
Cover Image: MICHAEL MCKINLEY

ISBN-13: 978-0-470-03857-4
ISBN-10: 0-470-03857-8

*To my family, for their love and support.*

 # Acknowledgments

So once again, events have allowed me the great opportunity to work with Sybex and Wiley to produce a book! And once again, while my name may be on the cover, I can't take all the credit for its realization. Without the support of my family and friends, the understanding of those I worked with to produce the book's artwork, and the hard-working assistance of my editors, this book would never have made it out of the idea phase!

Great thanks once again to Steve Garcia, who contributed the ace concept art for all four of this book's major projects. He was able to take a few sentences of description and create some fantastic pieces of art that I and the other artists were able to really have a blast making!

Speaking of which, huge thanks to Gary Bergeron, David Russ, Leif Robles, and Evan Calderaro, who worked with me to create the models and textures used in this book's projects. I couldn't have done it without you guys!

Great thanks to my good friend Sarah Stacy for helping me out at the last minute by providing her voice for the lip synching chapter.

Thank you very much to Jacque Reimer for performing the sometimes-embarrassing gunslinger moves for the video reference and lugging those heavy pistols around!

Thank you as well to Michael Morlan for helping me with the video reference filming. A great feature of this book wouldn't have been possible without his expertise and equipment. Check out his impressive body of work (and maybe hire him for some) at www.Michael-Morlan.net.

Big thanks to everyone I worked with at Feverpitch Studios. I've never worked with a greater group of people, and I'd count myself blessed to get the chance to work with any of you again in the future!

And, of course, I have to thank everyone who withstood my bickering e-mails and finally conceded to contributing their profiles to this book. Floyd Bishop, Scott Ruggels, Kiel Figgins, Grayson Chalmers, Adam Houghton, and my good buddy Steve Garcia—thank you!

I have to acknowledge the great people at Sybex, Wiley, and Alias who helped me so much in the creation of this book. While my writing skills perhaps have improved slightly since my first book, without their help I'm sure this thing would have been made with cardboard and crayons! Willem Knibbe, Heather O'Connor, Keith Reicher, and Daria Meoli, thank you very much! Is book number three in the future?

And last, but certainly not least, my parents and family. Without your constant support and encouragement I would never have accomplished as much as I have. I love you all!

Philippians 4:13

# Contents

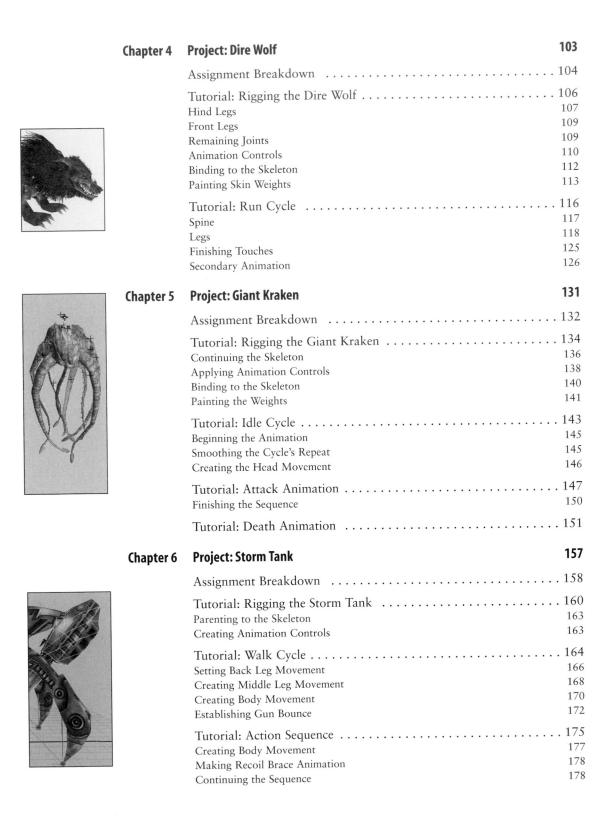

# Introduction

Welcome to *The Game Animator's Guide to Maya*! Whether you're a current animator in the game industry or looking forward to becoming one, this book will help you learn the skills and techniques you need to become successful.

When I first began to use Maya, the greatest learning tool I ever found was studying the work of those actually doing the job I wanted and striving to be like them. None of the books or tutorials I found really conveyed this same principle—of actually teaching me how to do a *job* and not just teaching me how to use a tool. When I was put in the position of instructing and mentoring up-and-coming artists, it became my goal to give the kind of instruction that a student will find really useful after school and long into their careers!

The lessons in this book are created with the actual job of a game animator in mind. Instead of lessons that teach the tools but do nothing to give you any real experience or knowledge useful in a career, these lessons are real-world tasks that you can expect to find given to you long after you've finished school and found your first job in the industry! And the techniques and tools you learn within are the same techniques and tools used on a day-to-day basis while working in the field.

## What You Will Learn from This Book

In *The Game Animator's Guide to Maya*, you'll learn about the game industry as a whole and the different artist positions that are generally available. I'll walk you through rigging and animating a variety of different character types for video games. Also, spread throughout the book, I've placed profiles of current industry professionals whose insight into the field can help answer some of the questions you aspiring artists and animators may have.

## Who Should Read This Book

Anyone who is interested in working as an animator in the game industry, has recently joined the field, or perhaps is a veteran of the industry interested in new game art possibilities will find the contents of this book very useful. It goes over real-life responsibilities that professional game animators have to deal with on a daily basis. As such, some basic Maya knowledge is good to have beforehand, such as basic interface navigation as well as basic knowledge of Maya's toolset.

## How to Use This Book

The content of this book falls into two categories: Introductory Information and Project Activities. In the opening two chapters, I focus on useful information about the game industry, how one might find employment within it, and about the background of animation, discussing the terms, tools, and editors that all animators should know before jumping into an animation assignment. Each of the five project chapters that follow go over an entire animation assignment, beginning with creating a skeleton and animation controls all the way through creating example animations for each project, giving a thorough introduction to the process as one might expect to find when employed as an actual game animator.

### How This Book Is Organized

Here are some specifics about the chapter breakdown for this book.

**Chapter 1: Careers in the Game Industry** Before delving into art production, this first chapter gives you a quick introduction to how the game industry and the game development pipeline works. I'll go over the differences between Developers and Publishers, and the many different artist jobs that are out there. I also include demo reel advice for when you're ready to get that game job!

**Chapter 2: The Ins-and-Outs of Animation** This chapter delves into the technical information behind animation—discussing the tools, editors, terms, and concepts in depth and at length.

**Chapter 3: Project: Calamity Jane** For the first animation project chapter of the book, I discuss the animation of Calamity Jane, a sci-fi/western gunslinger character that would serve as the major focus character of a real game project. The focus of the lesson is to go over rigging and animating a biped, humanoid character.

**Chapter 4: Project: Dire Wolf** In this project chapter, you'll animate Dire Wolf, a carnivorous, nasty wolf-like monster that would serve as a standard enemy in a real game project. The focus of the lesson is to give you a background in the rigging and animation of a quadruped creature.

**Chapter 5: Project: Giant Kraken** This chapter covers the animation of the Giant Kraken, a huge octopus-like sea monster that would serve as a "boss" encounter in a real game project. The focus of the lesson is to go over the rigging and animation of a spinal creature made up of multiple tentacles.

**Chapter 6: Project: Storm Tank** In this project chapter, I discuss the animation of the Storm Tank, a spider-legged mechanical vehicle that would serve as a fantasy military vehicle in a real game project. The focus of the lesson is to go over the rigging and animation of a non-organic, mechanical object.

**Chapter 7: Lip Synching** In this chapter, you'll learn about the importance of acting when animating characters. We'll also create the different mouth shapes necessary for forming the vowel and consonant sounds to synch a character's face to the audio. The chapter's project takes Calamity Jane from Chapter 3 and goes over how to create a conversation animation using provided audio from the included with the book CD.

**Chapter 8: Other Animation Tasks** For the final chapter, I cover three other common animation tasks: animating wings, a blobby material, and a standard vehicle suspension system.

**Artist Profiles** Throughout the book I've added sidebars that profile current game art professionals from all over the country. I think you'll find their perspectives on the industry and how Maya is used in it inspiring.

## Hardware and Software Considerations

Maya is quite the athlete these days, as the program is capable of running on many different operating systems and computer setups. Autodesk provides specifics as to what hardware and software are compatible with Maya at their website:

www.autodesk.com/maya

In general, though, the faster the computer, the better; a nice, fast processor, a good chunk of RAM (memory), and a capable video card are all must-haves. A sizeable hard drive for storage is also very desirable. Some good numbers to shoot for are:

- At least 3–3.5 Ghz processor
- 1 GB–2 GB of RAM
- A nice video card, such as the nVidia Quadro or ATI FireGL series
- 200+ GB Hard drive

## The Companion CD

I've stocked the companion CD for this book with all sorts of useful files for you to complete the projects in the text as well as supplemental materials that you will find useful in your own projects. Here's a rundown of what's included on the CD:

**Images** This folder contains the concept art of each of the book's projects as well as many sample high-resolution images of photo sources provided by the fine folks at www.3d.sk, one of the best human anatomy sources on the internet. These images can be useful for anatomy reference or as texture sources.

**Project Files** This folder is divided into each chapter's specific section. Each chapter folder has the Maya project directories for the tutorials in question, which include saved stages of the projects at each major step for the reader's convenience. The project directories for each chapter contain a scenes and sourceimages folder containing the Maya files and their textures respectively.

**Audio** This folder contains a variety of sample audio files as well as the audio used in Chapter 7's lip synching lessons.

**Video** Divided into a couple sections, the video folder has a Gallery and Reference folders. The Gallery simply provides some sample game animations from the projects within the book as well as other sources to serve as examples. The References folder contains many sample videos of movement from www.3d.sk as well as other sources that can be used in your own projects as well as the Calamity Jane project in Chapter 3. The generous folks at DivX (http://www.divx.com) have graciously granted us permission to supply you with a trial version of DivX Player 6.1 so you can access the video files on the CD.

**Maya Personal Learning Edition 7** Also on the CD is the Maya Personal Learning Edition 7 (Maya PLE 7), the free version of Maya that gives you access to Maya Complete for non-commercial uses. Everything in the tutorials is capable of being done with this free version, and the software runs on Windows 2000/XP Professional and Mac OS.

> **Note:** For the Chapter 2, "The Ins-and-Outs of Animation," files on the CD, you can find a few supplemental files, such as a run-and-climb animation sequence as well as a bouncing ball animation. These extra files serve as examples that will help you understand the principles of animation discussed within Chapter 2.

## About the Author

Michael McKinley is a 3D Artist for Buzz Monkey Software (www.buzzmonkey.com), a game developer in Eugene, Oregon. He can often be found helping out with Maya questions online at www.simplymaya.com. More information about Michael and his past and future projects can be discovered at his website: www.mtmckinley.net. Feel free to track him down at either location to say hello and ask any Maya or general video game questions.

# Careers in the Game Industry

*For many aspiring digital artists, a job in the game industry is the dream of a lifetime. Whether it's fashioning fantastic worlds and characters from scratch or painstakingly re-creating accurate World War II submarines, the life of a game artist can be greatly rewarding. A game artist's career comes with its fair share of challenging times, however. The more you know early in your career, the better off you will be. Before you delve into the ins and outs of art production, it's important to understand not only what is expected of you as a game artist but also what the game industry is all about.*

**1**

**In this chapter, we'll discuss the following topics:**
Developers and Publishers
Artist Jobs in the Industry
Demo Reels
The Game Development Pipeline

## Developers and Publishers

More often than not, games are created through a partnership between two distinct companies known as a *developer* and a *publisher*. The developer actually creates the game. The publisher takes that game, markets it, and distributes it throughout the rest of the country or world.

The relationships between developers and publishers have evolved in many ways. These relationships are normally divided into three categories: first-party developers, second-party developers, and third-party developers.

**First-party developers** These developers are entirely owned by their publishers. One example is Nintendo. In addition to being the originator of the Nintendo brand gaming consoles (Game Boy Advance, Nintendo Revolution, and Nintendo DS), they are also the developer. Their trademark games, such as *Super Mario Brothers* and *The Legend of Zelda*, are games they create themselves using teams of developers under their employ.

**Second-party developers** These independent developers are not owned by a publisher. They have, however, signed agreements giving a specific publisher the exclusive right to publish their titles. An example is Naughty Dog, the developer of popular titles such as *Crash Bandicoot* and *Jak & Daxter*. They have signed exclusive publishing rights with Sony to develop their games for the Playstation2.

 **Note:** The defining line between first-party and second-party developers is a thin one. Generally, a first-party developer can be considered an in-house department of the publisher, while a second-party developer is a separate entity.

**Third-party developers** These developers are the most common type. They sign contracts with a publisher on a per-game basis. In fact, many third-party-developed games are released on multiple gaming platforms. An example studio would be Neversoft. Their game *GUN* was developed and released on the Microsoft Xbox, the Microsoft Xbox 360, the Nintendo GameCube, the Sony Playstation2, the Sony PSP, and the PC. For this game, Neversoft partnered with a publisher known as Activision, a company that arranges distribution deals for all major game platforms.

There are many pros and cons to being a first-, second-, or third-party developer. For instance, third-party developers have a lot more freedom to develop a larger variety of projects for a larger variety of platforms because they aren't constrained to a certain publisher or platform. Once a project ends for one publisher, they can sign another project for a completely separate publisher if they so desire. However, a third-party studio is always on the lookout for its next project and is constantly trying to get that next deal. Sometimes there can be long gaps of time between projects—and thus between paychecks! These gaps in revenue often result in having to cut costs—and subsequently employees.

First- or second-party developers, because the studio is owned by the platform for which they are developing (or because the studio has been given exclusive rights to their games), do not necessarily have to worry as much about where that next project will come from. However, there can be a lack of variety in the work and a greater chance of creative burnout in such environments. There are also far fewer first-party developers in the industry, and therefore they can be much more difficult to find employment with.

All in all, typical rookie game artists may not be terribly concerned with this information since they're just trying to get their feet in the door. As you gain both experience and a more discerning eye for the kind of work you want to do in the future, keep in mind these distinctions.

## Artist Jobs in the Industry

As an artist in the game industry, you will eventually work for a developer of some sort. But what jobs are available for someone of your talents? A variety of jobs are available in the art departments of game developers—anything from junior artist and 3D artist to art director.

One thing about the modern working world in general that's true about the gaming industry in particular is that you may end up wearing a lot of hats under one job title. It's becoming more and more common to find game developer positions combined into a single job. For example, most modelers are also expected to be very capable texture artists. When browsing a studio's help wanted list, always keep the other job criteria in mind. Make sure that you are at least familiar with the whole process that goes into creating a piece of game art, since you never know when you may be called upon to pick up the slack in another department.

Now let's discuss these positions in depth.

**Note:** The positions at game studios vary greatly. For instance, a 3D artist at one studio may have a completely different set of responsibilities or duties than a 3D artist at another. I can, however, give you a general idea of what you might expect in such positions. These generalizations should help you better understand the kinds of jobs available to you in this industry.

## Junior Artist

A junior artist is typically an entry-level position in the industry. With little or no prior game experience, a junior artist is usually hired into a company primarily to create background elements for the developing games and to learn the development process.

Many studios hire junior artists on a temporary basis. These positions are used to ramp up the art staff to handle the stress period of the development schedule, which eventually ramp back down as the game nears completion. You must prove that you are a capable and talented artist during these kinds of arrangements so that you can increase your chances of becoming a permanent employee.

## 3D Artist

The position of a 3D artist (or staff artist) is fairly generic in title if not in duty. As unexciting as this position might sound, it could very well be the job with the most exciting variety of duties. As a 3D artist, you could be called upon to create just about anything—vehicles and weapons, structures and environments, characters and creatures, planets and star fields, and beyond. In most cases, 3D artists make up a large percentage of a studio's art department, and the position can be divided into three main categories: modeler, texture artist, and animator.

**Modeler** A modeler is an artist responsible for creating the *geometry*, or the surfaces, of an object in a game.

**Texture artist** A texture artist takes the completed 3D model and creates *textures*, or surface details, for the object. In most cases, the same person acts as both the modeler and the texture artist.

**Animator** An animator is an artist who is responsible for rigging and animating the characters, creatures, and moving objects found in a game. Animators rarely are involved with the modeling or texturing of a game model. Instead, they focus on that model's movement.

## Concept Artist

Concept artists are responsible for creating the look of the game world. A concept artist illustrates the big-picture ideas of the game, such as environments, characters, creatures, and vehicles. These designs, once approved, are then given to the 3D artists to develop into the game.

## Character/Environment Artist

A character or environment artist is a specialist who is responsible for creating (and sometimes animating) the characters and creatures or the environments and structures found in a game. Such specialized positions are generally found at larger studios, where there are enough people to make such positions viable.

### FX Artist

An FX artist (or effects artist) is responsible for creating the many particle effects found in games. These can range from weather effects such as rain and snow to action effects such as the flash of a gun barrel. The vast majority of such effects are generally composed entirely of *sprites,* small images that are affected by dynamic forces such as gravity, wind, or turbulence.

### Technical Artist

A technical artist is a combination artist and programmer. While such persons have the creative responsibilities of an artist, they also have the scripting and programming skills necessary to create scripts and plug-ins for Maya or other applications to make the artists' jobs easier and more efficient.

A technical artist can also be responsible for creating setup tools, such as a common animation rig that is used for all of the characters in the game.

### Senior Artist

A senior artist is someone who more than likely has been in the industry for a number of years or who has a couple of finished games on his résumé and a proven track record. They are generally the ones given the more important responsibilities, such as creating the main characters or other critical elements, in a game project.

### Lead Artist

Lead artists are put in charge of a group of artists within a team. They ensure that their group follows instructions and accomplishes its goals on time. They are generally the first people who review a finished art asset before it is sent along on the approval process. While lead artists incorporate more management into their roles than most other artists, they also tend to have at least some art production duties. Depending on the size of the team, a project can have any number of lead artists.

### Art Director

The art director holds the top position in the artist chain of command. Responsibilities of this position include managing and scheduling the rest of the art staff, hiring and firing, and other such managerial duties. In general, art directors have a lot of experience in the game industry and usually work their way up from the position of lead artist.

**Note:** How much money does a game artist make? The answer is highly relative. The latest results (as of this writing) from the Game Development Salary Survey can be found on the Features page at http://www.gamasutra.com.

## Demo Reels

Getting your foot in the door of a game development studio can be challenging. It's mostly a matter of the quality of your portfolio, but applying for the right job at the right time and having a little bit of luck can also be factors. If you don't have any luck in your first few attempts to find a job, have patience and keep trying. With a quality portfolio and the willingness to relocate, you should eventually find a job.

Your portfolio is the most important tool you need to get that first job. I also recommend creating a website to display your portfolio online. Even something simple containing only your portfolio of images and animation and an e-mail address is better than nothing. A website will give possible employers something that is easy to click through, so they can get a good idea of your potential. Preparing a demo reel is definitely a good idea. A demo reel is a video presentation of your portfolio. Here are some demo reel tips:

**Keep it short and sweet.** Try to limit the length of your reel to two or three minutes. As it approaches the four-minute mark, no matter how good the work is, potential employers may start looking at their watches. Get their attention with a short, high-quality reel. If you have additional work, you can direct them to your website or have them request more samples from you.

**Don't make your opening too long.** An opening sequence that shows your name and contact info is fine, but don't make it too long. Two or three seconds should be enough. Don't forget that a viewer can pause it. Try to make sure any blank, silent time before the reel starts is as short as possible. Reel reviewers can be pretty impatient, and if they don't see something within a few seconds, they might just discard the reel before it starts.

**Put your best work first.** You may feel like you want to end your reel with a bang by showing your very best work last, but many reviewers might not have the time or patience to view an entire reel. Putting your best work up front will grab their interest early, which may entice them to watch the rest of the demo. If a weak piece is the first thing they see, they may not wait to see the awesome work you display later.

**Use a pleasant music track.** A reel doesn't necessarily need to be an audio extravaganza, but you should put some sort of music to your reel to involve the viewer's ears. Silence during a reel's playback can seem boring, even if the work being shown is good. Adding a little audio can make your reel more appealing, which is always a good thing!

**Don't dwell too long on a single piece.** When your reel is short, focusing on a single piece for thirty seconds or more may seem conspicuously like padding your reel for length. Don't be afraid to have a shorter reel, but make sure the work is your best.

**Keep your reel focused.** Customize your reel for the job for which you are applying. If you are applying for a modeler or texture artist position, don't have too much animation or other off-topic work. Otherwise, you're just wasting the employer's time. If you're applying for different kinds of jobs, make multiple reels that focus on the jobs in question.

**Label your work accurately.** Make sure that the employer understands what your contribution is to the work you submitted. If you collaborated with a group to complete a certain piece of work, send a *breakdown sheet*, a description of the reel that details the project title, what the piece was used for, and your role in its creation. This way, the employer can focus on your work and not someone else's. If you did all the work yourself, say so.

**Be kind. Rewind.** Possibly the most frequent mistake that job candidates make is forgetting to rewind their reels before sending them to potential employers. Don't forget to rewind your VHS reel before you submit it.

**Note:** Make sure you carefully read the submission requirements of a job ad. Many will specifically ask for a website or a VHS reel rather than other more-modern media. CDs and DVDs are not as desirable because of the many different DVD brands and audio/video codecs out there that potentially won't work on their players. In contrast, a VHS tape works with any VCR.

## Art Tests

Studios frequently ask applicants to complete an art test. This is usually a good sign, because it means they are interested in you for the job and they want to see how you perform a given task.

Art tests are also given to make sure that the work you are taking credit for is actually yours. If you deliver an out-of-this-world demo reel, but your art test results are poor, they may call into question your truthfulness.

In most cases, however, the art test is to gauge your performance for their current project. After all, you may have shown in your demo reel that you can create awesome skyscrapers and motorbikes, but can you do just as well with a knight on horseback or a post-apocalyptic robot? The art test will find out. Make sure you're prepared.

### Crunch Time

The thought of creating games is obviously very appealing. One common misconception, however, is that working at a game studio means you're just playing games all day. That could not be further from the truth! In fact, your game-playing time might dwindle because of the amount of work that is involved. It *can* be fun work, but it *is* work just the same.

Most people interested in game development have heard of the dreaded *crunch time*. This refers to a period of time in a game's development schedule where overtime is mandatory in order to meet fast-approaching deadlines. What was once a fairly mild eight- or nine-hour day suddenly balloons to twelve, fifteen, or more hours a day. Crunch time can potentially last weeks or even months on end.

The best way to avoid massive amounts of crunch time is to do your best to get things done efficiently, accurately, and on schedule during your normal workday. Some crunch time should probably be expected. However, if everyone on a project works together and makes full use of their time, it can be minimized.

Of course, crunch time doesn't necessarily have to be all bad. A good employer will reward such hard work with extra pay or bonuses!

## The Game Development Pipeline

The art production pipeline is the path that a game object takes from beginning to end, from conception to effects. This path actually comprises only one facet of the overall game development pipeline. Understanding the pipeline processes early is a great asset to potential employers, as it gets you that much closer to being able to contribute to it. The average development pipeline is as follows:

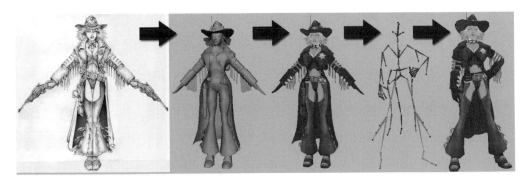

**Design** In the design stage of the production pipeline, writers and designers play a crucial role in the development of a game. They are the ones who actively give birth to the idea that eventually becomes a game you see on the shelf. They come up with the story, script, and the overall game play. When the writers and designers are ready, they pass their ideas on to the concept artist.

**Concept art** Concept artists receive the documents that describe the game's characters and world. They visually interpret the ideas, creating dozens of sketches and paintings before they finally find that perfect look for the game. This is an important step in the development of a piece of game art. When a concept has been completed and approved by the art director, it moves on to the modelers.

**Modeling** A modeler takes the approved concept art and uses that information to create a 3D model, or *art asset*, that can ultimately be used in the game. Before it does, however, it must go to texturing.

**Texturing** Once modeled, the 3D object must be textured. Textures are primarily created with a 2D program such as Adobe Photoshop. After textures are applied, the model continues on to be rigged, if necessary.

**Rigging** To create movement, models need to be rigged. Rigging can be done either by a specialized technical artist or by the animator. *Rigging*, as described throughout this book, is the creation of animation controls that the animator uses to create movement. Once the controls are in place, the character can travel to the animator, so to speak.

**Animation** With the animation controls in place, animation can commence. The animators will perform any number of actions with the model, as if they were manipulating a marionette—a highly complex, digital marionette, but a puppet just the same. When the finished model's performance actions are approved, the model can then go to the FX artists.

**Special FX** All that is left in the art production part of this pipeline is adding the eye-candy effects. The FX artists can use any number of tools to jazz things up. They usually use custom tools developed for the game in question. Once the model's journey through the art pipeline has completed, the model is exported to the programmers.

**Programming** While the artists were hard at work creating this model, the programmers were plugging away at their own workstations. They created code for the express purpose of giving the completed model the necessary attributes to make it behave and react as expected. Before an art asset can be utilized in a game, however, it must make one more trip—this time to the level designers.

**Level design** Using custom tools, the level designers place the newly completed character into a level in the game, ready to meet the players who later will purchase the finished product.

Thus ends the life cycle of an art asset. Make way for the next one. Now that you understand how games and game assets are made, let's get started on one of your own.

## Artist Profile: Floyd Bishop

**Job Title** Creative director/owner
**Studio** Bishop Animation
**Credits** *Rise of the Kasai, SOCOM II: U.S. Navy SEALS, Ice Age* (feature film)
**Personal Site** http://www.bishopanimation.com

**Q.** How and why did you get into the game industry?

**A.** I have a degree in communication design. About halfway through school, I decided that I didn't like graphic design enough to do it as my career. I bought a bunch of books and talked to as many animators as I could to get feedback on my work and improve my skills. I moved around a lot and tried to meet as many CG artists as I could.

My big break as an animator came when I was hired at Blue Sky as a character animator on the first *Ice Age* film. I learned a lot there, and it really opened my eyes to the realities of the industry. After *Ice Age* wrapped and most of the crew was let go, I freelanced around Manhattan for a while. I worked mostly on commercials and television shows at this point. I got together with a few friends to take on bigger projects and got to work on my first game project, which was *SOCOM II*.

I was then asked by Sony to work for them full time on-site in San Diego. After only three or four weeks of work, I was let go because the title I was working on got canceled (the realities of the industry). I had a job interview the next morning and was hired at Bottlerocket Entertainment in Del Mar, California, only eight hours after being laid off at Sony.

At Bottlerocket, I really learned all about games and what goes into making them. It was there that I worked on *Rise of the Kasai* for the PS2. It was a great experience. In addition to animation, I was responsible for the bulk of the effects in the game (both in-game and cinematics).

In April of 2005 my family and I left California and moved back to our home state of Pennsylvania, where I started up Bishop Animation.

**Q.** Describe your role at your studio.

**A.** Well, I'm the owner/creative director here. I have a small in-house crew and an extended network of freelancers that I use for specific projects from time to time.

**Q.** What has been the most inspirational to you in regard to your artwork?

**A.** In the summer of 2004, I got the chance to meet Frank Thomas and Ollie Johnston. A friend and I spent an afternoon at Frank's house. They looked at some of my work and gave me feedback on my animation. They also filled my head with stories of their careers, their views on the future of animation, and stories of working with Walt Disney (the man). It was very inspiring. They also signed my *Illusion of Life* book, which is the copy I bought to teach myself animation. Frank also drew a Mickey Mouse in my *Nine Old Men* book. Whenever I get bummed out or stuck on a specific shot, I think of that day or take a look at the Mickey Mouse, drawn with a shaky hand. It gets me going, and I can work through the worst creative blocks that way.

**Q.** What is your favorite style of animation to work with?

**A.** I really enjoy animating things that are cartoon-like in nature. A realistic guy running with a football doesn't excite me too much as an animator. Now if it was a cartoony *octopus* running with a football, then I'd get excited.

**Q.** What is your favorite kind of game?

**A.** I really enjoy the openness of the *Grand Theft Auto* series. I also like the First-Person Shooters (FPS) such as *Unreal* and *Call of Duty*. Some of the longer games, such as *The Legend of Zelda: Wind Waker*, are beautiful as well, but man, do they take a long time to complete!

**Q.** Which Maya animation tool, command, or editor could you not live without?

**A.** It sounds like it's not a big deal, but I use the += and -= commands constantly. [In the Graph Editor (Window > Animation Editors > Graph Editor), selecting a keyframe and typing += or -= and a number in the Stats input areas will decrease or increase the key's value by that amount.] I also like to scale my keyframes quite a bit. I work out nearly all my timing while sitting at the workstation. I'll playblast [Window > Playblast], adjust, playblast again, and adjust until I get things working the way I want them.

**Q.** What advice might you have for the up-and-coming animator?

**A.** Don't rely only on books for your studies. Study animated films as well as live-action films. Go outside and watch animals in the park. Go to the food court at your local mall and watch people eat their food or shop.

Another thing I see a lot of in animation reels from beginners is bad animation in regard to weight. Heavy things need to feel *heavy*. A walk cycle involves a lot more than just forward movement and swinging arms and legs. Get up out of your seat and act it out. What happens to your hips when you walk? How does your weight shift from foot to foot? If you're looking at your animation, and something doesn't look quite right, nine times out of ten it has to do with the way you are animating the weight distribution and balance of your character.

Also, don't be afraid to push things. The worst comment I hear from time to time is "It's just a game." I hate that. You're asking an audience to spend hours and hours with your game. The least you can do is make sure the animation looks good. In an action game, someone is going to watch several hours of that run cycle you're animating. Make it look great!

# Animation

*Animation is a very robust and challenging art form that is rooted deep in art's history. While the technology has advanced greatly since pen first met paper eons ago, many of the same techniques and terminology from the early animation days are still widely used today. In this chapter, I will focus on not only the general terms and techniques used in animation but also the tools and commands that Maya provides animators with to accomplish their goals and how that knowledge relates to animation in game work.*

**In this chapter, we'll discuss the following topics:**

Animation Concepts

3D Animation Terminology

Rigging Tools and Commands

Animation Tools and Commands

Animation User Interface

Upcoming Lessons

## Animation Concepts

Obviously, most of us are familiar with the many classic films of the famous Walt Disney or the hilarious Saturday morning cartoons of Warner Brothers, but just what is animation anyway? *Animation* is officially defined as "the state of being alive." So what we are essentially doing through animation is creating the illusion of life! Whether it is a simple flipbook or a feature-length animated film, we make what was at first a simple series of drawings explode into life before the audience. Of course, the process of creating that life has grown and expanded greatly since the days of *Snow White and the Seven Dwarves*!

Through the advances of the computer, we are now able to create life in the third dimension, giving our animations the visual depth and space that take us from simply watching the animation unfold to experiencing the action as if we were there. And through video games, we are not only there in the thick of things, but we have become the stars of the show, dictating the results of the action.

As the art of animation has grown and evolved over the years, certain common terms and techniques have been developed along the way. We'll discuss these terms and techniques in the following sections.

### Timing

*Timing* is utilized in many aspects of animation. In general, it is the overall identifier of a subject's speed and weight, as well as how long a particular action or sequence of actions should last. If not properly timed, an animation may seem to be in slow motion or zipping by too fast, depicting the action and the animated subject's mass and weight incorrectly. What was intended to be a slow, lumbering elephant would obviously get quite a different reaction if it sprinted through the scene like a gazelle!

Timing can also refer to the *pacing* (or beat) of an animation, especially when character movement is involved. Any professional comedian will tell you that a large part of why a joke is funny is the pacing of its delivery. The same can be said of most animation.

Another aspect of timing is the *ease-in* and the *ease-out* of a movement. When a football player runs up to kick the ball, he pulls back his foot in anticipation of the action. As his foot arcs down to come into contact with the ball, it starts out relatively slowly, picks up speed through the point of impact, and then slows again at the end of the arc. (See Figure 2.1).

### Emphasis

*Emphasis* refers to using exaggeration and dynamism to make certain that every action is easily understood and readable to the audience (See Figure 2.2). This is especially important in games, as you have to ensure that the player is able to tell what is going on at all times in order for him to make the game-play decisions he deems necessary to achieve the game's goal. Realistically, a skilled martial artist may be able to punch or kick so quickly that a viewer or even a camera would have difficulty seeing each move clearly. In a video game fight scene, however, allowing two players to play against each other with faster-than-sight moves would quickly become frustrating!

**Figure 2.1** The swinging of the leg slows down as it pulls back in anticipation of kicking the ball

The leg swings quickly through the ball's position

The swing slows down as it completes the follow-through of the arc after kicking the ball

**Figure 2.2** Emphasis can make a boring animation...

...much more exciting!

'Emphasis also comes into play when dealing with character-driven dialogue. If a character doesn't move as she speaks, she comes across as very stiff and lifeless. Visually emphasizing the character's emotional highs and lows and effectively conveying body language can greatly improve an audience's reaction to a scene.

Every animation tells a story. Make certain that the emphasis you build into your animation does what it is designed to do—draw the viewer's eye to the motion's story. Emphasizing and exaggerating too many details at once will only succeed in confusing the viewer and making him miss what you are trying to show him.

## Secondary Motion

*Secondary motion* can mean many things, but in general, any movement that is a result of a primary movement or that leads up to a primary movement is considered secondary motion. The flopping ears of a rabbit as it jumps and the recoil of a character after firing a weapon are examples of secondary motion.

## Anticipation

*Anticipation*, as hinted at with the kicking example above, is movement that leads up to a primary action. A character leaping across a chasm, for example, wouldn't just suddenly spring across the gap. She would first bend down and draw her arms back to help build momentum for the push forward.

## Follow-Through

A movement that is a result of or directly follows a primary movement is an example of *follow-through*. Once the above cliff-leaper has made her jump and come safely to the other side of the chasm, for example, she may tumble forward upon landing, extending her hands to catch herself before coming to a stop (See Figure 2.3.)

**Figure 2.3** Secondary motion of anticipating the leap

The primary leaping motion

The follow-through directly after the leap

## Overlapping Action

*Overlapping action* can bring a lot of realism to an animation. A character wearing loose-fitting shoulder pads is one example. If he were to jump up and down, the shoulder pads would continue on the upward movement for a beat or two before following the character's downward movement. Other examples of the kinds of objects that would warrant overlapping animation would be any sort of flexible antennae on an alien's head or even the holster hanging from a cowboy's belt. When these characters walk, run, or make any sort of body movement, these secondary objects react with overlap.

## Arcing Motion

Especially in living, organic characters, nearly all movement should have an *arc*, or curve, to its motion path. Whether it's swinging one's arms when walking, throwing a grenade, or even turning one's head (See Figure 2.4), the movement is never in a straight line from one point to another.

**Figure 2.4** Even the simple act of turning your head is done in a small arcing movement

As she turns, her head dips and she might blink to refocus her eyes

She finishes the turn and acknowledges what she noticed

## Squash and Stretch

Flexibility or stiffness can be very effectively conveyed through the principle of *squash and stretch*. The classic example of this concept is a bouncing rubber ball. A rubber ball will squash (or compress) when it strikes the floor and stretch (or extend) as it bounces back. The stiffer an object is, the less change it will experience (See Figure 2.5).

Make sure you don't mistake squash and stretch with shrink and expand. No matter how flexible an object may be, it will never realistically lose or gain mass or volume.

**Figure 2.5** It's easy to tell how flexible these two dropped balls are by how they react to the impact

The more flexible ball compresses upon impact

And stretches upward as it bounces back

## Settling and Resting

When a movement comes to an end, it can't just stop. It needs time to *settle* into a stop. Also, between major movements (depending on the movement in question) times of *rest* are important to help differentiate between motions and to prevent an unnatural "floating" of two movements blending into each other.

## Straight-Ahead Animation

*Straight-ahead animation* is the technique of just starting at the beginning and seeing what happens as you animate your character through the scene. There are many pros and cons to this method. One of the main advantages is spontaneity; you never know what kind of surprises you might stumble upon. However, the lack of planning could be a disadvantage—especially if you have very specific constraints for a particular action!

## Pose-to-Pose Animation

*Pose-to-pose animation* is the opposite of straight-ahead animation. Instead of just starting from the beginning and animating through the scene, you plan it out by setting up the key poses at important moments throughout the scene. There are pros and cons to this technique also. Among the advantages, you do have a plan, so things can stay on track and not get too far out of control. Advance planning also saves a bit of time. However, a disadvantage is that you don't have that element of suspense anymore, which could detract somewhat from the experience.

A good alternative would be to try to incorporate a little of both straight-ahead *and* pose-to-pose as you work. Plan out the major, story-driven keyframes to act as your guide through the scene, but remain flexible with them, going through the scene and animating major parts one at a time—animate the feet, then the arms, adding in the spine rotation and so on in individual passes as you work through the scene.

Now let's delve into the more technical terminology involved with computer animation.

## 3D Animation Terminology

In addition to the animation techniques and concepts that have been around since animation began, 3D animation must deal with technical concepts that are specific to the digital world. In the following sections I'll introduce these concepts. Keep them in mind as we go through the lessons in the rest of the book.

### Keyframes

In traditional 2D animation, a *keyframe* refers to a major pose in an animation. Usually, you would have one group of artists drawing each major keyframe in a sequence while another group would go through and draw the frames that blend one keyframe into another (a process called *in-betweening*, or *tweening*).

*Keyframes* (or keys) are also used in 3D animation. Setting a key in Maya will imprint the selected object's position at that frame in time. Setting another key on a later frame will cause the movement to blend from one keyframe to the other. This is known as *keyframe animation* and is the standard way of animating nearly anything.

### Interpolation

Luckily, 3D animation doesn't require a team of people to do the in-betweening work because the software will automatically compute the movement to blend between set keyframes. The in-betweening of keyframes in 3D animation is called *interpolation* and can be handled many ways to create different kinds of movement transitions, such as the ease-in and ease-out animation described earlier. We'll talk more in depth about how to do this later in the chapter.

### Rigging

*Rigging* is the process of setting up the controls on a model to allow it to move and be animated. In most cases, you use a skeleton to set up a rig. A *skeleton* comprises a hierarchy of *joints* (or bones) that you consciously disperse throughout the model (Figure 2.6). The joints act as a structure on which animation can take place, like a digital puppet. We'll definitely be going more into the specifics of this process in this book's upcoming lessons.

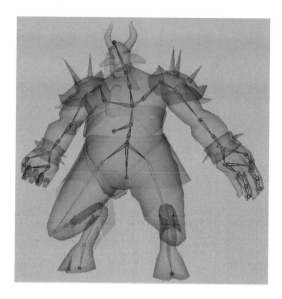

**Figure 2.6**
A skeleton rig for a character

## Binding

Attaching a model to a skeleton for animation is called *binding*. This process associates individual vertices of a mesh to nearby joints. When a joint is moved or rotated, the associated bound vertices move accordingly. The degree of influence a joint has on a bound vertex is called *vertex weight*. The type of binding we are interested in is *smooth binding*.

Smooth binding allows a vertex to be affected by multiple joints. So a vertex in the middle of a character's back, for example, can have a percentage of its total weight affected by multiple joints along the character's spine, allowing for a smoother deformation.

## Articulation

With any kind of mesh deformation, such as the bending at stress points like the knee or elbow, it's important that the geometry has enough surface detail to allow for the bending. The degree of freedom of movement allowed to an animator is known as *articulation* (See Figure 2.7). This is commonly decided early on when discussing the limitations of a game project.

For instance, how much articulation should be built into the hands? Will characters have all five fingers completely modeled and bendable? Or do the project's *polycount* limitations (the limited amount of geometry for a specific model, most commonly described using triangle faces, or *tris*) require that the character models instead have what are known as *mittens* (or *mitts*)—a thumb and a large mass representing the four fingers?

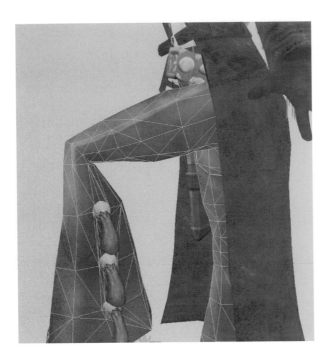

**Figure 2.7**
The geometry built into the knee allows
for good articulation

The geometry built into a character's face allows for much more "acting" to take place

## Forward and Inverse Kinematics

*Forward kinematics (FK)* and *inverse kinematics (IK)* are two skeleton-manipulation techniques used to control the bending of joints along the chain. Forward kinematics is a method of manipulating joints in order *down* the hierarchy. Inverse kinematics affects joints *up* the hierarchy.

For example, a typical arm skeleton is made up of three joints in a connected chain: shoulder joint → elbow joint → wrist joint. Using forward kinematics, rotating the shoulder joint will also move the elbow and wrist. Rotating the elbow will affect the wrist and so on. Using inverse kinematics, when you move the wrist, the movement will automatically adjust the rotation of the elbow and shoulder joints.

Another form of IK is called *spline IK*. This uses a curve that runs through a series of joints. Manipulating the flow of the curve affects the flow of the joints. This is most useful for flexible, tube-like forms, such as the joints that make up a character's spine or an octopus' tentacles.

## Vertex Animation

*Vertex animation* is an animation type that actually animates the individual vertices of a mesh individually without the use of a skeleton. One common example of vertex animation in games is the player-creation interfaces in many sports games and role-playing games. In order to create a character with the specific look the player desires, the game includes sliders and buttons that change the shape of a character's nose, mouth, and other parts of the body.

## Blend Shapes

The most common form of vertex animation used in games is facial animation using *blend shapes* (also known as *morph targets*). By creating copies of a character's head and manipulating it to form different facial expressions, mouth forms, and the like, you can blend the mesh between these different shapes to create facial animation, such as lip synching and showing emotion.

> **Note:** Not all game engines support the use of vertex animation. As with any project, your supervisor will inform you about the specifics related to the task at hand.

## Animation Cycles

In video game animation, everything that a character does on the screen is controlled somehow through the input of a player. By pressing the control stick forward, a player initiates some kind of animation cycle, based on the type of character being shown on the screen. An *animation cycle* is an animation sequence that has the option to play continuously in a loop.

The most common example is a character's walk or run cycle. The player telling the character to move forward triggers the character's walk cycle. The main reason why actions such as the walk cycle are short looping animations rather than long sequences is because at any time the player needs to be able to break the character from the walk animation and go into, say, an attack animation when an enemy character confronts him.

### Set Driven Key

*Set Driven Key* (Animate > Set Driven Key) is an alternative animation method that involves setting up certain relationships between the attributes of two or more objects. For example, we can set up a relationship between a car and a garage door, so that whenever the car approaches the door, the door will automatically open and close behind it without our having to manually tell it to do so every time the player wants the car to enter or exit the garage. This will be explained more thoroughly later in the "Animation Tools and Commands" section.

Now that we've gone over terms, techniques, and concepts of animation in general as well as those that apply specifically to computer animation, let's get really specific and start talking about what tools and commands Maya has available for rigging a model for animation.

## Rigging Tools and Commands

Since you are now familiar with the basic concepts behind animation, let's focus on the more common rigging tools and commands, along with their available options. In addition to the general explanations given here, I'll demonstrate more specific uses of tools throughout the lessons found later in this book. All of the tools I discuss in the following sections can be found under Maya's Animation menu set (F2).

### Joint Tool

The Joint Tool (Skeleton > Joint Tool) is used for creating and placing joints in order to create a skeletal hierarchy. As with most direct-placement tools, I recommend using this tool while viewing your scene through one of the orthographic views, such as the side, front, or top cameras.

When placing joints, keep in mind that each additional joint you place will automatically be a part of the current joint chain and a child of the previously placed joint. Joints are points of articulation on a skeleton, so make certain that you position the joints at locations where bending is likely to occur.

Once you have completed a joint chain, press the Enter key to exit the tool. If you want to continue the chain elsewhere, with the Joint Tool still active, left-click an existing joint. It should now be highlighted, indicating that the next joint you place will become a child of the currently selected joint.

Notice that the bone that is created between each joint is wider at one end than the other. The narrow end of a bone indicates the direction of the joint chain down its hierarchy.

To connect two separate joint chains, select the top joint (or *root joint*) of the child chain and then Shift+select the end of the second chain where you want the connection to occur. Go to Edit > Parent (or press P on the keyboard). This connects the first joint to the second's hierarchy. Edit > Unparent (or Shift+P) disconnects the selected joint and its chain from the hierarchy.

## IK Handle Tool

The IK Handle Tool (Skeleton > IK Handle Tool) sets up a chain of bones to use inverse kinematics.

1.  While the IK Handle Tool is active, left-click the joint that will serve as the base joint to be affected by the IK.

2.  Left-click the end joint that will serve as the handle.

For example, to set up IK for a typical hip → knee → ankle joint chain, you would click the hip first and then the ankle joint. The IK handle will appear at the location of the ankle joint.

In the tool's options, the main one you'll need to worry about is the Sticky option. By default it is unchecked. Turning Sticky on will make the IK-enabled feet stay level with the ground plane, allowing such things as footsteps without the feet sliding through the floor.

> **Note:** If the joints or IK handles in your scene are too large or too small, you can change their size by going to Display > Joint Size or Display > IK Handle Size, respectively.

## IK Spline Handle Tool

The IK Spline Handle Tool (Skeleton > IK Spline Handle Tool) creates a curve through the joint chain. Manipulating the curve's *control vertices (CVs)* to adjust the path of the curve's shape allows the joint chain to follow the same path.

1.  With the IK Spline Handle Tool active, left-click the joint that will serve as the base joint in the chain.

2.  Left-click the joint at the tip of the desired joint chain. The curve will form through the indicated chain of joints.

Of the options, the most important one to consider is the number of *spans* (or divisions) that the curve has. The more spans, the more CVs the curve will have available to use.

IK Spline is most useful for things like spines, tails, whips, tentacles, and other similar organic structures.

### Paint Skin Weights Tool

Very rarely is a binding considered complete simply after applying it. Nine times out of ten, you'll need to do some kind of weight editing to repair any unwanted stretching and deformation that inevitably occur. In the case of smooth binding, this is predominantly done by painting the weight distribution using the Paint Skin Weights Tool (Skin > Edit Smooth Skin > Paint Skin Weights Tool).

To get started, select a mesh that is smooth-bound to a skeleton, and activate the Paint Skin Weights Tool. The selected mesh will turn black while the active joint's influence of weight is displayed on the mesh as an area of white (Figure 2.8). The Paint Skin Weights Tool icon will appear at the bottom of the toolbar (beneath the Show Manipulator Tool). Double-click the tool icon to open the tool's option panel (or open the option panel by going to Skin > Edit Smooth Skin > Paint Skin Weights Tool > Options).

The Brush settings of the option panel control the shape of the brush:

**Radius(U) and Radius(L)** These two radius sliders control the upper and lower radiuses of the brush, respectively. The upper radius slider controls the main, visible radius of the painting brush, indicated by a red circle.

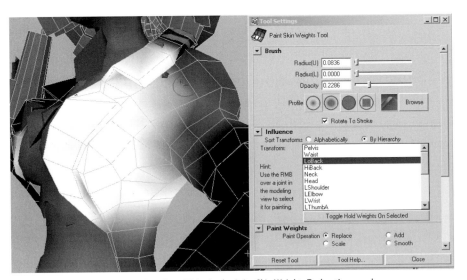

**Figure 2.8** The area of influence of a selected joint in the Paint Skin Weights Tool option panel

The lower radius slider is active only when a stylus with pressure sensitivity is being used as the input device—the lighter the pen stroke, the smaller the radius of the painted effect. Adjusting the lower radius controls the minimum radius the stroke will shrink to.

**Opacity**  The Opacity slider adjusts the strength of the brush's painted affect.

**Profile**  The Profile setting offers a selection of basic brush shapes and allows you to browse for your own custom shape.

> **Note:** To interactively scale the upper radius of your brush, while in your scene hold the B shortcut key and left-click and drag.

The large list in the Influence section of the option panel displays all of the joints within the skeleton to which the selected mesh is bound. Selecting a joint in the list displays that joint's active weight distribution on the selected mesh as a white gradient and allows that distribution to be edited.

The Toggle Hold Weights On Selected button ensures that the weights of the selected joint are not changed when other joints in the list are edited.

Within the Paint Weights section of the option panel is the Paint Operation setting, which controls the method of weight distribution the brush utilizes with each stroke. There are four methods:

**Replace**  This method replaces the existing weight with the current weight settings of the brush.

**Add**  This method increases the influence of nearby joints.

**Scale**  This method decreases the influence of distant joints, scaling the effect toward the brush stroke.

**Smooth**  This method smoothes out the influences of surrounding joints.

While all four of these paint operations have viable uses, I recommend mostly using the Replace operation. The Add, Scale, and Smooth operations all adjust the weights with rather hard-to-specify results, especially the Smooth operation, which I find rather random. And since game art is predominantly *low-poly* (comprised of limited geometry), it usually isn't too hard of a task to edit the weights on a vertex-by-vertex level.

The Value setting adjusts the maximum percentage of weight each brush stroke will apply to a vertex, ranging from 0 to 1 by default, where 1 is equal to 100 percent weight. Increasing or decreasing the Min/Max Value will suitably affect this percentage, increasing or decreasing it.

The Flood button will apply the current weight settings for the currently selected joint to the entire selected mesh.

## Clusters

One useful technique to make manipulating the CVs of the IK spline curve easier is to use clusters. *Clusters* (Deform > Create Cluster) are control handles that allow you to manipulate points (vertices, CVs, etc.) either individually or in groups.

1. Right-click the spline curve and choose CVs from the marking menu that appears. This puts you into component mode.

2. Select a CV. Go to Deform > Create Cluster. A handle will appear where the CV is located, allowing you to manipulate the CV easily without having to access component mode each time.

3. Repeat for the other CVs for which you want to add cluster handles.

## Mirror Joint

As its name suggests, this command mirrors a joint chain. This is obviously useful for arms and legs. After setting up the joint chain for one side, you can simply mirror the chain for the other side.

In the Mirror Joint options (Skeleton > Mirror Joint > Options), adjust the Mirror Across option to coincide with the axis you want to mirror. The standard character orientation is to face the positive Z direction in XYZ space. In that case, choose the YZ option to mirror across the character's body.

The Replacement Names For Duplicated Joints section of the option box allows you to rename the mirrored joints with a handy search-and-replace function. For instance, Left_Shoulder can be mirrored and become Right_Shoulder.

Make certain that you select only the top joint in the chain that you want to mirror. For instance, if you want to mirror an arm chain of joints (typically shoulder joint → elbow joint → wrist joint → hand joints) that is attached to the body through the spine from the left side of the body to the right, select the left shoulder joint to mirror and not the spine joint to which it is linked. If the spine joint is selected when the mirroring takes place, it will also be duplicated, resulting in a branching spine, which, in most natural organic shapes, is impractical, difficult to work with, and just plain incorrect.

## Smooth Bind

As described earlier, smooth binding allows each vertex of a mesh to be affected by multiple joints to allow a smoother deformation when bending.

In the Smooth Bind options, there are two main settings that you need to pay close attention to—Max Influences and Dropoff Rate.

The Max Influences setting indicates the maximum number of joints that can affect a single vertex. The Dropoff Rate setting determines how close a joint can be to a vertex and still have influence on it. The higher the Dropoff Rate, the closer a joint must be to have any effect.

I personally like giving myself as much control as possible over how the weighting is dispersed around the skeleton, so I generally recommend beginning with a low Max Influence of 2 and a high Dropoff Rate of around 8. This is just to get the geometry bound to the skeleton. Later, we can be as meticulous as we want in controlling how the weight is shared among the vertices.

To bind a mesh to a skeleton using smooth binding, follow these simple steps:

1. Select all of the geometry that is to be bound to the skeleton.

2. Shift+click the skeleton's root joint.

3. Go to Skin > Bind Skin > Smooth Bind, and set the options as you want them.

## Detach Skin

As it sounds, the Detach Skin (Skin > Detach Skin) command unbinds the selected mesh from the skeleton, returning it to its original position. Be careful when using this, as you will lose all vertex weight adjustments that have been made prior to the detachment.

## Go to Bind Pose

The Go to Bind Pose (Skin > Go to Bind Pose) command returns a skeleton with a bound mesh to its position at the time of its original binding.

Occasionally, this command will run into difficulties, and the skeleton will refuse to return to the bind pose. Most of the time, this is because the IK handles and other such constraints are preventing it. To fix this, simply go to Modify > Evaluate Nodes > Ignore All. Anything that is preventing this command from working will be turned off. Once you achieve the bound pose, you can turn the IK handles and other such things back on with the Modify > Evaluate Nodes > Evaluate All command.

Now that you are familiar with the tools and commands used for rigging a model, we'll focus on those tools and commands that are used for the actual animation.

## Animation Tools and Commands

There are a number of tools, commands, and editors available to give an animator many more options when going about the process of creating an animation. Many of these are common tools and commands used in the general day-to-day process, such as setting and manipulating keyframes. Others can be used specifically to help automate a complex set of actions.

In the following sections, I'll introduce these tools and also demonstrate a few examples of how you can integrate many of them into your own workflow.

### Setting Keyframes

There are multiple ways of setting a keyframe in Maya. Here are three of the more common methods: Set Key, Set Transform Keys, and Key Selected. Let's discuss these in greater detail.

**Animate > Set Key**  Set Key (or pressing the S shortcut key on the keyboard) sets a keyframe for each keyable channel in the channel box for the selected object. This method is not necessarily the most efficient, however, as you  generally don't need to have a key set for all of an object's channels.

**Note:** To remove unnecessary keyframes from unchanging attributes, select the object(s) in question and go to Edit > Delete by Type > Static Channels. Any unneeded sequential keyframes that do not change in value will be removed.

Instead of setting keys for all channels, you can be a bit more efficient and set keys only for certain groups of channels, as described with the next three commands:

**Animate > Set Transform Keys > Translate**  This command (also accessible with the Shift+W shortcut) sets a keyframe for all three (X, Y, and Z) translation channels.

**Animate > Set Transform Keys > Rotate**  This command (also accessible with the Shift+E shortcut) sets a keyframe for all three rotation channels.

**Animate > Set Transform Keys > Scale**  This command (Shift+R) sets a keyframe for all three scale channels.

**Key Selected**  In order to key individual channels separately, select the desired channel(s) in the channel box (be sure to select the channel *name* and not the value input box) right-click and hold, and choose Key Selected from the Channels menu that appears.

**Note:** To prevent having to manually set a key each and every time you make a movement, you can turn on Auto Key by toggling the key icon in the lower right of the Maya user interface, near the range slider. Once you set an initial keyframe for an attribute, each change made to that attribute farther down the time line will automatically set a key for it. Auto Key can be a big time-saver but can also flood your scene with unwanted keyframes if you aren't careful!

Keep in mind that if you want something to remain still (or *at rest*) for any length of time, you will need to set a keyframe at the beginning and at the end of the time period of no change. Animate > Hold Current Keys sets a keyframe with the selected object's current keyframe values.

### Opening Files from Different Versions of Maya

The Maya scene files found on the CD of this book are all in the Maya ASCII format (.ma), which differs from the standard Maya scene format of Maya Binary (.mb) files. If you were to open the same Maya scene in .mb and .ma formats in a text editor, such as Notepad or Wordpad, you'll notice right away the major difference.

Maya Binary is the Maya application specific protocol for defining Maya objects and scenes. Only the Maya application can understand these files, therefore if you open them in a text editor, you will see lots of mumbo jumbo.

On the other hand, Maya ASCII is the same Maya file information but in a standard text format. With this in mind, it generally is possible to open Maya files from later versions of the software in an earlier version, but only if it is saved as an .ma file.

Here's how it works.

1. Right-click on a Maya .ma file and choose Open With > Choose Program....

2. Choose Notepad from the list that appears (Any text editor will work.).

3. You'll see a file full of text and numbers open in Notepad. At the beginning, you can usually see something like the following:

   ```
   //Maya ASCII 7.0 scene
   ```

   So, the only thing that prevents a Maya 7.0 file from being opened in, for example, Maya 6.5, is that the file itself designates it as such in this text file.

4. In the text file, place your cursor at the beginning of the file, before the first character.

*Continues*

**Opening Files from Different Versions of Maya** *(Continued)*

5.  In Notepad (other applications should have a similar feature, but differing wording), go to Edit > Replace.

    In the Find What: box, type the version of Maya your .ma scene is currently using. In the case of the files on this book's CD, that'd be 7.0.

    In the Replace With: box, type in the version of Maya you are using, such as 6.5 or 6.0.

6.  Click the Find Next button. The first thing that should highlight is the 7.0 mentioned earlier that is at the beginning of the text file. Click the Replace button. After clicking Replace, the 7.0 gets switched with your version and automatically highlights the next "7.0" in the text file.

    Do NOT click the Replace All button!

7.  Continue to do this throughout the text file. However, take every precaution to read what is highlighted. If the highlighted 7.0 is not in relation to the version of the file, don't replace it. Realize that there are *lots* of numbers in this file that all have to deal with the construction of your scene and you're liable to get a lot of 7.0 combinations that are a part of larger numbers.

8.  When you come to the end of the file, save it (preferably as a new file and not over your old one) making sure to maintain the .ma file extension.

When complete, your file should be readable in an earlier version of the Maya software! However, keep in mind that because this is a manual text edit of the file, there's always the possibility that it may not work for one reason or another. Also, if the Maya scene file in question is dealing with anything that is specific to a version of Maya, such as the new Full-Body IK system in Maya 7.0, it will not work properly in earlier versions because those versions would not have support for such new features. None of the files I've provided on the CD are making use of anything specific to Maya 7.0, so they all have the potential to work properly when making this change. Good luck!

## Set Driven Key

Set Driven Key allows you to create a relationship between two or more attributes so that one will directly affect (or "drive") others automatically. You can do this for any number of reasons. One common use is to create what is essentially a "remote control"—a dummy object that contains lots of sliders and settings that affect the animated character or object in some way—to avoid a lot of repetitive, time-consuming work.

For instance, you can create hand controls that will automate the constricting of a fist, a trigger finger position, or any other finger configuration once you have set them properly, each with a slider, so that you won't have to manually adjust each finger joint every time.

When we use the Set Driven Key tool in the book's upcoming lessons, we'll go over the situation-by-situation specifics that the lessons call for, but here we'll just go over how it works in general terms. We'll use the simple example given earlier as our scenario: a garage door that automatically opens at the approach of a car. Let's get started.

1.    Navigate on the CD to Project_Files/Chapter_2/Set_Driven_Key/Scenes and open the file garagedoor.ma. In this file, you'll find a primitive car object as well as a "garage door."

2. Select the garage door object. Go to Animate > Set Driven Key > Set > Options.

3. Having the garage_door object selected when you opened the Set Driven Key options automatically placed the garage_door in the Set Driven Key window's Driven panel. If you didn't select the object at the outset, you can select the door now and press the Load Driven button to achieve the same thing.

4. On the left side of the Driven panel is the name of the object, in this case, the garage_door. On the right side of the panel are all of that object's keyable channels. We want the garage_door to open up along its Z-axis. Select and highlight the RotateZ channel.

5. Select the car object. In the Set Driven Key window, click the Load Driver button. The car object appears in the Driver panel. Select and highlight the TranslateX channel on the right side of the Driver panel.

6. In the Set Driven Key options, press the Key button. You've now begun to set up a relationship between the car and the garage_door, based on the settings of the highlighted attributes in both the Driver and Driven panels.

7. With the car object selected, input 13 into the TranslateX channel, which moves it 13 units toward the garage_door object. Rotate the garage_door -100 degrees on the Z-axis (Figure 2.9). Again, press the Key button in the Set Driven Key options.

8. Input 26 into the TranslateX channel of the car, which moves it past the garage_door. Rotate the garage_door back down to 0 degrees on the Z-axis. Press the Key button.

Now when you move the car to and from the garage_door, the door will automatically open and close behind the car.

To remove this relationship, select the garage_door, highlight the Driven RotateZ channel in the channel box, right click, and choose Break Connections from the Channels menu that appears.

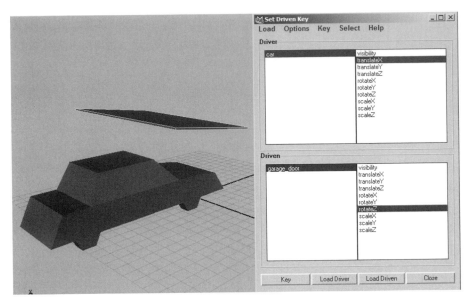

**Figure 2.9** The car in position through the garage door, with the Set Driven Key panel open

## Blend Shapes

Blend shapes are a form of vertex animation that allows you to manipulate the position of individual vertices on the mesh without the use of bones. This is very commonly used for facial expressions and mouth shapes for lip-synching.

When you create blend shapes for the purposes of lip-synching to audio, a number of core mouth formations are used for audible vowel and consonant sounds. These are known as *phoneme shapes*. For a comprehensive list of the different phoneme shapes used for accurate lip-synching, take a look at http://www.garycmartin.com/phoneme_examples.html. In addition to these phoneme shapes for lip-synching, you can also create various facial expressions to show emotion: smile, frown, raised eyebrows for surprise, and so on. Blend shapes can also help with rather mundane things like blinking.

Blend shapes can be tricky at first, but once you get the hang of them, they can be quite fun to make! Let's try them next.

1. Browse on the CD to Project_Files/Chapter_2/Blend_Shape/Scenes and open the file Cowgirl_Head_Start.ma. In this scene, you will find the head of Calamity Jane, although admittedly in a rather unfinished state. It's in a good positionfor learning the basics of blend shapes, though (Figure 2.10)!

2. In your scene, select Jane's head and duplicate it (Edit > Duplicate, or Ctrl+D). Move the duplicate to the side about two units.

3. While the duplicate is still selected, press Shift+D. This is the keyboard shortcut for Edit > Duplicate with Transform. This command duplicates the selected object and moves it in the same way the previous duplicate command did. You should find that it duplicated and moved a new head to the side.

4. Now, switch back to the first duplicated head. Manipulate the points around the mouth to form an O shape.

5. Select the second duplicate and duplicate it once again, and then move the third duplicate to the side. Adjust the vertices of the second head into a smile. Continue doing this as much as you'd like, creating new and different mouth and head shapes (Figure 2.11).

Duplicating the head before adjusting the vertices to create an expression or phoneme shape will ensure that you always have a clean head in its default pose ready for the next shape target you want to create.

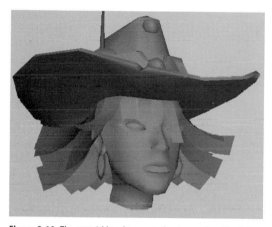

**Figure 2.10** The cowgirl head to use to begin creating blend shapes

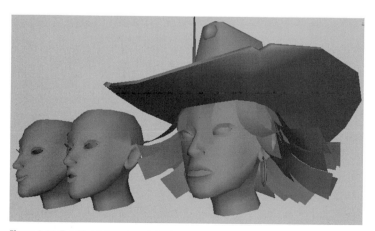

**Figure 2.11** Two blend shape targets in place

**Note:** Do not use Freeze Transformations (Modify > Freeze Transformations) on any object that you want to become a blend shape target because it will interfere with the blending calculations. This command makes all transformation information of an object (including the vertices we're trying to animate) go to zero without actually changing the shape.

**6.** When all of your blend shape targets are ready to be applied to the original head as blend shape modifiers, rename them to be called the expression or shape they are depicting: Smile, O, and the like.

**7.** Select all of the duplicated heads that you want to apply. Shift+click the original head last.

**8.** Go to Deform > Create Blend Shape. The blend shape targets are now all influencing the original head, albeit with no visible effect.

**9.** Open the Blend Shape Editor under Window > Animation Editors > Blend Shape.

Now that we have created some blend shape targets, we'll need to actually control them. That's where the Blend Shape Editor comes into play.

### Blend Shape Editor

The Blend Shape Editor window allows you to control the applied blend shapes in the entire scene without having to select the objects in question to gain access to the controls. This editor contains a slider for each blend shape target object that you applied in the scene, along with a series of buttons.

The sliders are labeled based on the name of the blend shape target meshes. In the case of the scene provided on the CD called Cowgirl_Head_Blends.ma, I have two: one for an O mouth shape and another for a smile expression. If you forgot to name your meshes, you can rename them here.

The sliders themselves are percentage sliders, representing how much influence the particular blend shape target has on the original mesh. For instance, you could have the smile blend shape affect the face only 25 percent of its total influence (Figure 2.12), giving you a smile that is slight and not nearly as overt as the actual target mesh (you can directly type in the percentage you want using the value input box below each slider). You can also combine blend shape targets. You could, for example, set the O mouth shape at around 25 percent as well, causing the character to open her mouth in a slight smile. Experiment with your sliders once you have a full array of combinations to work with; you can really get a lot of mileage out of just a few different shapes if you're clever about it!

The Key button below each slider allows you to set a keyframe for the slider's current position at the current frame.

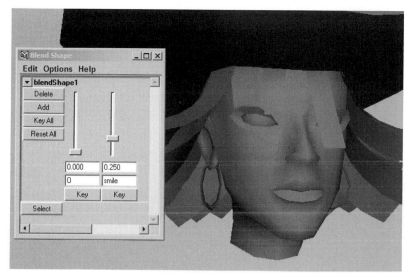

**Figure 2.12** The Blend Shape Editor

In addition to the controls for each individual blend shape slider, you also have controls for the entire group of blend shapes on the left side of the editor. Which blend shapes are included in the grouping is determined by which blend shape target meshes were selected when you applied the blend shape.

**Delete** This control deletes the entire group of blend shapes from the original mesh.

**Add** If there's a particular blend shape combination of sliders that you really like and would like to use again, you can create a new slider for it with the Add button. Using the above example, position both the O and smile slider at 25 percent. Select the original mesh and click Add. A new target mesh will be created on top of the original mesh, and a new slider will be added to the blend shape group in the editor.

**Key All** This control sets a keyframe for all of a group's blend shape sliders at the current frame.

**Reset All** This control resets all of the group's sliders to 0.

**Select** This control selects the blend shape group node. It is useful for selecting the blend shape group as a Driver or Driven object for use in Set Driven Key, among other things.

> **Note:** If you have a lot of blend shape sliders, you can arrange the orientation of each slider to horizontal (rather than the default vertical) to save screen space. This is done in the Blend Shape Editor under Options > Orientation > Horizontal.

## Graph Editor

The Graph Editor (Window > Animation Editors > Graph Editor, as shown in Figure 2.13) is the primary editor used during animation. It has controls not only for setting and manipulating keyframes but also for manipulating different methods of interpolation, or how keyframes blend together. Here, we'll go through many of the options and settings that are available and explain what they do. During this book's upcoming lessons, we'll go over more specific uses of the Graph Editor based on the projects in question.

The main area of the Graph Editor, the graph view, displays all of the keyframes, animation curves, and key tangents of the selected objects, and their keyable attributes appear on the left side of the Graph Editor in the graph outliner. An *animation curve* represents motion and shows how keyframes interpolate. Each keyframe on each animation curve has *key tangents* that manipulate the flow of the animation curve's *in tangent* (the flow of the curve into the key) and *out tangent* (the flow of the curve out of the key), adjusting the interpolation.

The standard move and scale tools can be used to manipulate the position of keyframes and key tangents in the graph view. Select the move tool from the Toolbox (or press W on the keyboard), then select a keyframe, and middle-click and drag to reposition the keyframe. Hold down the Shift key to constrain the keyframe's movement to a straight line. To scale, select the scale tool from the Toolbox (or press R on the keyboard), select the range of keyframes that you want to scale, and middle-click and drag from the point from which you want to scale.

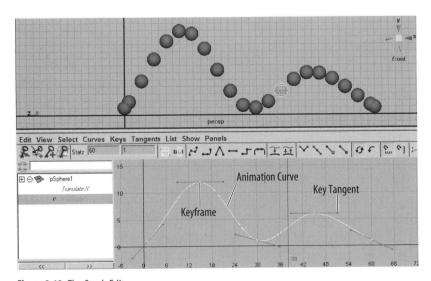

**Figure 2.13** The Graph Editor

You can also directly input positional and value information for a keyframe. When a keyframe is selected in the graph view, two numbers appear in the Stats section on the Graph Editor's toolbar. The number in the left input box indicates the frame position of the selected key, while the number in the right input box indicates the value of the selected key. Both numbers can be directly edited here.

## Deformation Order

One error that can sometimes creep into your files when rigging a character that uses blend shapes is its deformation order. When you deform something, you are changing its shape in some way. Maya allows you to deform an object many ways all at the same time; however, it calculates each deformation separately, usually in the order that they were applied.

For example, rigging a character with a skeleton is considered a deforming action, as you are changing the mesh's shape when you bend the elbow or the knee or any of the other joints in the skeleton. If you were to then apply blend shapes on top of that, the skeleton would deform the mesh first and then the blend shape.

However, occasionally you may experience a situation where you notice that when you raise a blend shape slider, the mesh suddenly pulls away from the skeleton or just acts strangely. More than likely, this is caused by Maya calculating the deformations in the wrong order. To correct the order, follow these steps:

1. Select the wayward mesh. Left-click and hold down the Inputs To The Selected Object button on the status line (to the right of the snapping toggles).

2. Select the All Inputs option from the menu that appears.

3. The List Of Input Operations window opens, showing each deforming action that is currently applied to the mesh listed in the order it is calculated, as shown in the illustration below. Middle-clicking and dragging an item allows you to rearrange that order and thus the order of deformation.

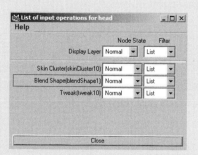

### Editing Interpolation

Interpolation can be edited manually using key tangents or by using provided tangent presets found under the Tangents menu or the shortcut keys in the Graph Editor's toolbar. The preset tangent types are as follows:

**Spline** A *spline tangent* (Figure 2.14) creates a smooth flow between the keys before and after the selected keyframe(s). This type of animation curve is good for creating smooth, fluid movement.

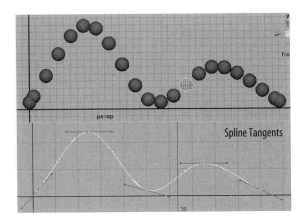

Spline Tangents

**Figure 2.14**
Using a spline tangent animation curve with a bouncing ball example

**Note:** An example of the bouncing ball file above, as well as a sample animation, can be found on the CD under Project_Files/Chapter_2/Scenes/Graph_Editor.

**Linear** A *linear tangent*'s flow is a straight line (Figure 2.15), joining two keys as directly as possible, with no delineation of the animation curve.

**Clamped** A *clamped tangent*'s flow has some similar elements of both the spline and linear tangents (Figure 2.16). When two adjacent clamped keys' values do not change very much, they will use a linear tangent flow. If the next adjacent key does change in a more dramatic fashion, a spline tangent will be used.

This type can be very useful for animating a character's feet placement during a walk or run sequence. When a character's foot makes contact with the ground, it remains on the ground at that spot until the other foot makes contact. At that point, the first foot rises to travel forward.

With a standard spline curve flow, there is a fluid "wave" pattern to the animation curve. Using the example of the character footstep, the planted foot would slip slightly, not maintaining its grounding. Using a clamped tangent can fix this error.

**Stepped** Using *stepped tangents* (Figure 2.17), a key's animation curve won't change its value until the next key. This works well for something you would want to react like a light switch. The moment you turn the light on, it stays on until the moment it's turned off, with no other change in between.

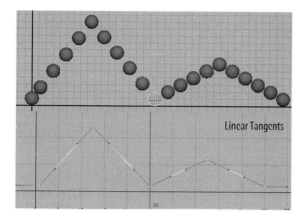

**Figure 2.15**
Using a linear tangent animation curve with a bouncing ball example

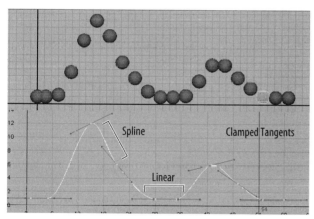

**Figure 2.16**
An example of a clamped tangent animation curve

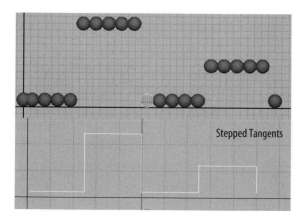

**Figure 2.17**
An example of a stepped tangent animation curve using the bouncing ball example

**Stepped Next** *Stepped next tangents* (Figure 2.18) are very similar to regular stepped tangents. However, instead of a value waiting until the next key's moment in time to make the applicable change, the value does so right away.

**Flat** *Flat tangents* (Figure 2.19) set the in tangent and out tangent of the keyframe to have a perfectly horizontal flow, with no slope. This causes the value of the keyframe to not change for a moment before and after the key, giving the animation a "hanging in place" look, such as the hang time of a kicked ball at its apex.

**Fixed** Setting a tangent as *fixed* allows a key's value to be edited without changing the key's tangents.

**Plateau** *Plateau tangents* keep a keyframe's animation curves from flowing past their values. In the case of a spline animation curve, for example, the animation curve's need to create a fluid transition from one key to another usually results in the value of the curve fluctuating higher or lower than what was set in the keyframe. Plateau tangents prevent that effect (Figure 2.20).

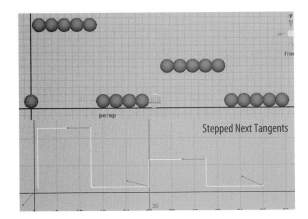

**Figure 2.18**
The opposite effect of stepped next tangents

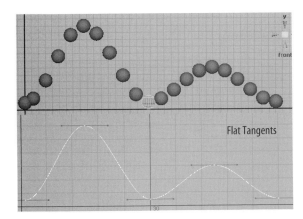

**Figure 2.19**
Flat tangents on an animation curve

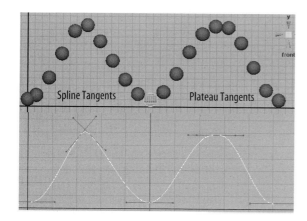

**Figure 2.20**
The difference between spline tangents (left) and plateau tangents (right)

### Manual Tangent Editing

There are multiple methods available for manually manipulating the tangents of a key. With a standard key selected, two handles emerge from the keyframe that indicate the flow of the animation curve coming into and out of the key. Selecting one of these handles and middle-clicking and dragging to move it will adjust that flow's direction and thus the interpolation. By default, both the in tangent and out tangent will maintain their relationship to each other when one or the other is adjusted. It is possible to change this relationship and adjust it more precisely.

With a key selected, you can set one of the tangent presets from the above list for the in tangent and a different one for the out tangent, changing the flow of the animation curve. Choose Tangents > In Tangent or Out Tangent and then choose from the available tangent presets. For example, you could have the in tangent set to linear, while the out tangent is set to flat.

With a key selected, you can also break the two tangent handles, allowing you to change one without it changing the other. This is done with the Keys > Break Tangents command. The tangent handles change colors to indicate the break. Now each side of a key's tangents can be adjusted independently. Keys > Unify Tangents reconnects the broken tangents.

By default, the tangent handles of keys are *non-weighted*; this provides simplified handles for manipulating the angle of tangents. Making the tangent handles *weighted* causes them to represent the amount of *tangent weight* (or the influence they have on the animation curve) and provide finer control. To do this, select a key, and in the Graph Editor, go to Curves > Weighted Tangents. The ends of the tangent handles will become thicker and shorten or lengthen based on the flow of the curve. To return a key's tangents to non-weighted, use Curves > Non-weighted Tangents.

Once the tangents are weighted, you can control the key tangents two different ways: with locked weights or with free weights. By default, the tangent weight is locked, allowing you to manipulate the tangent angle without changing the tangent weight. To affect the tangent weight as well as the angle, use Keys > Free Tangent Weight. To lock them again, use Keys > Lock Tangent Weight.

All of the commands we discussed are available simply to give you the most control over how your keyframes blend together (Figure 2.21). It may seem complicated at first, but believe me, it's much faster than having squadrons of animators draw each in-between by hand!

**Note:** To get the "ghosting" result as seen in the previous figures, with your animated object selected, go to Animate > Ghost Selected > Options. In the options, you can adjust to what degree you want the ghosting affect to be visible.

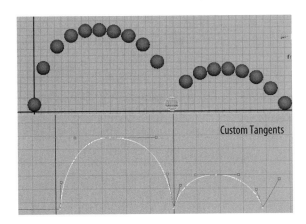

Custom Tangents

**Figure 2.21**
A true bouncing ball result after manually adjusting key tangents with Free Tangent Weights

## Dope Sheet

The Dope Sheet (Window > Animation Editors > Dope Sheet, as shown in Figure 2.22) is an alternative animation editor that can accomplish many of the same things that the Graph Editor can; however, its design is primarily geared toward easy keyframe moving as opposed to the interpolation of animation curves.

The selected animated objects, such as a skeleton hierarchy, appear on the left side in the Dope Sheet outliner. In the Dope Sheet view area, each key is represented by a

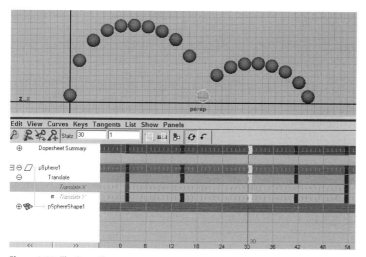

**Figure 2.22** The Dope Sheet

small block. You can select blocks individually or select an entire group of them using the Select Keyframe Tool from the Dope Sheet toolbar. Just as in the Graph Editor, the move and scale tools can be used to reposition a keyframe or group of keyframes.

## Trax Editor

The Trax Editor (Window > Animation Editors > Trax Editor) is Maya's nonlinear animation tool. Nonlinear animation refers to being able to take your animation sequences and manipulate them in a way that is not as straightforward as simply setting keyframes one after another. You can take different animation sequences and blend them, intersect them, or reorder them.

Whether or not this is useful or even usable to your project is really dependent on what the game project requires. For example, many games import their animations as individual files. Others have a character's entire library of movements in a single file all laid out one after another in the timeline.

The Trax Editor's tools work only for character sets. A *character set* is a way for Maya to put all of a character's animation controls together under one handle rather than have you hunting through a skeleton looking for that missing joint. Once a character set is created, the movements of the included joints and objects can be converted into clips. A *clip* is an animation sequence that the Trax Editor can use.

While the Trax Editor can be very useful, I actually very rarely use it in my work in games. For a more extensive look at the Trax Editor and its uses, take a look at *The Game Artist's Guide to Maya* (Sybex, 2005), my previous title.

### Selection Sets

An alternative to character sets that I use pretty often is *selection sets*. A selection set creates a node in the Outliner (Window > Outliner) that will list the desired objects, and creating one is much less time consuming and allows for easier selection access than a typical character set. To create a selection set, follow these steps:

**1.** Select all of the joints, groups, handles, and so on for which you want easy access.

**2.** With the selection active, go to Create > Sets > Set.

**3.** In the Outliner, at the bottom of the list, you'll now find a new node called Set1. Expand the node by clicking the + icon. Your selected objects now are listed cleanly for your access.

## Animation User Interface

The Maya user interface for animation is very straightforward and user friendly, and it is located at the bottom of the screen. It consists primarily of three areas: the Time Slider, the Range Slider, and the playback controls (Figure 2.23).

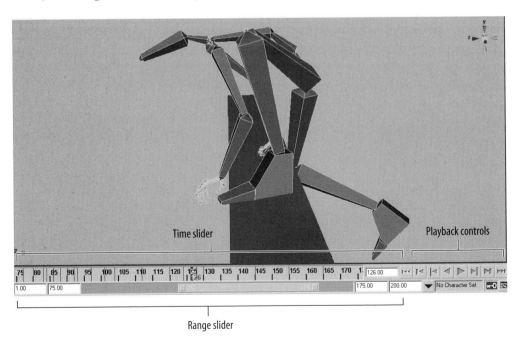

**Figure 2.23** The Maya animation user interface

## Time Slider

The Time Slider displays the playback range as well as the keys in the scene. Keyframes are displayed as red ticks or hash marks on the time slider. (You can change the appearance of key ticks in the preferences if you'd like.) The current time is indicated with a black box that can be dragged back and forth (or *scrubbed*) to actually run through the animation backward and forward in your active view. Within the Time Slider, you can edit keyframe positions much as you do in the Graph Editor or Dope Sheet. For example, you can cut, copy, and paste by right-clicking on the Time Slider and choosing the command from the menu that appears.

You can also move and scale keys from the Time Slider. If you press the Shift key and left-click and drag along the Time Slider, a red selection area will appear, highlighting the keys that you want to manipulate. The selection area will display an arrow at both ends as well as a double arrow in the center. Left-click and drag on the center arrows to move the selected keyframes. To scale them, left-click and drag on one of the arrows at either end.

## Range Slider

The Range Slider controls the playback range of available frames that the Time Slider will display. For example, if you had over 1,000 frames in your scene, it'd be far too difficult to view them all in the Time Slider. The Range Slider lets you display only a particular section.

There are two input boxes on either end of the Range Slider. On the left are the Start Time and Playback Start Time, while on the right are the Playback End Time and the End Time.

The Start and End Times indicate how many frames are in the entire animation from start to finish.

The Playback Start and End Times indicate how many frames are displayed in the Time Slider.

## Playback Controls

The playback controls are in the lower right of the interface and are very similar to typical VCR controls, but there are a few Maya-specific additions. From left to right, the controls are these:

**Go To Start** The Go To Start button returns the animation to the start of the displayed frames in the Time Slider.

**Step Back Frame** This button moves the animation backward one frame in time.

**Step Back Key** This button moves the animation backward to the next available keyframe.

**Play Backwards** This button plays the scene's animation backward, like a typical rewind command. While the animation is playing, this button changes into a Stop button.

**Play Forwards** This is a typical Play button, playing the scene forward. While the animation is playing, this button changes into a Stop button.

**Step Forward Key** This button moves the animation forward to the next available keyframe.

**Step Forward Frame** This button steps the animation forward one frame in time.

**Go to End** This button moves the animation to the end of the animation playback range displayed in the Time Slider.

## Upcoming Lessons

Animation in video games is really not all that different from animation in other media. The main differences are in the actual animations themselves. As mentioned in the beginning, most animations in video games are animation cycles or small sequences. These sequences can be as simple as a looping walk or run cycle that is used continuously or as complex as a scripted event that happens only once in the entire game.

Now you're familiar with the majority of the basics of animation concepts, techniques, tools, and commands that are used not only in games but in nearly all animated media. The following sections of this book will give you a real animation project to work on. Think of yourself as an animator in a studio, and you've just been handed a finished model and given the task of bringing that model to life.

There are four main projects included in this book, representing four basic archetypal animated forms:

**Biped** A biped character is a typical humanoid character with two arms and two legs. The Calamity Jane project in Chapter 3 will focus on this form.

**Quadruped** A quadruped character is a typical animalistic character, with four legs and a tail. In the Dire Wolf project in Chapter 4, I will discuss this form.

**Spinal** A spinal character isn't technically a basic archetype as much as a particular case where long sinewy forms are used, such as an octopus. Chapter 5 will focus on this form with the Giant Kraken project.

**Inorganic** An inorganic character could be most anything, but in this particular case, we'll be animating a mechanical, robotic, fantasy vehicle. In Chapter 6 I'll discuss this form in the Storm Tank project.

In addition to these four main project scenes, in Chapter 7 I'll go over lip synching and and acting and how it is used in animation. For Chapter 8 I'll focus on some miscellaneous special-case forms and situations—wings, blobby movement, and a standard vehicular suspension.

I hope you enjoy these projects!

## Artist Profile: Scott Ruggels

**Job Title** Senior animator

**Studio** Castaway Entertainment L.L.C.

**Credits** *Johnny Mosely: Mad Trix, Army Men, Army Men II, Army Men: Toys In Space, Army Men: World War, Army Men: Green Rogue, High Heat Baseball*

**Personal Site** http://www.rdwarf.com/ruggels

**Q.** How and why did you get into the game industry?

**A.** I got into the game industry oddly enough as a favor to friends. I had always wanted to be a classical animator growing up. Anything that wasn't a cartoon didn't hold my interest, and that view of television and movies persisted into college. My parents would not spring for the tuition for me to go to Cal Arts, so I went to San Jose State and sort of put the idea of being an animator to the side…until I flunked out of college.

At that point, I had to get a day job, and it was a series of crappy contract security jobs at hospitals and Silicon Valley computer companies, doing freelance illustration and inking comic books on the side. All the while, I'm still taking animation and computer art classes at night. In December of 1991, while I was a guard at Apple Computer Inc., former associates of mine from Hero Games, a publisher of paper-and-pencil–based role-playing games, approached me to do animated sprites and background art for a computer realization of their superhero game. The project was called *Champions: The Computer Roleplaying Game*, and after getting the cover of Computer Gaming World in March of 1993, the project became the biggest vaporware product of the time and was suspended shortly after, without a word to the world or the press. I think *Duke Nuk'em Forever* has now taken the title, but for a while *Champions* was the epitome of vaporware.

**Q.** Describe your role at your studio.

**A.** Castaway Entertainment L.L.C. is a small developer of about 25 people based in Redwood City, California. I am one of four people in the character team, the people responsible for the characters and creatures used in our game. There are also an environments team, a design team, and an engineering team. In the character team, the roles are pretty loose, and as our project continued over the past year and a half, my duties have evolved. At first I would model characters, based on the concept art of the art lead, Rick Macaraeg. Since the models were to be animated, my emphasis in making the geometry was in ensuring that there was enough mesh around the joints so the character wouldn't "beer can," or collapse when it moved. I'd then apply the skeleton and paint the weights on the model, and while it was being rigged, I would work on the textures. Then, depending on the current workload, I'd either animate the character or hand it off to Kelly Johnson to animate. At the beginning, people were responsible for the characters from the time they were handed the concept art to the point they were imported

*Continues*

## Artist Profile: Scott Ruggels *(Continued)*

into the game engine. This was inefficient, and over time the team organized around their strengths. While I was a fast and good modeler, I was not very good at painting texture maps, was pretty good at painting weights, but apparently was a superior animator. So eventually I ended up mostly animating and doing research projects for the engineers for the animation and AI systems they were coming up with in the Unreal 3 engine.

**Q.** What has been the most inspirational to you in regard to your artwork?

**A.** Just about everything that moves. I am easily distracted by movement. I had one of those lousy jobs, driving an armored car through the crime-infested streets of downtown Oakland, California. When we stopped to make a pick up or delivery, I'd have to be extra observant, watching all the people around me. In doing so, often my animator's instincts would take over and I would observe the "walk cycles" of the people. You'd see the hip sway and precise "heel toe" of the young women trying to look good. Or you'd see the jog/walk of the businesspeople in a hurry, the unhurried rhythmic swagger of the teenage hip-hop males. Then there were the walks of the infirm and the homeless who would pass by, lurching like broken robot toys. It was basically a good job to observe people and animals closely, as if your life depended on it, because in a way, it did.

In terms of other artistic inspirations, of course Ray Harryhausen, *Star Wars*, but also classic Warner Brothers, and the economy of sixties' Hanna-Barbera adventure cartoons. These days, I am always impressed with the accuracy and honesty of the emotional portrayals in Pixar's work, but then they always have rock-solid stories as well. But for me, a lot of the effects work and digital characters appearing in live-action film [inspire me]. I am also inspired by the work of people I see at the Massive Black workshops, my peers on Polycount.com, and also comic books. Like I said, just about anything is inspirational.

**Q.** What is your favorite style of animation to work with?

**A.** I don't really have a favorite style, but my preference is "away" from the silhouette pantomime and "circularity" of classic Disney, as it doesn't seem to work really well in 3D since it plays to an audience assumed to be in a theater, rather than to an audience that could be viewing the action from any angle. But in most cases you will be animating to what your project needs, whether it is a style lacking in any anticipation but having a profligate follow-through such as for a fight game, so that the move occurs precisely when the player presses the button, to the broadly played animation of action RPGs so that the characters look epic and their actions will read even if they are only a few pixels tall on the screen. You also may be required to enhance or fix motion capture data by fixing foot slide and adding finger, hand, and face animation to prerecorded sequences. You sort of can't have a favorite if you want to do the best for each particular project as it comes along.

**Q.** What is your favorite kind of game?

**A.** To play? That's easy. Give me a good First-Person Shooter (FPS). Right now it's *Battlefield 2* and *Unreal Tournament 2004*, and I am drooling in anticipation of *Quakeworld* and *Unreal 2007*. As you can tell, these are PC games rather than console titles. I really prefer the precision of mouse and keyboard controls. I also like to tinker with FPS games and add custom characters. That was how I found Polycount.com. I don't have the patience for massive multiplayer online games as I think that simulating labor by farming and grinding should result in them paying me, because it is real time I am burning doing the boring stuff. Also, I come from an age where role-playing means playing a role other than yourself in a game, to immerse yourself into another character's thoughts and deeds, but in these games, it's just a Halloween party with swords. Might be fun to work on a game like that. I also like to play flight simulators, but I'm really bad at them. Real-Time Strategy (RTS) games make me panic and hide under the table, because I cannot juggle a lot of variables in a stress situation. Just give me a mess of bullets and a target, and I am a happy camper.

**Q.** Which Maya animation tool, command, or editor could you not live without?

**A.** That's easy: Pose2shelf. Without that, making game animations that link up properly would be a nightmare. Next to that would be the Graph Editor and the Dope Sheet in tandem, because I am one who believes in keeping their curves and keyframes clean. If you can edit a curve instead of putting in another key, you can edit your work so much easier. Also, with the Dope Sheet I can play with the timing of the animation and edit it without messing the curves up. Also, the way it can scale time and select all the keys on that particular frame—heaven.

**Q.** What advice might you have for the up-and-coming animator?

**A.** If you are just starting out, there is no better training than getting a pad of stationary and a pen or pencil and drawing flipbooks so that you learn the basics of motion and timing. Play with it so that you can figure out how things look when you move with different numbers of frames or directions. It also helps if you have a DVD player that has a jog shuttle or single-frame capability forward and backward so you can analyze cartoons and other animated fare. Watching how others do it is a good learning tool, but few things beat hands on. If you don't have Maya right now, go get a cheap program like Hash: Animation Master, just so you can get the experience in animating characters; Hash has the best animation tools for the money. If you have Maya already, do as many tutorials as you can on animation, and once you feel confident about that, then volunteer with a video game modifications [or MODs] team as an animator, learn the editor, and start making the characters dance. If the MOD is bad, you will have learned something. If the MOD is good, you may get a job from it as well as the respect of your peers.

But above all, let your passion for it pull you along, through the tedium of learning curves and tutorials, the bad day jobs, and the frustrations with the software puzzles and issues. If you love animation, let it pull you through. If you don't love it, then you may want to look at another career.

# Project: Calamity Jane

**3**

*Your first animation assignment is to rig and animate Calamity Jane, one of the main playable characters for a next-generation console game, a sci-fi/Western shoot-'em-up action title. This game character is going to have all the bells and whistles, with very few restrictions.*

**In this chapter, we'll cover the following topics:**

Assignment Breakdown

Tutorial: Blend Shapes

Tutorial: Rigging Calamity Jane

Tutorial: Walk Cycle

Tutorial: Action Sequence

## Assignment Breakdown

Calamity Jane is a higher resolution model than what has been considered a typical character in the past. With the advancements that consoles such as the Sony Playstation3 and the Microsoft Xbox 360 give us, as well as the increased power of the gaming PC, we suddenly find ourselves with a lot more flexibility.

To get our feet wet and really delve into this first project, we won't be too terribly restricted as to what we can use to control Jane. The controls include plenty of joints for fully articulated fingers as well as an adequate number of joints for the flowing movement of Jane's coat (I'll explain this further in the sidebar below). In a real project, you'd definitely have to conform to a limited number of joints.

## Tutorial: Blend Shapes

The first step is to get Jane's face ready for animation by creating a series of blend shape target meshes. Each one will control a different aspect of the character's facial movement, such as eye blinking, mouth movement, and facial expressions.

1. 💿 Browse on the CD to Project_Files/Chapter_3/Calamity_Jane. Copy the Calamity_Jane directory to your hard drive. Open the file Calamity_Jane_Start.ma from the Scenes directory.

   This file contains the modeled and textured geometry for the Calamity Jane character model.

2. Select the following items: Head, LEye, REye, REyelash, LEyelash, Tongue, UpperTeeth, and LowerTeeth.

3. Go to Edit > Duplicate > Options. In the options, choose Edit > Reset Settings. This resets the Duplicate command's options to their default settings, just in case they might have been set differently from an earlier project.

4. Click the Duplicate button. Your selected geometry will be duplicated right on top of the originals and will remain selected. Move these duplicates to the side, away from your model, so you can get to them easily.

5. Duplicate them again (Ctrl+D). Move this second duplicated set farther to the side, out of the way (Figure 3.1).

 **Note:** Make certain that you do not use the Freeze Transformations (Modify > Freeze Transformations) command on the duplicated heads that you intend to use to make blend shapes, because it will cause the blending to react negatively.

## Behind Calamity Jane

Calamity Jane is designed to be the main playable character of an action video game. Because she is featured and central to her game, she is a bit more complicated than a typical video game character, both in her design and in her construction. She has fully articulated fingers and face, allowing for wide freedom of movement in these areas. The coat she wears presents an interesting challenge as it will need to be constantly acting and reacting to Jane's movements during game play.

She consists of approximately 9,000 polygons and currently uses four higher-resolution textures for this book's printing and display purposes (two $1024 \times 1024$ and two $512 \times 512$ resolution textures). In an actual game project, the texture resolutions a model would use would usually be lower and would be combined to make as few needed texture tiles as possible (just one $1024 \times 1024$ or just two $512 \times 512$ resolution textures, for example). However, because Jane is designed to be a main playable character, we'll give her some leeway since she will literally be on the screen at all times and with different costumes and weapons as the game progresses.

Jane's pistol consists of approximately 550 polygons and uses one $512 \times 512$ resolution texture, again for the purposes of printing. In an actual game, this texture would more than likely be reduced to a much smaller $256 \times 256$, and unless it is a major weapon in the game, its *polycount* (or the number of polygons it is made of) could be lowered as well.

Your art lead will make any art limitations and requirements known to you in a real project, of course.

Jane was designed by Steve Garcia and built by Michael McKinley, the author.

Concept art by Steve Garcia

**Figure 3.1** Duplicated heads in preparation for creating blend shape targets

## Creating Blend Shape Targets

The eyes and teeth won't actually play any part in the creation of the blend shape targets you are about to make, but having them in position will make it easier to know where they should be when you make the targets. This way, you won't accidentally have the face intersect the eyeballs or teeth during their animation.

There are many standard blend shape targets you will want to make, depending on what your character is designed to do. These mostly are *phoneme shapes*, which consist of major vocal forms for the mouth to utilize during lip-synching for dialogue. Others are simple facial expressions, such as blend shape targets for blinking, opening and closing the mouth, smiling, frowning, and so on.

6. On the first duplicated head, manipulate the vertices to produce a look suitable for Jane's mouth being open, as if for a yell or yawn.

   As you can quickly tell, you will need to move the duplicated LowerTeeth1 and Tongue1 objects to accommodate this change in the character's jaw position.

7. Go ahead and reposition the LowerTeeth1 and Tongue1 objects to get a feel for where the actual teeth and tongue will eventually need to go for the actual model (Figure 3.2).

8. Rename this modified head (just the head itself and not the other items that make up the duplicated face) **MouthOpen**. For organizational purposes, you can select all the objects that make up the MouthOpen face and group them (Ctrl+G); name this group **MouthOpen_Group**.

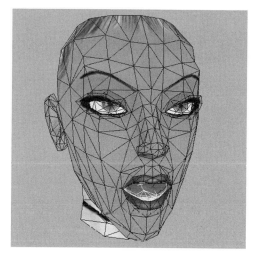

**Figure 3.2** The open mouth blend shape target with repositioned teeth

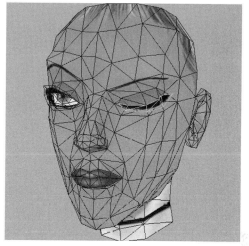

**Figure 3.3** The left eye closed with the eyelash and surrounding skin modified to match

9. Select the set of objects that make up the second duplicated head, duplicate them all again (**Ctrl+D**), and move this third set to the side.

Each time you start to create a new blend shape target, you'll want to have a newly duplicated clean copy to the side. This way you will always have an unmodified head to start from in case you think of a new blend shape target that you want to make later on.

10. Modify the second duplicated head to close the left eyelid. Keep in mind the position of the left eyeball.

11. Obviously, like the teeth, the left eyelash won't go with your modifications automatically, so grab its vertices and adjust them to fit with the closed eyelid (Figure 3.3). Don't forget to adjust the features surrounding the eye to accentuate the blinking and make it seem more real. The left brow should lower and the skin directly beneath the eye should lift upward, for example.

12. Once you have it the way you want it, rename this head mesh **LEye_Close** and the modified eyelash **LEyelash_Close**. Select all the pieces that make up this head and group them together (Ctrl+G); name the group **LEye_CloseGroup**.

13. Grab the fresh, unmodified head that you made earlier, duplicate it once again, and move the copy to the side. You'll do this between each new blend shape target that you make!

14. Modify duplicate 3 to show the right eye closed, just like we did for the left eye. Then name the applicable objects **REye_Close**, **REyelash_Close**, and **REye_CloseGroup**.

Continue to make more blend shape target heads as desired, modifying the eyelashes and positions of the teeth and tongue objects as necessary. Also, rename each modified mesh to indicate what that blend shape target is actually doing. Lastly, group each set to make them easy to find and identify and to keep them separate from their counterpart objects on the actual model.

One rule of thumb to keep in mind is to not modify the eyes and the mouth (or another part of the face that moves) in the same blend shape target. This way, you can have multiple combinations of eye movements and mouth movements to easily create many new expressions. This gives you the flexibility and freedom to create a greater number of facial expressions but with fewer targets.

 The file Calamity_Jane_Blends.ma found in the Project_Files/ Chapter_3/ Calamity_Jane/Scenes folder will show you how far I took the blend shapes (Figure 3.4). You could go much further depending on how complex you want the character's facial movement to be.

**Note:** You can duplicate a previously modified blend shape to create new blend shapes as well. For example, if you want to create an expression that is similar to that of the MouthOpen shape target, you can duplicate it and modify it further to create a new one rather than starting from scratch.

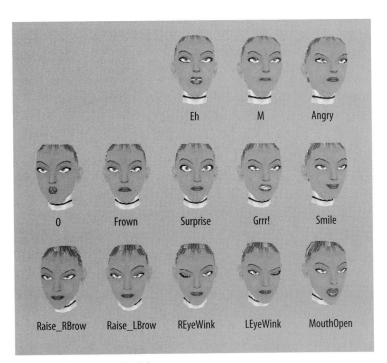

**Figure 3.4** Calamity Jane's blend shapes

## Assigning Blend Shapes

Now, once all your blend shape targets are created, you can assign them to the character's face.

**1.** Select each modified head (not the modified eyelashes or any other meshes). Shift+click the original head *last*.

**2.** Go to Deform > Create Blend Shape > Options in the Animation menu set (F2). Here, name the BlendShape node **Face_Blends**. Click Create.

**3.** Now select each modified *left* eyelash. Make certain that you select only the left eyelashes you have modified and not any unmodified LEyelash objects and not any of the REyelash objects.

If you are starting with the Calamity_Jane_Blends.ma file from the CD, these would be LEyelash_Close, LEyelash_Surprise, and LEyelash_Angry. None of the other LEyelash objects were changed for their blend shape targets, so you don't need to use them.

**4.** With the modified LEyelash objects selected, Shift+click the original LEyelash object *last*. Go to Deform > Create Blend Shape > Options. Name the BlendShape node **LEye_Blends**.

**5.** Repeat this with the REyelash objects. Make sure that you are selecting only the ones that you modified and not the unmodified eyelash objects. Also, be certain that the original mesh that you want to apply these blend shapes to is selected last. Name the BlendShape node **REye_Blends**.

All of the blend shape targets are now applied. Go to Window > Animation Editors > Blend Shape. Here in the Blend Shape Editor you can see sliders that correspond with each blend shape target applied in the scene (Figure 3.5).

**Figure 3.5**

The Blend Shape Editor window with the applied blend shapes in the scene

Feel free to play with the sliders and see how the model reacts. You may notice that when the eyes close, the eyeballs peek out from behind the lids. If that's the case, you can modify the blend shape target to adjust how the geometry deforms and fix any intersection problems.

## Setting Up Set Driven Key

As it now stands, you have to adjust two sliders in order for the eyelid and the eyelash to close. Let's see if we can make that happen automatically using Set Driven Key.

1. In the Blend Shape Editor, press the Select button for the set of blend shapes called LEye_Blends. This selects that set of blend shape targets.

2. Go to Animate > Set Driven Key > Set > Options. Because you had the LEye_Blends set selected when you opened the Set Driven Key options, it automatically is placed in the Driven section of the options window.

3. Back in the Blend Shape Editor, press the Select button for the set of blend shapes called Head_Blends. This selects the head's blend shapes. In the Set Driven Key options, press the Load Driver button. This places the Head_Blends set in the Driver section of the options window.

4. In the right side of the Driver's section of the options are all of the attributes of the Head_Blends, including the blend shapes themselves. Select the LEye_Close blend shape in the Driver section.

5. In the right side of the Driven's section of the options, select the LEyelash_Close blend shape. Press the Key button. This sets a key for the current relationship between the Driver and the Driven, in this case, the LEye_Close and LEyelash_Close blend shapes.

6. Raise the LEye_Close blend shape slider all the way up. This will close the head's left eye. Now, raise the LEyelash_Close blend shape slider all the way up. This will obviously close the left eyelash. Back in the Set Driven Key options, press the Key button again.

7. Raise and lower the LEye_Close blend shape slider and test to see if the Set Driven Key operates properly. You should see the obvious result of the left eyelash opening and closing along with the eye.

Repeat these steps for both eyelashes, linking the following together:

| Driven | Driver |
| --- | --- |
| REyelash_Close | REye_Close |
| REyelash_Surprise | Surprise |
| LEyelash_Surprise | Surprise |
| REyelash_Angry | Angry |
| LEyelash_Angry | Angry |

### Teeth and Tongue

Now, we're going to use Set Driven Key to make the teeth and tongue move automatically along with the mouth movements, just like the eyelashes with the eye movements.

**1.** Select the LowerTeeth object. Go to Animate > Set Driven Key > Set > Options. Just like before, the LowerTeeth object is automatically placed in the Driven section.

**2.** Select the Head_Blends blend shape from the Blend Shape Editor. Click the Load Driver button in the Set Driven Key options.

**3.** In the right side of the Driver's section, select the MouthOpen blend shape attribute. In the right side of the Driven's section, select all three Translate attributes and all three Rotate attributes.

**4.** Lower the MouthOpen blend shape slider to 0 if it isn't there already. Press the Key button.

**5.** Now, raise the MouthOpen blend shape slider back up to 1, which opens the mouth all the way. Reposition the LowerTeeth object, setting it in a location that would work for the new lower jaw position.

**6.** Repeat for the tongue, setting a key (in the Set Driven Key options) with the MouthOpen slider set to 0 and the tongue in its original position, and set another key with the slider at 1 and the tongue repositioned (Figure 3.6).

Repeat these steps with the teeth and tongue objects for any other blend shapes that have the mouth open and require movement of the teeth and/or tongue, such as the Eh mouth shape in my provided file.

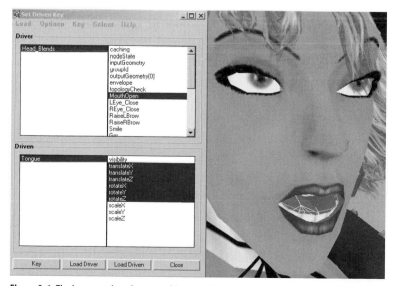

**Figure 3.6** The lower teeth and tongue objects in place

**Blinking**

At the moment, to do a simple blink, we have to raise both the LEye_Close and REye_Close blend shape sliders. Let's create a new one for a quick Blink blend shape.

1.  Raise both sliders to close both eyes. Select the original Head mesh. In the Blend Shape Editor, click the Add button under the Head_Blends section.

2.  A new duplicate of the head's current state is created on top of the original. Move it to the side and rename it **Blink**. In the Blend Shape Editor, a new slider has been added. Rename it **Blink** as well by typing in the input box that contains the name.

3.  Repeat the Set Driven Key steps listed previously to have both eyelashes close with the blinking motion.

If you find other blend shape combinations that you really like, you can repeat these steps with those elements to create a single slider that will result in the facial expression you want easier and quicker access to.

Once you've finished, the controls for the facial animation should all be in place! Have fun playing with the sliders, making different combinations of facial expressions. You may be surprised at the kind of combinations you can make (Figure 3.7)!

Now would be a good time to save your file!

 **Note:** It's a general rule of thumb to never save over your previous files but to always save new files numbered sequentially as they are made. That way, if CalamityJane_4.mb suddenly became corrupted or lost, you at least have CalamityJane_3.mb to fall back on—as opposed to losing it all!

**Figure 3.7** "You're making me wear *that*?"

## Tutorial: Rigging Calamity Jane

Now, let's focus on setting up Calamity Jane's skeleton. We'll start with the spine.

1. Activate the Joint Tool under Skeleton > Joint Tool. From the Front view, place the first joint in the pelvis region, about 4.88 units high from the floor plane. Hold the Shift key and place three more joints about 0.3 units apart, up the spine in a straight line.

2. Place the next joint a little above the clavicle beneath the base of the neck.

3. The next joint should go at the top of the neck, about even with the lower lip in the front view.

4. Place the last joint at the top of the head.

5. Now, switch to the Side view. The joints we've just placed for the spine are going up in a straight line, but we want them to curve along the back.

6. Press the Insert key on the keyboard. This activates edit pivot mode. For geometry and most other objects, this will let you reposition an object's pivot point. For joints, however, this will let you move the joint without moving other joints within the chain.

7. Position each of the previously placed joints as shown in Figure 3.8, setting them along the path of the spine.

8. Rename these joints **Pelvis, BackWaist, BackLow, BackMid, BackHigh, Head,** and **Hat**, in the order they were placed.

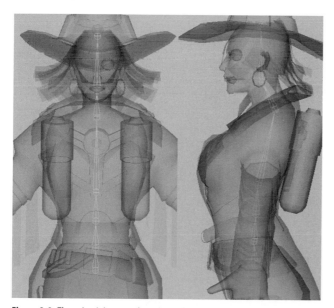

**Figure 3.8** The spine joints set along Jane's back

## Creating Leg and Feet Joints

We'll continue the skeleton by placing the leg and feet joints.

1. In the Front view, place a joint at the approximate location of the left hip.

2. Place the next joint at the middle knee and a third at the ankle.

3. Switch to the Side view and, much like with the spine, reposition these joints as shown in Figure 3.9, with a slight bend in the knee.

4. Rename these joints **LHip**, **LKnee**, and **LAnkle** in the order they were placed.

5. Select the LHip joint and Shift+click the Pelvis joint. Go to Edit > Parent (or the **p** shortcut key) to parent (or link) the leg joint chain to the spine's hierarchy.

 **Note:** To unparent something, select it, and press P (Shift+p) or go to Edit > Unparent.

6. In the Side view, place three joints in a horizontal line, the first at the base of the heel, the second at the point where the toe starts to bend upward, and the third at the tip of the toe.

7. Rename these **LHeel**, **LBall**, and **LToe**, respectively. Select the LHeel joint and Shift+click the LAnkle joint. Press **p** to parent the foot joint chain to the leg's hierarchy (Figure 3.10).

8. Back in the Front view, you can see the newly placed joints positioned at the origin, between the character's legs. Move these to the right, centering them in the foot.

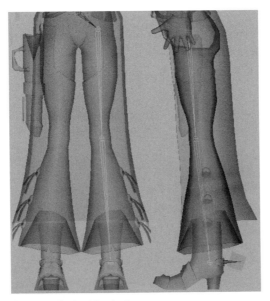

**Figure 3.9** The leg joints in place

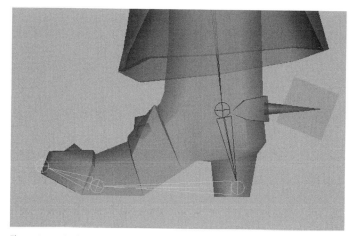

**Figure 3.10** The foot joints in place

## Set Preferred Angle

Eventually the knee will need to bend, and we want it to bend naturally. The best way to make it do so is to directly tell it what angle we want it to bend. We do this by setting a joint's preferred angle.

1. Select the LKnee joint. Rotate it backward, as if Jane was pulling her leg back.

2. Right-click and hold, which opens the joint's marking menu. Move your cursor up and select the Set Preferred Angle option.

3. Rotate the knee back to its original position.

## Setting Up the Arm Skeleton

Next, we'll place the joints for the arms and hands.

1. In the Front view, place a joint at about the left-middle chest.

2. Place a second joint where the arm merges into the coat, the next at the elbow, and one more at the wrist.

3. Rename them **LClavicle**, **LShoulder**, **LElbow**, and **LWrist**, respectively.

4. Parent the LClavicle joint to the BackMid joint to attach it to the skeleton's hierarchy.

5. Go to the Persp view now, and you can see that the arm joints are behind the arm geometry. Move them forward and rotate them to place them within the arm's mesh. Take a look at Figure 3.11 and note the slight bend in the elbow.

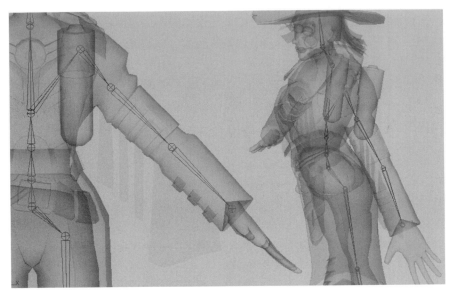

**Figure 3.11** The arm joints placed along the arm mesh

### Hand Skeleton

For Jane's hands, we'll use full articulation. This method creates an individual three-joint chain for each finger.

1. In the Front view, place four joints along the approximate locations of the three major knuckles and the tip of the finger, as in Figure 3.12. In the Persp view, reposition the joints to run along the middle finger.

2. You didn't read the above wrong. We *are* going to use three-joint chains for the fingers. The reason why the fourth joint is placed is to line up the previous three to run along the finger. The last joint in the chain is generally not aligned like this, so setting one extra joint along the chain aligns the previous one. There are ways of realigning a joint's rotation, but this is a bit of a shortcut. Now that we've placed four joints along the finger, we can select and delete the fourth joint, leaving the aligned three-joint chain behind.

3. Rename the joints **LFinger2A**, **LFinger2B**, and **LFinger2C** in the order they were placed.

4. Duplicate (Ctrl+D) the joint chain and move it to the index finger, repositioning the joints to align with the new finger's knuckles. Rename these **LFinger1A**, **B**, and **C**, respectively.

5. Duplicate the chain two more times, placing them along the ring finger and little finger, aligning the joints with the finger knuckles. Rename the ring finger joints **LFinger3A**, **B**, and **C**. Rename the little finger joints **LFinger4A**, **B**, and **C**.

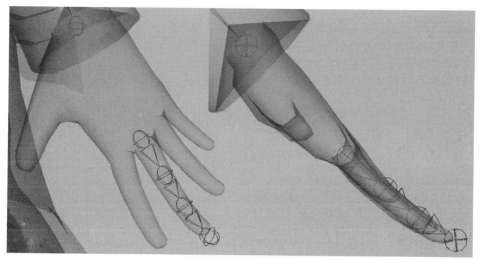

**Figure 3.12** A four-joint finger chain in place

**6.** Duplicate the chain one more time, and position this new joint sequence along the thumb.

Unlike the fingers, the thumb only has two major rotation points—where it connects to the palm and about halfway up the thumb. So, with this in mind, delete the third joint in the chain, as only the two joints are needed.

**7.** Rename these joints **ThumbA** and **ThumbB**.

**8.** To connect all these fingers to the hierarchy, select each of the fingers labeled as A: LFinger1A, LFinger2A, LFinger3A, LFinger4A, and LThumbA. Shift+click the LWrist joint and press the p shortcut key, parenting the finger joint chains to the wrist (Figure 3.13).

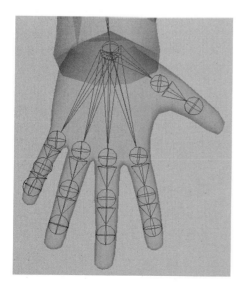

**Figure 3.13**
The completed hand skeleton

## Hand Skeleton Formations

Depending on a game's limitations, a character's hands can be rigged several ways, all giving you different levels of control for different game-play scenarios.

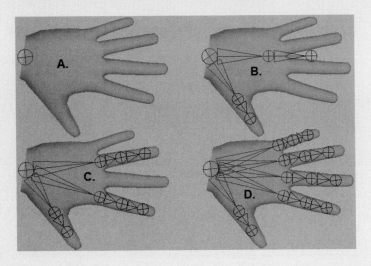

**A. No articulation** This hand rig is seldom done these days, except in lower-powered 3D hand-held games and Real-Time Strategy (RTS) games that have potentially hundreds of characters on the screen at once. This essentially is simply parenting the entire hand to the wrist, with no finger articulation at all. In this case, the hands are generally modeled to resemble a fist, since it isn't quite as strange visually if a character in a game has his hands in fists the entire time.

**B. Single chain** This hand setup is generally used when a hand's mesh consists of *mits* (or mittens). In this setup there are no individual fingers but a sectional piece of geometry that makes up all four fingers, looking much like a mitten.

**C. Trigger finger** In a game where the majority of the action takes place with projectile weapons, many times only the trigger finger of the four fingers would be rigged individually, while the remainder make use of a single chain of joints. In such cases, the three fingers might not be modeled individually either, depending on what kind of polycount the game in question gives to its characters.

**D. Full articulation** And of course, there is full hand articulation! This is what we'll use for Jane.

### Local Rotation Axis

We laid out an extra joint for the fingers to align the rotation of the last joint we wanted to keep on the chain. We didn't do that for the arms, however, so the wrist joint is *not* currently aligned with the rest of the chain. Select the LElbow joint, for example. Notice that the rotation handles are aligned with the path of the arm joints, letting you rotate the elbow naturally.

Now, select the wrist joint. Do you see the difference? The wrist joint's rotation handles aren't aligned with the wrist's angle, so rotating it is unnatural and can be confusing to animate. Let's change the joint's local rotation axis to align with the arm for easier animation.

1. Select the LWrist joint. Press the F8 key to enter component mode, or press the Select by Component Type button in the status line of the interface. The skeleton will turn blue, indicating the switch to component mode.

2. To the right of the Select by Component Type button in the status line are the component selection masks. These determine what kind of components you are able to manipulate based on which are enabled. To select and manipulate the local rotation axis of an object, you'll need to enable the Select by Component Type: Miscellaneous mask, indicated by the question mark icon. Disable any other active masks.

3. You'll notice that the LWrist joint as well as each of the attached finger joints have a small translation axis at their positions. This small axis indicates the orientation of a joint's local rotation axis. Select the axis located on the LWrist, and rotate it to be aligned with the arm's orientation, as the finger joints are (Figure 3.14).

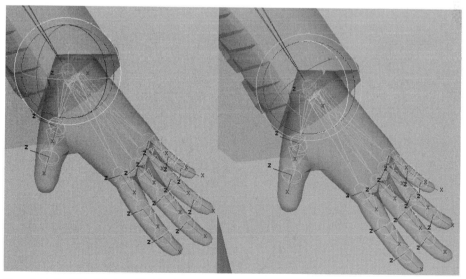

**Figure 3.14** The LWrist joint's modified local rotation axis

## Mirroring Joints

Now that we have the basic skeleton for the spine, left arm, and left leg complete, we can mirror the joint chains for the arm and leg on the right side.

**1.** Select the LClavicle joint. Go to Skeleton > Mirror Joint > Options. In the options, set the following:

- Mirror Across: YZ
- Search For: L
- Replace With: R

The Mirror Across option tells the selected joint chain to mirror across the YZ axis, from the positive X to the negative X.

The Search For and Replace With options rename the mirrored joints, changing the L to an R.

**2.** Repeat the process with the LHip joint.

You should end up with a completed basic skeleton, with the right arm and leg in place and renamed with an R prefix.

## Creating Specialized Joints

Calamity Jane is composed of a number of different unique components not found on a generic character: the fringe hanging from the arms of the coat, the tassels on the lower legs, the holster, not to mention the coat itself. We'll have to accommodate these things in the rigging of the character if we want to animate them accurately, especially for secondary animation as described in Chapter 2.

Let's start with the fringes under the arms. They need at least two bones: one for the fringe under the upper arm, another for the fringe under the forearm.

**1.** In the Front view, use the Joint Tool (Skeleton > Joint Tool) and place a joint at about the center of the leather fringe under the character's left upper arm. Press Enter.

**2.** Place another joint under the left lower arm, again at the center of the fringe. Press Enter.

**3.** Make sure they are positioned accurately in the Persp view. The ideal place for them would be at the point where their geometry is divided.

**4.** Rename these joints **LLeather1** and **LLeather2**, respectively. Parent the LLeather1 joint to the LShoulder joint. Parent the LLeather2 joint to the LElbow joint (Figure 3.15).

**5.** You can repeat these steps with the right arm's fringe, or you can delete the right arm and remirror the left arm across with these new joints added to the chain. Either way, make sure you rename them with an R prefix rather than the L.

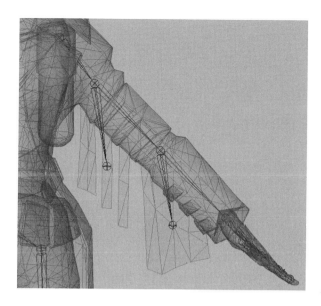

**Figure 3.15** The leather fringe joints in place under the left arm

Watch out for the Search and Replace feature of the Mirror Joint command renaming your objects RReather1 rather than the desired RLeather1!

### Holster

The holster is a loose object that is attached near the character's hip. When Jane eventually moves around, we'll expect the holster to react with secondary motion. So, let's create a joint that will control this motion.

1.  In the Front view, place a single joint in the middle of the strap holding the holster to Calamity Jane's chaps. Press Enter.

2.  In the Persp view, reposition this joint to be centered on the strap, and rotate it to align with the holster's orientation.

3.  Rename this joint **Holster_Joint**, and parent it to the Pelvis joint.

### Leg Tassels

The lower legs each have three cloth tassels. Depending on what kind of joint limitations we may be dealing with for a real project, we could either have a single joint for all six or just have two joints, one for each side. Since this project is primarily to get your feet wet, we'll go ahead and give a joint to each tassel.

1.  In the Front view, using the Joint Tool, position a single joint (pressing the Enter key after each one) at the point where each tassel meets the leg.

2.  In the Persp view, reposition the joints to be centered and rotate them to align them along with the orientation of their respective tassel.

3. Rename them **LLeg_Tassel1, 2, 3** and **RLeg_Tassel1, 2, 3**, as applicable.

4. Parent the left tassel joints to the LKnee joint. Parent the right tassel joints to the RKnee joint (Figure 3.16).

### Earrings

Small details like the earrings may not always be high on the priority list of things to devote joints to, but again, in this case, we're not worrying about restrictions.

1. In the Front view, position a single joint (pressing the Enter key after each one) at the point where each earring meets its ear.

2. In the Persp view, reposition them to be centered and rotate them to align their orientation with the rotation of the earring objects.

3. Rename them **LEarring_Joint** and **REarring_Joint** as applicable.

4. Parent both joints to the Head joint.

### Hair

The hair isn't always rigged either, unless it's long. Calamity Jane's hair looks like it could have some good bounce to it, though. We'll use one or two simple joints to add some subtle secondary hair movement to our animation.

1. In the Side view, this time position a single joint near the back of Jane's head, within the thickness of her hair. Press Enter.

2. Place a second joint near her forehead for the bangs. We'll have those strands of hair animate separately from the main clump of hair. Press Enter.

3. Rename these joints **Hair1** and **Hair2**, respectively. Parent them to the Head joint (Figure 3.17).

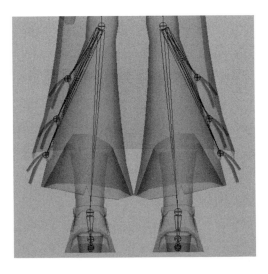

**Figure 3.16**
Leg tassel joints at their final positions

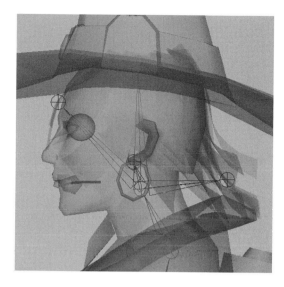

**Figure 3.17**
The hair joints positioned on the head

### Chest

Let's face it, as a woman with Jane's ... physical characteristics ... runs, walks, and so on, certain parts of her anatomy tend to have a bit of secondary bounce to them. Now, obviously, we don't need to go crazy and be obscene with it (as some games that I'll fail to mention here *have*, in my opinion), but for the sake of that all-important dynamism, we'll add a joint for such control. Believe me, you *will* be asked to accommodate this type of secondary animation in your rig somehow on some occasions in an actual job, depending on the game project in question.

1. In the Side view, place a single joint near the chest area of the character. Rename it Chest.

2. Parent it to the BackMid joint (Figure 3.18).

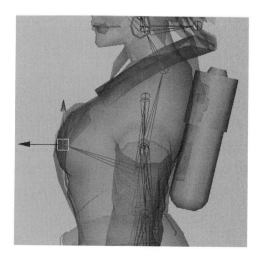

**Figure 3.18**
The Chest joint in place

### Coat

Now for the coat, probably the most complicated addition this character presents to an animator that a typical character doesn't have. It's almost like a separate character unto itself that is constantly reacting to the movements Jane makes!

I think the best way to handle it is to completely ignore it until you are happy with Jane's actual body movements. Then go back and animate the coat to react to them. If you animate the coat right along with the body, you'll soon find that as you go back and make changes and tweak keyframe positions and values for Jane's body movement, you'll constantly be going back and forth, changing the coat reaction to accommodate the changes.

Before we worry about that, however, we need to set up the coat's skeleton. We'll want to place the joints at points where the geometry has a division to allow for movement. The easiest way to see this is to turn on Shading > Wireframe on Shaded as well as Shading > X-Ray from the viewport menus.

1. In the Side view, start a chain of seven joints behind Jane's waist, and work your way down the back of the coat's profile, placing joints along the way at points that allow deformation (Figure 3.19).

2. Rename these joints **CoatBack1–7**. Select CoatBack1 at the top of the chain and parent it to the BackWaist joint.

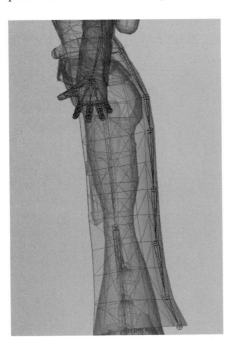

**Figure 3.19**
A joint chain positioned along the back of the coat.

**3.** With CoatBack1 selected, duplicate the joint chain (Ctrl+D), and move it to Jane's left side. Position these joints along the left side of the coat, making sure to position them on the same edge loops on which the back joints are positioned.

Also, make sure to rotate the joints (or adjust their local rotation axis) to align their orientation with the flow of the coat.

**4.** Rename these joints **LCoat1–7**.

**5.** Use the Mirror Joint command to create the right side of the coat's chain of joints. The Find and Replace option should automatically rename them **RCoat1–7** (Figure 3.20).

We've now completed our skeleton rig (Figure 3.21). As you can see, we have quite a few joints, typically many more than a generic game character would have. However, because Calamity Jane is the playable, key character for our "game" and we're also making this character as if for a high-end game engine, with lots of bells and whistles, she isn't too unusual, as no other character in the game would be like her.

For a typical enemy character or non-playable character (NPC), however, we'd be going a bit overboard here and would need to figure out how to reduce our joint count considerably. The most obvious joints we could sacrifice are some of the specialty joints we've created, such as the tassel joints on the lower legs, the earring joints, and the hair joints. None of them are really necessary. We could also sacrifice a bit of articulation in the coat, perhaps limiting the joint chains used there to four rather than our seven.

Save your file.

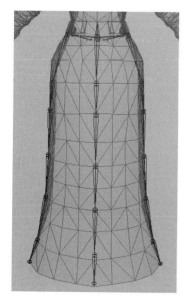 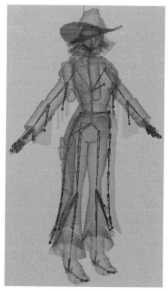

**Figure 3.20** The completed coat rig    **Figure 3.21** The completed skeleton

## Setting Animation Controls

Creating the skeleton isn't all we can do to prepare a model for animation. We can also create a number of controls for a variety of things, such as easier selection and more options for movement. The first thing we'll do is add IK handles for the legs and feet.

**Note:** To start from an already built skeleton, use the Calamity_Jane_Skeleton.ma file from the Project_Files/Chapter_3/Calamity_Jane/Scenes directory. The values for positioning in the following tutorials are assuming this file is being used. Your own scene's positional values may vary.

1. Go to Skeleton > IK Handle Tool > Options. In the options, check the Sticky check box. Close the options window.

   With the sticky attribute enabled, the feet will stay in their set position when keyframes are set.

2. With the IK Handle Tool active, left-click the LHip joint. Then, left-click the LAnkle joint. An IK handle will appear extended between the joints. Rename it **LLeg_IK**.

3. Create another IK handle, first clicking the LAnkle joint and then the LBall joint. Rename this one **LBall_IK**.

4. Create one last IK handle, clicking the LBall joint and then the LToe joint. Rename this one **LToe_IK**.

5. With the LToe_IK handle selected, group it to itself, with Edit > Group (or Ctrl+G). Rename the group **LToe_Group**.

6. Press the Insert key on the keyboard, enabling edit pivot mode. Point snap the group's pivot to the LBall joint. Do this by holding the V key (or toggling the Snap to Points button on the Status Line) and clicking and dragging the Move Tool handle to the joint. Press the Insert key again to exit edit pivot mode.

7. Edit the group's local rotation axis to point upward toward the toe joint.

8. With the LToe_Group selected (not the IK, but the IK's group), Shift+click the LBall_IK handle. Group these again. Rename this group **LHeel_Group**. Point snap this group's pivot to the LHeel joint.

9. Lastly, with the new LHeel_Group selected, Shift+click the LLeg_IK handle. Group this one last time and name the group **LFoot**. Point snap this group's pivot to the LHeel joint as well.

This LFoot group is going to be the main object that controls the movement and rotation of the left foot. If you open the Outliner (Window > Outliner), you'll see a list of all groups and objects in your scene. Find the LFoot group and Shift+click the [+] icon next to it, expanding the group. If everything above was done correctly, you should see the LFoot group listed as in Figure 3.22.

Repeat the above steps for the right leg, substituting the R prefix for the L.

### Knee Control

If you try to lift one of the feet groups right now, you might find that the knee bends rather awkwardly. We can fix this by giving the knee something to point at.

1. Go to Create > Locator. Move the locator in front of the left knee. Duplicate it and move the new locator in front of the right knee. Rename them **LKnee_Locator** and **RKnee_Locator**, respectively.

   A *locator* is like a dummy object that, on its own, does nothing. However, you can select it in your scene and give it any number of purposes. In this case, we'll make the locators an aim point for the knees.

2. Select LKnee_Locator. Shift+click the LLeg_IK handle. Go to Constrain > Pole Vector.

**Note:** The leg tassel joints may shift slightly when the Pole Vector constraints are in place. You can simply move them back to their original positions.

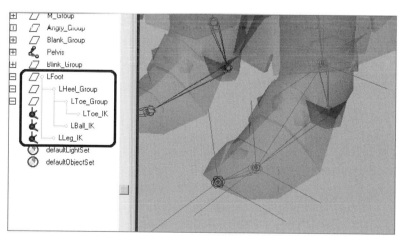

**Figure 3.22** The LFoot group in the Outliner

### Selection Handles

As things are now, the LFoot and RFoot groups are kind of a pain to actually select. You have to grab one of the elements within the group, such as the LLeg_IK, and then press the Up arrow key on the keyboard to select the top node of the LFoot hierarchy. Let's simplify this selection process, as well as the selection process of a few other joints around the skeleton, giving you easy control.

1. Select the LFoot Group.

2. Go to Display > Component Display > Selection Handles.

   A small crosshair will appear at the LHeel joint, where the LFoot group's pivot is. This is its selection handle, a small nonrenderable object that you can use as an alternative item to select something—in this case, the LFoot group.

   This is great, but right now it's within the geometry, on top of a joint! Not exactly any easier to get to. Let's do something about that.

3. Press the F8 key to enter component mode, or press the Select by Component Type button in the status line of the interface.

4. This time, enable the Select by Component Type: Handles selection mask. Disable the others.

5. Now you should be able to select the LFoot group's selection handle and move it to an easier access point, a few units outside the foot (Figure 3.23).

   We can repeat these steps for nearly any joint, object, or group for which we want easier access. I'll do it for the following: LToe_Group, RFoot, RToe_Group, Pelvis, BackWaist, BackLow, BackMid, BackHigh, Head, Chest, LClavicle, and RClavicle (Figure 3.24).

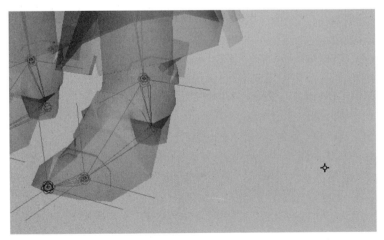

**Figure 3.23** The LFoot group's selection handle, outside the area of the geometry for easy access

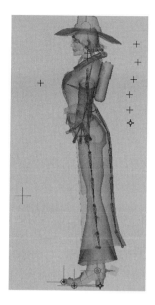

**Figure 3.24**

All of Calamity Jane's displayed selection handles in place

## Arm IK

Sometimes I want to use forward kinematics (FK) and sometimes inverse kinematics (IK) with a character's arms, depending on the situation. It also depends on the game engine being used. For example, some engines don't allow for IK at all, and we have to use FK for the arms and legs.

However, assuming IK is allowed, it is possible to switch between IK and FK during animation. So, we'll go ahead an add IK handles to the arms for the situations that call for them.

1.  Go to Skeleton > IK Handle Tool > Options. This time, we want to *uncheck* Sticky. Close the options. This will make the IK handles follow the wrist joints when they are disabled, as opposed to being left behind.

2.  With the IK Handle Tool, left-click the LShoulder joint. Left-click the LWrist joint next. An IK handle is created between the two joints. Rename it **LArm_IK**.

    With the LArm_IK handle still selected, look over in the Channel Box at all of its displayed attributes. The last one on the list is IK Blend. This is the attribute that allows you to switch between FK and IK. With the IK Blend attribute set to its default value of 1, IK is enabled. If we lower it to 0, IK is disabled and FK can be used.

3.  Go ahead and lower IK Blend to 0 for now.

4.  Repeat with the right arm, creating an RArm_IK handle with its IK Blend attribute lowered to 0 and Sticky turned off.

    Save your file.

### Full Body IK (FBIK)

New to Maya is the Full Body IK set of tools, mostly found under Skeleton > Full Body IK. This is a new pseudoautomatic method of setting up a skeleton with animation controls. In games, it's mostly a viable option only when the game engine in question is able to export joint positions on a per-frame basis and ignore all other input (or if the programmers in charge of your game's exporter are able to program in support for FBIK export).

For FBIK to work, the skeleton must conform to a few standards. The skeleton must be positioned in a T formation, with the arms out straight from the sides and facing the positive Z direction in the scene.

Also, the joints must be named and labeled in order for the FBIK tools to know what each joint is.

We aren't going to use FBIK for Calamity Jane because of the number of specialized joints she requires, with the coat, fringe, and so on. However, it's definitely something worth becoming familiar with.

To read more about FBIK in the Maya Help Files (F1), go through the Help File's navigation links on the left to Animation, Character Setup, and Deformers > Character Setup > Skeletons > Use Full Body IK.

## Binding the Skeleton

**Note:** To start from an already built rig, use the Calamity_Jane_Setup.ma file from the Project_Files/Chapter_3/Calamity_Jane/Scenes directory. The values for positioning in the following tutorials are assuming this file is being used. Your own scene's positional values may vary.

Now that we have the skeleton created and the animation controls in place, we can start the process of binding the character to it, allowing it to be deformed by the skeleton's movement. However, not all of the character needs to be bound, as not all of it is going to be deformed or change shape, such as the hat or holster. These kinds of objects will be parented to their respective joints instead.

There are exceptions to this, however. If something is in direct contact with a deforming piece of geometry, it may be better to go ahead and bind it to the skeleton as well to minimize the possibility of geometry intersecting in an ugly way. An example of this kind of thing would be the badge on the collar of the coat or the lace on the shirt.

1. Select the holster. Shift+select the Holster_Joint. Press **p** (Edit > Parent) to parent the holster to the Holster_Joint.

**2.** Using this same method (selecting the child object first and Shift+clicking the parent joint second), parent the following as listed. Hide (Ctrl+H) each one as you finish.

> **Note:** You can parent multiple child objects at once by simply selecting them all and Shift+clicking the parent last before using the Parent command.

| Child (object) | Parent (joint) |
| --- | --- |
| Hat | Hat |
| REye | Head |
| LEye | Head |
| REyelash | Head |
| LEyelash | Head |
| UpperTeeth | Head |
| Tie | Head |
| REarring | REarring_Joint |
| REarring_bolt | REarring_Joint |
| LEarring | LEarring_Joint |
| LEarring_bolt | LEarring_Joint |
| Backpack | BackMid |
| RArm_misc | RElbow |
| LArm_misc | LElbow |
| RLeg_leather1 | RLeg_Tassel1 |
| RLeg_leather2 | RLeg_Tassel2 |
| RLeg_leather3 | RLeg_Tassel3 |
| LLeg_leather1 | LLeg_Tassel1 |
| LLeg_leather2 | LLeg_Tassel2 |
| LLeg_leather3 | LLeg_Tassel3 |
| L_spur | LAnkle |
| R_spur | RAnkle |

The Tongue and LowerTeeth objects will need to be handled a little differently. Right now, their positioning is being driven by Set Driven Key. If you parent them to the head joint and then raise the MouthOpen blend shape, for example, you may see them suddenly repositioned far outside of the mouth.

**1.** To get around this, select both the Tongue and LowerTeeth objects and group them together. Name this new group **MouthStuff**.

**2.** Now, parent this group to the Head joint.

### Binding Geometry

When you've finished and have hidden all of the child objects, the geometry that is left visible is all of the geometry that is going to be bound to the skeleton.

1.  Select all of the visible geometry that makes up Calamity Jane: Hair, Head, Coat, Body, Lace, Badge, LHand, RHand, RLowerArm_leather, RUpperArm_leather, LLowerArm_leather, LUpperArm_leather, Belt, Holster_Connector, LBoot, RBoot. Make sure you *don't* select the pistol (it may be hidden within your scene).

2.  Shift+click the Pelvis joint. Go to Skin > Bind Skin > Smooth Bind > Options.

3.  In the Smooth Bind Options window, set the following:

    *   Max Influences: 2. This option limits the number of joints that can affect each vertex to only two.
    *   Dropoff Rate: 8.5. The higher the dropoff rate, the less influence a joint will have over distance.
    *   Remove Unused Influences: Disabled. If Remove Unused Influences is kept on, the blend shapes that aren't active right now will suddenly all be removed. And we wouldn't want that!

    If you want, you can disable Colorize Skeleton, but that's mostly a matter of preference.

4.  Click the Bind Skin button.

    We should test to make certain that the blend shapes of the head are not conflicting with the binding. Rotate the Head joint a bit and raise the MouthOpen slider in the Blend Shape Editor. It should react as you'd expect, with no visible unwanted deformation.

    However, if you should see the head suddenly stretch back to its original position, or any other strangeness, you might need to change the deformation order of the blend shapes and the binding, as described in Chapter 2. You can unhide everything now (Display > Show > Show Geometry > Polygon Surfaces). You might want to hide the pistol again for now, though.

### Painting Skin Weights

If you were to play with the rig a little bit, it'd soon be obvious that we still have a bit of work to do. The rigging does work, but the body deforms and stretches in many places in ugly ways, such as under the arms, the pelvis area, and the neck (Figure 3.25).

1.  Let's start with the left shoulder area. Rotate the LClavicle joint in the RotateZ channel 28 degrees. Rotate the LShoulder joint in the RotateZ channel 11 degrees.

2.  Select the coat and go to Skin > Edit Smooth Skin > Paint Skin Weights Tool > Options. This opens the Paint Skin Weights Tool options window. The coat will turn black.

**Figure 3.25**
Obviously, something isn't quite right.

3. Let's isolate the coat from everything else by going to Show > Isolate Select > View Selected. Everything but the coat will disappear.

4. In the Paint Skin Weights Tool Options, select the BackHigh joint. A white area will appear on the mesh to show how the selected joint influences the geometry. Lower your brush's Opacity to a manageable amount, like 0.3.

   Carefully brush across the vertices, adding influence from the BackHigh joint to them where it is needed.

5. Continue doing this, switching between other joints in the list, such as the LClavicle and the LShoulder, adding influence where needed to create a smooth transition with the arm in its current position. If your opacity doesn't add enough or adds too much influence on a stroke, adjust it as needed.

### Mirroring Skin Weights

Once you have the left shoulder region's skin weights painted to your satisfaction, you can attempt to mirror the skin weights over to the right side.

1. Select the coat. Go to Skin > Edit Smooth Skin > Mirror Skin Weights > Options. In the options, choose the XY angle to mirror across, just as we did when we mirrored the skeleton joints for the right arm and leg.

2. Press the Mirror button. This command usually doesn't work perfectly, but it should at least get the opposite side of your geometry's skin weights close to where you have them set up on the side you worked on. They should also be to the point where you can clean them up manually rather than starting from scratch.

Continue editing weights all over the body in this way. I usually bend a joint or chain of joints to see how bad the deformation is, isolate the object, and then meticulously paint the weights until the deformation is clean. This can be very time consuming and tedious but is very necessary for clean deformation.

One rule of thumb is to not totally remove joint influence from a vertex. If you totally remove influence from a vertex, even if by accident, it can be difficult to add that influence back in later. And if you were to add it back only partially, then you could have vertices that are only partially bound to the skeleton, and they'd move strangely.

Therefore, I recommend instead replacing the influence of a vertex or adding the influence of a different joint to a vertex.

It can be very challenging to paint the skin weights for Jane's coat and different special elements, but eventually you should start to see them come together nicely (Figure 3.26).

Save your file.

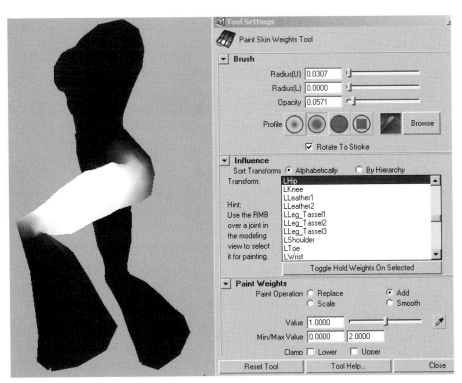

**Figure 3.26** The unwanted deformation getting under control

## Tutorial: Walk Cycle

Different game engines handle animation sequences differently. Some engines are able to blend between sequences themselves, while others require the sequences to animate to a common pose to avoid a visible switch between sequences. Some engines require each animation sequence to be in its own file; others have every animation set one after the other in one long sequence in one large file.

For this particular project, we won't worry about manually blending the animations together, and we'll assume that the game will be able to blend between sequences itself. We'll focus more on blending in an upcoming project in this book.

An animation in a game is usually either a *cycle* or a *sequence*. An animation cycle, when triggered, is designed to be a repeating animation that can play over and over again. An obvious example of this would be a walk or run animation. An animation sequence or event is an animation that, when triggered, isn't necessarily designed to immediately repeat but to play once and come to an end.

Another point about animation in games is that 90 percent of the time, the character doesn't actually make any forward movement in the Maya scene file. For our upcoming walk cycle, for example, the character will literally be walking in place. The reason is that it's the game engine itself that controls a character's direction and rate of movement based on input from the player.

For our first animation project, we'll create a walk cycle. Walking is essentially a series of controlled falls. You are pushing your body forward and catching yourself with your feet as you move.

**Note:** Make sure your scene is set to play at 30 frames per second (fps). Set this under Window > Settings/Preferences > Preferences. In the Preferences window, look under Settings and set the Time attribute to NTSC (30 fps). Under Timeline, set the Playback Speed attribute to Real-time (30 fps).

1.  To start with a provided Calamity Jane already fully rigged, open the Calamity_Jane_WalkStart.ma file from the Project_Files/Chapter_3/Calamity_Jane/Scenes folder. The values for positioning in the following tutorials are assuming this file is being used. Your own scene's positional values may vary.

    In this scene are the completed rigged model of Calamity Jane, a ground plane to serve as reference for the floor, and a video reference plane of a walk.

    The video should be used only as a reference and not as a guide. Your goal isn't to copy the poses you see in the video but to use it as a reference for how a real person walks. However, what you are making isn't a real person but a video game character. Therefore, you have to conform to the game's visual style, which more often than not is a very visually *interesting* style. Make sure you keep visual dynamism in mind for your animations.

2.  Go to frame 1. Manipulate the pose of your model's skeleton to be midstride, as in Figure 3.27. Don't concern yourself with the coat and other secondary animation objects (leather fringe, holster, and so on).

    As you position the body how you want it, set keyframes for its positions, either rotation and/or translation as applicable.

**Figure 3.27** Midstride pose at frame 1 to start the walk cycle

**Note:** To set translation keys, press Shift+W. To set rotation keys, press Shift+E. To set scale keys, press Shift+R. See Chapter 2 for more keyframing methods.

There are a few things to take note of with this pose in a walk cycle:

**A.** Notice the curvature of the spine. The waist is tilted, with the high side being the side with the leg extending backward, while the low side is the side with the leg extending forward.

As you go up the spine, it will curve back around until eventually, at the shoulders, the tilt will be the opposite of that of the waist—the shoulders tilted high on the side with the leg extended forward and low on the side with the leg extended backward.

**B.** During a standard walk, the feet will be placed closer to the centerline of the body when they make contact with the ground. Especially for a female character, you may want to exaggerate this foot placement (like a fashion model walking a catwalk), depending on the visual style and mood of the walk you are going for.

3. Let's forget about the arms for now and focus on the legs. Go to Frame 13. Position the body as you see it in Figure 3.28. Again, let's take a look at this pose. (Remember, we're focusing on the legs for now. We'll return to the arm animation once the legs are situated.)

**A.** Straighten up the spine in this pose when the legs pass each other so that there is no tilt. The spine joints can still curve forward or backward, depending on what kind of look you are trying to achieve.

**B.** Raise up the Pelvis joint, straightening the leg that is in contact with the ground.

**C.** The LFoot that is raised up and passing the right leg should move outward, giving itself room to make the pass around the RFoot that is still set inward, toward the center line.

4. Go back to frame 5 now and rotate the RFoot down to lay the sole of the boot flat on the ground, and raise the LFoot to have it stand on the toe (Figure 3.29).

**Figure 3.28**
Passing feet at frame 13

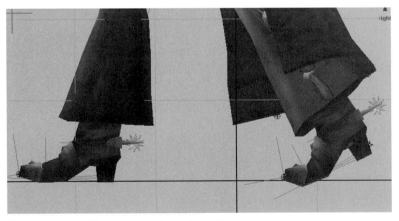

**Figure 3.29** Lay the RFoot down and raise the LFoot at frame 5.

5. At frame 23, continue the forward movement of the LFoot, reversing the feet position from frame 1; this time the LFoot is forward and the RFoot is back. Similarly, we'll want to tilt the hips and the shoulders to be the opposite from frame 1 (Figure 3.30).

**Figure 3.30**
The opposite stride pose at frame 23

**A.** As before, the waist is tilted so that the high side is on the RFoot side with the leg extended back, while the low side is on the LFoot side with the leg extended forward. The spine curves around to the opposite direction at the shoulders.

**B.** Once the LFoot makes contact with the ground, it should again be toward the center line.

You should now see a nice walking step if you scrub through the timeline.

6.  At frame 36, we'll do the opposite pose from what we did on frame 13, with the RFoot passing the LFoot (Figure 3.31).

    **A.** Again, the spine has very little tilt to the side.

    **B.** As before, raise the Pelvis joint up to straighten the left leg as the RFoot makes its pass.

    **C.** The RFoot moves outward to have room to pass the LFoot.

    The last major position of the legs and feet is actually the same position as the first.

7.  We're going to want to duplicate the pose from frame 1 and put it at frame 48. Go to frame 1. *Middle*-click and drag on the timeline to frame 48. You'll notice that time did not move forward in the scene. So, here at frame 48, the pose from frame 1 is visible in the scene.

    Select all of the elements that we are animating (the feet, pelvis, and spine) and reset all of their keys at their current positions. What this does is set keyframes at frame 48 that are equal to the values of the keyframes that were set at frame 1!

    Play the animation at its current state. You should see Jane's legs moving as if on a leisurely stroll.

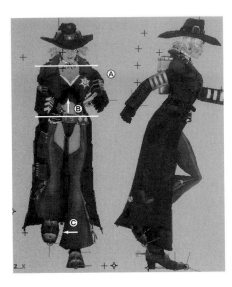

**Figure 3.31**
The feet pass again at frame 36.

### Establishing Arm Movement

Now that we have the leg movement to a satisfactory state, let's focus on the arms. We positioned them for a good pose at frame 1 but haven't moved them yet for the rest of the cycle.

1.  We already know that the pose the arms are in at frame 1 is going to be the same pose we want at frame 48, so let's go ahead and key their current positions a second time at frame 48.

2.  At frame 23, position the arms to be in the opposite pose from frames 1 and 48—the left arm swung back (the left leg is extended forward right now) and the right arm swung forward (the right leg is back).

3.  At about frames 9 and 40, when both arms are near the sides of Calamity Jane's torso, you may need to rotate the arms outward slightly to prevent them from passing through the chest.

4.  For a bit of secondary animation, animate the wrists similarly to what you see in Figure 3.32. The momentum of the arm's swing and its change in swing direction cause the wrist to follow through the movement, creating an arcing motion.

    We're now closer to a basic walk cycle. You may notice that the movement plays a little clunky when it repeats after frame 48. You may also notice a slight stutter at the end.

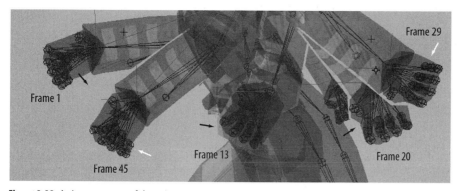

Frame 29

Frame 1

Frame 45

Frame 13

Frame 20

**Figure 3.32** Arcing movement of the wrist

## Ensuring Smooth Cycling

For one thing, we have the same body position at frame 1 and at frame 48. So, when we allow the animation to play over and over, we essentially are experiencing two frames that have no movement between them at the end and beginning of the cycle.

In an actual game project, when the time comes to export this animation to the game, you'd actually export only the animation from frames 1–47, leaving off the last frame. This way, the animation doesn't play two frames side by side that have no change and instead has a smoother flow of movement. So, to alleviate this stutter for now, simply change the playback end time to 47.

We could also adjust the animation curves to smooth the transition between the last and first keyframes of the cycle.

1. Select the Pelvis joint. Open the Graph Editor under Window > Animation Editors > Graph Editor (or click the Persp/Graph button on the left side of the UI, beneath the toolbar, to display the Persp view and the Graph Editor within the UI).

2. Here, you can see the animation curves of the selected joint. Select all of the keyframes at frame 1. Shift+click the keyframes at frame 48.

3. Within the Graph Editor, go to Tangents > Flat, or click the Flat tangents button in the Graph Editor toolbar. The curves will flatten out at the beginning and end of the animation, which will smooth the transition as the animation repeats.

4. Repeat these steps for every animating joint, flattening the tangents at frames 1 and 48 to smooth their transition.
Save your file.

## Incorporating Secondary Animation

Now that the basic body movement is at a good point, we can go through and start incorporating the secondary animation of the reactive parts of the character, such as the coat.

1. At frame 1, move the coat to a good position, such as that shown in Figure 3.33, with the coat whipping up and to the side. Set rotation keyframes for each coat joint.

2. At frame 48, key the joints again.

3. At frame 23, have the coat joints whip to the opposite side.

4. Because Jane is just walking and not moving all that quickly, the coat shouldn't always be extended out as if she's moving at a great speed. At frame 13, have the coat drape downward against the back of her legs (Figure 3.34).

5. Repeat at frame 36, having the coat drape downward.

6. Flatten the tangents of the first and last frames (at frame 1 and 48) in the Graph Editor to smooth the cycle transition for all the coat joints, as described in the previous section.

If we play the animation at this point, we can see if the coat moves realistically. I noticed, for example, that the upward flip to the side that I have my coat doing is a little too strong for Jane's slow walking movement, so I'll tone down the upward movement of the coat at frame 1 (and 48) and at frame 23.

**Figure 3.33** Positioning the coat at frame 1

**Figure 3.34** The coat drapes downward at frame 13.

7. After toning down the flipping motion to an acceptable degree, we can fine-tune the movement a bit by delaying the flip to happen more suddenly as opposed to the gradual change that happens now. Select all of the coat joints (the easiest way to do this is to select the joints in the Outliner).

8. Go to frame 13, where the coat joints hang down. Then, middle-click and drag to frame 18 in the timeline. Press Shift+E to set a new rotation key at frame 18 using the rotation values set at frame 13 for all the coat joints.

9. Repeat this action, going to frame 36. Middle-click and drag to frame 41 and set a new rotation keyframe here, using the same values from frame 36.

The coat should now flip up more quickly as Jane walks.

## Holster

Now we can start looking at the additional secondary animation items, such as the holster. The main thing we need to know is that the holster *wants* to just follow gravity's pull and hang straight down.

1. Let's start at frame 1 and rotate the Holster_Joint to point the holster down (don't forget to key this same position at frame 48).

2. Play through the animation and watch how the holster moves. Go through and periodically rotate the holster to make it seem like it is swinging back toward its straight position, trying to follow gravity's pull. I set keys at frames 14, 26, and 38.

3. In addition, I'd like to add a little moment where the holster bounces off Jane's leg as it is passing by. At frame 22, rotate the holster outward a bit. It gets pulled back in from the keyframe we set at frame 26. Move to frame 28 and move it back out a little again.

You can now see the holster bounce slightly against Jane's thigh as she walks. You don't want these kinds of secondary movements to be too noticeable, as they are literally repeating over and over again and can seem unnatural if not done carefully.

## Leather Fringe

Just like the holster, the leather fringe hanging off the arms wants to constantly hang down toward the ground.

1. With that in mind, set keyframes for the left and right arm leather joints at frames 1, 23, and 48 (with frames 1 and 48 being the same), with the fringe hanging down from the arms (Figure 3.35).

2. At frames 13 and 37, have the fringe extend from the arm in the direction from which the arms are swinging. For example, the fringe on the right arm at frame 13 should point toward the back and at frame 37 point toward the front.

As Jane walks now, the fringe should flip back and forth in momentum with the arms.

**Figure 3.35** The leather fringe hanging from the arms at frame 23

### Chest

As we continue with the secondary animation, we'll add a slight counterbounce motion to the Chest control.

1. At frames 13 and 37, as Jane rises upward, lower the Chest joint about 0.1 unit from its original position.

2. At frames 21 and 45, a few frames before her stepping motion makes ground contact, raise the Chest joint about 0.1 unit from its original position.

3. At frames 25 and 48 (which will be copied to frame 1), a couple frames after the step, lower the Chest joint back to its original position.

### Leg Tassels

Using the same bounce idea from the Chest joint, let's have the tassels hanging from Jane's legs perform a similar action.

Now don't forget, we're walking in place, so while it looks like the right leg is moving backward from frame 1 to frame 25, it's actually planted on a spot on the ground and the character is pushing forward from that point. With that in mind, make sure you have the tassels reacting to true leg movement and not just perceived movement.

1. Select the RLeg_Tassel1 joint. At frame 24, rotate it so it is draping downward, and set a rotation keyframe.

2. At frame 40, when the right leg has moved forward to take a step, rotate the tassel to point backward, reacting to the forward movement of the leg.

3. At frame 48 (which will be copied to frame 1), rotate the tassel upward, reacting to the downward motion of the leg.

4. Since the animation now cycles back to the beginning, we need to show gravity taking back control of the tassel near the beginning of the cycle.

   At frame 6, rotate the tassel to be similar to the position at frame 24, showing the tassel coming to settle as the body pushes forward from the planted right leg.

5. Repeat this type of reactive animating with the rest of the leg tassels, keeping in mind what is true leg movement and not just perceived movement.

**Earrings**

With the hair and earrings, we can achieve a similar counterbounce motion using many of the same techniques as we did with the chest and tassels.

1. At frames 15 and 34, with Jane rising upward in her stride, keyframe the rotation of the two earrings at their positions, hanging downward toward the ground (the tilt of Jane's head may require you to rotate the Earring joints a bit to make them point more downward).

2. At frames 21 and 45, a few frames before Jane's feet make contact with the ground, rotate the Earring joints to be outward as in Figure 3.36, as if they are falling downward as well.

3. At frames 25 and 48 (and thus also frame 1), rotate the Earring joints back to pointing downward.

**Figure 3.36** The earrings rotated outward at frames 21 and 45

### Hair

The hair counterbounce actually works exactly like the chest counterbounce does. In fact, replace the word *Chest* with *Hair* and you can follow the chest steps exactly. You can do this with both the Hair1 and Hair2 joints.

Once all of the secondary animation is to your satisfaction, your walk cycle is complete!

 **Note:** You can see my finished walk cycle by opening the Calamity_Jane_WalkFinish.ma file in the Project_Files/Chapter_3/Calamity_Jane/Scenes folder.

## Tutorial: Action Sequence

For the second animation tutorial using the Calamity Jane model, we'll work on an animation sequence that is not designed to cycle or repeat but to play once and come to an end. For this particular case, we'll have Jane perform a pistol quick draw and fire.

1. To start with a provided Calamity Jane already fully rigged, open the Calamity_ Jane_DrawStart.ma file from the Project_Files/Chapter_3/Calamity_Jane/Scenes folder. The values for positioning in the following tutorials are assuming this file is being used. Your own scene's positional values may vary.

   In this scene are the completed rigged model of Calamity Jane, a ground plane to serve as reference for the floor, and a video reference plane of a quick draw. Once again, the reference is mostly useful for timing and general movement reference and isn't meant to be matched pose-to-pose. Remember the all-important dynamism!

2. Manipulate the rig to get an initial starting pose that you like, similar to Figure 3.37. Set a keyframe for each element for rotation and/or translation where applicable. You can go ahead and pose the coat and the Holster_Joint, but don't worry about the other secondary animation elements just yet. (You can give Jane an applicable facial expression, too, if you'd like!)

**Figure 3.37**
Calamity Jane is ready to draw.

## Setting Pistol Constraints

Before we go too much further, we need to figure out how we're going to transition the pistol from the holster to the right hand. In a real game engine, objects can be coded to constrain to a certain joint, such as the Holster_Joint or the RWrist, and be triggered to switch between them. In our Maya scene, however, we'll have to do it manually to get the effect we're looking for.

By default, in the DrawStart scene, I had the pistol parented to the Holster_Joint so it would follow your model while you posed it. Now, we need to unparent it and create our constraint system.

1. Select the pistol and press Shift+p (or Edit > Unparent) to unparent the pistol from the Holster_Joint.

2. Create a locator (Create > Locator). Rename it **Holster_Constraint**.

3. Select the pistol at its place in the holster and Shift+click the Holster_Constraint locator. Go to Constrain > Point. The locator will snap to the pistol's current position.

4. Unselect everything and perform the selection again: select the pistol first and Shift+click the locator. This time, go to Constrain > Orient. The locator is now at the same point and orientation of the pistol within the holster.

5. We now want to remove the constraint of the locator to the pistol so that we can constrain the *pistol* to the locator later on. Select the Holster_Constraint locator. You can see in the Channel Box that the Translation X, Y, and Z and the Rotation X, Y, and Z channels are highlighted blue, indicating their being constrained by another object.

6. Select the six constrained attributes in the Channel Box. Within the Channel Box region, right-click and hold, which brings up the Channel Box menu, and choose Break Connections, which removes the constraining influence.

7. Parent the Holster_Constraint locator to the Holster_Joint.

8. We want to do the same thing with another locator for the pistol's position in Jane's right hand. Position the pistol in Jane's right hand how you want it.

9. Create another locator and name it **Hand_Constraint**. Again, we want to Point and Orient constrain the locator to the pistol's current position, following the same steps as before (Figure 3.38).

10. Once the locator is constrained to the pistol, break the connections of the translation and rotation channels to break the constraint, and parent the locator to the RWrist joint.

**Figure 3.38**
The Hand_Constraint locator in place
where the pistol fits into the hand

**11.** Now we want to constrain the pistol to the two locators. Select the Holster_ Constraint locator and Shift+click the pistol. Create a Point and Orient constraint between the two.

**12.** Repeat, creating a Point and Orient constraint between the pistol and the Hand_ Constraint locator. You'll notice that the pistol floats between the hand and the holster. Not exactly what we want it to do.

**13.** Select the pistol. In the lower panel of the Channel Box, under the SHAPES section, you can see the two constraints listed as Pistol_pointConstraint1 and Pistol_orientConstraint1. Select one or the other. Listed in both constraints' attributes are two called Holster_Constraint W0 and Hand_Constraint W1.

At the moment, both are set to 1. This means that both constraints are fully active, and the result is an averaging of the constraints' effects, causing the pistol to float between the hand and the holster.

**14.** At the beginning of the animation, we want the gun to be in the holster, so turn the Hand_Constraint attribute of both the Pistol_pointConstraint1 and the Pistol_orientConstraint1 to 0, effectively turning off the Hand_Constraint. The gun will snap to the holstered position.

## Continuing the Animation

Now that we have the pistol constraints put together, we can continue with the animation.

**1.** Go to frame 12 and position Jane in a quick-draw pose after the pistol is drawn, as in Figure 3.39.

**2.** The pistol will intersect the holster, but it shouldn't be too big a deal because of the speed of the draw, but to help some, we can go to frame 9 and raise up the arm as if in the act of drawing the weapon (Figure 3.40).

**Figure 3.39** *left* The quick-draw pose at frame 12

**Figure 3.40** *right* Drawing the weapon from the holster

3. At frame 6, set a keyframe for the Holster_Constraint W0 and Hand_Constraint W1 attributes of the pistol by selecting them in the Channel box, and right-click and hold. This brings up the Channel Box menu; choose the Key Selected option.

4. At frame 9, reverse the constraint, switching the pistol to the hand, and set another key for the Holster_Constraint W0 and Hand_Constraint W1.

5. The pistol is now drawn from the holster and pointing at our "target." We want Jane to pause for just a moment before she actually fires the gun. Go to frame 30 and set another keyframe for each element using the Animate > Hold Current Keys command so that she holds her position from frame 12 to frame 30. We don't want her to be perfectly robot-still, though.

6. In the Graph Editor (Window > Animation Editors > Graph Editor), select the keyframes of the objects at frames 12 and 30 and go to Tangents > Spline. This causes the animation curves between the two keys to use spline tangents and not to be completely straight, thus giving her some slight movement during the pause.

7. At frame 33, the gun fires! Position Jane in a proper recoil pose like the one in Figure 3.41.

8. At frame 50, we can begin to reholster the weapon. The easiest method is to start by copying the keyframe positions from frame 6. Go to frame 6, middle-click and drag to frame 50, and begin setting keyframes for all of the elements of the rig, effectively copying their values from frame 6 to frame 50.

9. At frame 48, set a keyframe for the pistol's current constraint attributes that are keeping the gun in the right hand. At frame 50, reverse them, constraining the gun to the holster, and set a keyframe for the change (Figure 3.42).

**Figure 3.41** The recoil pose at frame 33

**Figure 3.40** Reholstering the gun at the end of the animation sequence

At this point, the only thing left to do is the secondary animation. Using what you've learned, animate the reactions of the coat, holster, arm leather fringe, leg tassels, chest, earrings, and hair to the main body's movements.

You can see how mine turned out in the Calamity_Jane_DrawFinish.ma file in the Project_Files/Chapter_3/Calamity_Jane/Scenes folder.

# Project: Dire Wolf

*For our next animation project, we'll face the challenges and differences that a creature with four legs gives us. We'll also start to bring some limitations into our workflow. This particular creature is designed for a more current-generation console, such as the Sony Playstation2 or the Nintendo GameCube, which doesn't have nearly as much power as Calamity Jane's game, which was designed for a much more powerful machine. Not only that, our creature is not a main character or even a main villain but a run-of-the-mill creature that the player will face dozens of times throughout the game's play or in a specific environment of the game, such as a dark forest.*

**In this chapter, we'll discuss the following topics:**
Assignment Breakdown
Tutorial: Rigging the Dire Wolf
Tutorial: Run Cycle

## Assignment Breakdown

For this project, the Dire Wolf needs to be rigged with as few joints as possible, unlike Calamity Jane, which had as many joints as necessary. Not only that, this "game" doesn't have support for vertex animation, meaning any facial animation we want will also need to be handled with joints. Therefore, we will need to be creative with our skeleton's layout to make efficient use of the available joints to get all of the animation controls we need for a quality rig.

### Behind the Dire Wolf

The Dire Wolf model is designed to be a "typical" enemy. Not only that, it's constructed for the purpose of having multiple wolves on the screen at once, allowing them to attack the player in a pack.

As you can see in the following image, the Dire Wolf has a lot of long hair. For the most part, actual strands of hair are still not a possibility in the majority of game engines. So, for these midrange polycount models, planes of geometry are used and applied with opacity-mapped textures to simulate thick tufts of hair.

The Dire Wolf consists of approximately 2,000 polys and is textured with two 512 × 512 textures—one for the body and one for all that hair. We also have one 256 × 256 texture for the armor that the wolf wears.

Before we begin the project, take a minute to read about the artist behind the Dire Wolf. His background will give you some insight into the obstacles he faced with the project.

### About the Artist

**Name** Gary Bergeron, age 28

**Personal website** http://www.garybergeron.com

**Describe your role at your current studio.** I am an environment artist, which allows me to create environment assets, textures, and the occasional character model. Outside of Maya, a good portion of my work is done in the [game's level editor], which includes some modeling, texturing, and lighting but is mostly set dressing.

**Did you face any significant challenges with the Dire Wolf model?** The area I was most concerned about on the Dire Wolf was the texturing of the hair. With a resolution of 512 × 512, I was left with only enough room to paint a couple of large patches of hair. I was then forced to make multiple polygons share the same section of the texture map. Making these polygons share the map in a way that didn't look redundant and so that the alpha was able to bleed off the edges was a bit of a challenge. When taking on a model like this and any other, the one thing that always poses a problem is creating the seams in spots that are least noticeable and then painting them away.

**Can you describe your basic workflow?** I started out with a shape that was a basic cylinder with two legs sticking out of the side. I cut it in half so that I could make it symmetrical and work on only half of the model. From there I went on cutting the polys to finish out the body of the wolf. After the body was complete, I moved on to make the major portions of hair, starting with the mane and the neck area first and then moving on to the smaller sections around the legs and the tail. The armor came last, as it needed to be fitted around the body and through the hair. The next step was to double-check my work, [flipping] edges and checking for inconsistency in the flow of the topology and making sure the joints were suitable for animation purposes. Last, but definitely not the least of the work, was the UV unwrapping and texturing.

Concept art by Steve Garcia

Game art by Gary Bergeron

## Tutorial: Rigging the Dire Wolf

Even the most powerful of game engines have limitations. The number of joints per character is just as important as the polycount per character or the texture per character.

For this rig, we want to be as judicious with the bones as possible, only using the bare minimum that we need. For that reason, we might have to sacrifice some of the more finely tuned animation controls for the sake of efficiency. For our wolf project, we're going to see how much we can do with fewer than 30 joints total. It's not unusual to actually have that number limited even more, closer to 20–25.

1.　　⊙　Browse on the CD to Project_Files/Chapter_4/Dire_Wolf. Copy the Dire_Wolf directory to your hard drive. Open the file DireWolf_Start.ma from the Scenes directory.

　　This file contains the modeled and textured geometry for the Dire Wolf creature.

2.　To lay out the spine of the wolf, in the Side view we'll place a six-joint chain using the Joint Tool (Skeleton > Joint Tool), as shown in Figure 4.1.

　　**A.**　Place the first joint near the hind legs and name it **Pelvis**.

　　**B.**　The next joint on the chain should be placed near the next geometry division of the wolf's back. Name it **Back1**.

　　**C.**　The third joint is placed near the shoulders of the front legs and named **Back2**.

　　**D.**　The next joint, named **Neck**, should be placed where the head meets the body.

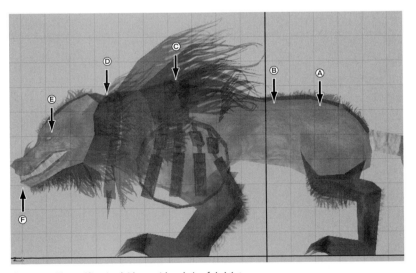

**Figure 4.1** The wolf's spine laid out with a chain of six joints

**E.** To animate the wolf's mouth, we'll place the next joint at the point of rotation of the jaw, as pictured. Name this joint **Jaw**.

**F.** And lastly, to help orient the previous joint on the chain, we'll place the sixth joint in front of the wolf's snout. Once it is placed, you can delete this joint.

**3.** We can continue the spine in the opposite direction to place the joints that we'll use to control the tail. With the Joint Tool, left-click the Pelvis joint.

Clicking an existing joint with the Joint Tool causes it to be the active joint. The next joints you place will then be included in the Pelvis joint's hierarchy.

**4.** In the Side view, lay out a three-joint chain for the tail, as pictured in Figure 4.2. Name these joints **Tail1**, **Tail2**, and **Tail3**, respectively.

We'll continue the skeleton by placing the leg joints.

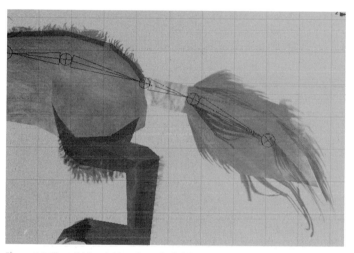

**Figure 4.2** The tail joints laid out from the Pelvis

## Hind Legs

The legs of a wolf are obviously not a typical human setup. However, if you take a look at Figure 4.3, you will find that the actual layouts of the two have a lot more in common than you might think. They both are composed of the standard hip → knee → ankle chains, as well as basic foot chains. It's the placement of those joints and how the IK handle reacts to them that differ the most.

**1.** Back in the Side view, place a five-joint chain as pictured in Figure 4.4, starting with the hip and working your way down to the toe. Name them **LHip**, **LKnee**, **LAnkle**, **LPaw**, and **LBackToe**, respectively.

2. Switch to the Persp view and make sure that the joints are positioned accurately through the left hind leg's geometry.

3. Select the LHip joint. Shift+click the Pelvis joint. Go to Edit > Parent (or press the **p** shortcut key) to add the left leg to the pelvis' hierarchy.

4. Select the LHip joint and go to Skeleton > Mirror Joint > Options. In the options, make sure that the L in the joint names is set to be replaced with an R, to designate the right side. Click the Mirror button. We now have both hind legs' joints in place.

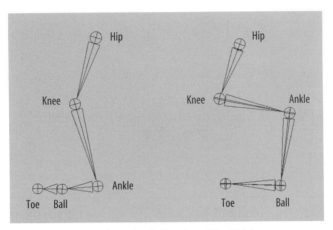

**Figure 4.3** Comparing a human leg (left) to the wolf leg (right)

**Figure 4.4** Placing the hind leg joints in the Side and Persp views

## Front Legs

The front legs will be placed in a very similar fashion. And just like a human arm, the front leg is composed of shoulder, elbow, and wrist joints.

1. In the Side view, place a four-joint chain as shown in Figure 4.5, starting with the shoulder.

2. In the Persp view, reposition the joints to run through the left front leg geometry. Name these **LShoulder**, **LElbow**, **LWrist**, and **LFrontToe**.

3. Parent the LShoulder to the Back2 joint.

4. Select the LShoulder joint and mirror the joint chain over, replacing the L in the names with an R.

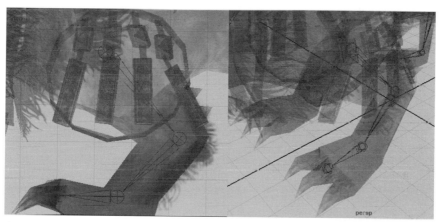

**Figure 4.5** Placing the front leg joints in the Side and Persp views

## Remaining Joints

If we count our joints now, we have 26 joints and we're already nearing our budget of 30. For our remaining four joints, we'll do what we can for secondary animation joint controls in the Dire Wolf's hair and on his shoulder armor.

1. For the hair, we'll add a two-joint chain. With the Joint Tool active, left-click the Back2 joint to make it the active joint. In the Side view, place the two joints for the hair as shown in Figure 4.6. Name them **Hair1** and **Hair2**.

2. For our last two remaining joints, we'll place a joint near each shoulder to control the armor straps that hang over the wolf's shoulders. In the Front view, place a single joint near the left shoulder, and position it in the Persp view, as shown in Figure 4.7.

3. Name it **LArmor** and parent it to the Back2 joint.

4. Mirror the joint, creating the RArmor joint on the other side.

**Figure 4.6**
The hair joints in place

110

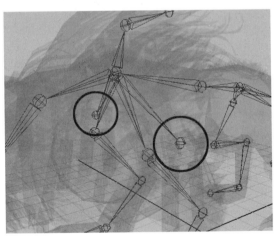

**Figure 4.7**
The armor joints

## Animation Controls

Just as with Calamity Jane, we'll go over the skeleton and add animation controls and selection handles to make the animation easier to do and the model easier to work with.

1. Select the Pelvis joint and choose Freeze Transformations (Modify > Freeze Transformations). This sets all of the joints into their current positions and ignores any rotation we have done to position the joints.

2. Using the IK Handle Tool (Skeleton > IK Handle Tool), left-click the LHip joint, and then left-click the LPaw joint. An IK handle is created between the two joints (make sure the IK handle's Sticky attribute is enabled). Name it **LLegIK**.

3. Create another IK handle between the LPaw and the LBackToe joints. Name this one **LBackToeIK**.

4. With the LBackToeIK selected, group it to itself (Edit > Group).

5. Press the Insert key on the keyboard to enable edit pivot mode, and point snap (V key) the group's pivot point to the LPaw joint. Press the Insert key again to disable edit pivot mode. Name the group **LBackToeGrp**.

6. With the LBackToeGrp selected, Shift+click the LLegIK handle and group the selection again. Point snap this group's pivot to the LPaw group as well. Name this group **LBackFoot**.

7. Repeat for the right foot, creating the RBackToeGrp and RBackFoot groups.

8. We can repeat these steps for the front legs as well. Create an IK handle between the LShoulder and LWrist joints. Name it **LArmIK**.

9. Create another IK handle between the LWrist and LFrontToe joints. Name it **LFrontToeIK**.

10. As we did before, we'll set up groups for the controls. With the LFrontToeIK selected, group it to itself. Point snap this joint's pivot point to the LWrist and name it **LFrontToeGrp**.

11. With the LFrontToeGrp selected, Shift+click the LArmIK and group them together. Point snap this group's pivot point to the LWrist joint and name it **LFrontFoot**.

12. Repeat these steps once again for the right side, creating RFrontToeGrp and RFrontFoot.

## Leg Orientation

To control the orientation of the legs, we'll use locators and Pole Constrain them, as we did with Calamity Jane, to control the aim direction of each leg.

1. Create a locator (Create > Locator) and put it in front of the left hind leg's knee. Name the locator **LBLeg_Locator** (with LBLeg standing for left back leg).

2. While the locator is selected, Shift+click the LLegIK and go to Constrain > Pole Vector. Now the leg will aim itself toward wherever the locator is positioned.

3. Repeat this with each leg, creating the RBLeg_Locator, LFLeg_Locator, and RFLeg_Locator. Pole Vector constrain each IK handle to its respective locator.

## Selection Handles

For easy access to joints and controls, we'll display selection handles for the following: Pelvis, Back1, Back2, Neck, Jaw, all four toe groups (e.g., LBackToeGrp), and all four foot groups (e.g., LBackFoot).

Once they are displayed, we can move them outside the body by going into component mode (by pressing the F8 key or by toggling the Select by Component Type button in the status line) and enabling the selection handle selection mask, indicated by a small + sign.

With the selection handles displayed and positioned for easy access, our animation controls are complete, and we can now bind the wolf to his rig (Figure 4.8).

**Figure 4.8** The completed skeleton with animation controls

## Binding to the Skeleton

As we did with Calamity Jane, we'll now bind the Dire Wolf to the skeleton, resulting in the rig driving the wolf's movement. Not everything will be bound to the geometry, though. Some elements that don't deform will be parented to their respective joints.

1. Select the Collar object. Shift+click the Neck joint. Go to Edit > Parent (or press the **p** shortcut key). The Collar object will be parented to the Neck joint.

2. Repeat these steps with the following objects, selecting the object to be parented first and then Shift+clicking the desired parent joint before parenting:

   | Child (object) | Parent (joint) |
   | --- | --- |
   | UpperTeeth | Neck |
   | LowerTeeth | Jaw |
   | Yoke | Back2 |

3. To bind the remaining geometry to the skeleton, select the rest of the unparented objects. Shift+click the Pelvis joint to add it to your selection last.

4. Go to Skin > Bind Skin > Smooth Bind > Options. We'll use the same settings as we did with our previous project:

- Max Influences: 2
- Dropoff Rate: 8.5
- Remove Unused Influences: Unchecked

## Centaur Rig

This book strives to give an example of each major kind of body arrangement an animator may be called upon to work with. There are certain specific creature types that are a bit rare but doable using what you have learned thus far.

A *centaur* is half-animal, half-human and is most typically represented by a human-horse combination, but there are others. In any case, the skeleton setup for such a creature is identical to that of any of the other creatures within this book, with the only obvious difference being that you are combining two rigs: the human half is rigged like Calamity Jane and the four-legged half is rigged like the wolf. You'd of course make room for minor adjustments as called for on a per-project basis.

## Painting Skin Weights

At this point, if you test some of the controls, you'll notice some unwanted stretching and deformation (Figure 4.9). Obviously, we have some weight-painting ahead of us!

1. Let's start with the head and jaw. Rotate the Neck joint to an extreme position, such as 50 degrees in the RotateZ channel. Select the WolfBody and go to Skin > Edit Smooth Skin > Paint Skin Weights Tool > Options. The Paint Skin Weights Tool options window will open with the options described in Chapter 2.

2. In the Influence section, select the Neck joint. You'll see the influence of the selected joint on the geometry indicated by a white gradient on the surface. With your circular red brush, paint more influence over the upper jaw and head, giving the Neck joint 100 percent influence over those areas. Do the same with the Jaw joint, giving the joint the complete influence of the lower jaw (Figure 4.10).

3. For the armor pieces, I chose to bind them to the skeleton as opposed to parenting them so that we can get the effect attaching the armor's straps to the yoke. Select the LArmor joint and move it away from the body.

4. You should see some parts of the wolf's body pull outward with the LArmor joint's movement. Paint these vertices with the LShoulder or Body2 joints, depending on where the deformation is occurring, to remove the LArmor joint's

influence on these areas. The LArmor joint should influence *only* the armor strap pieces and nothing on the body itself!

5. Select all four LStrap objects. Isolate them through Show > Isolate Select > View Selected, through the camera's view panel menus. This hides the rest of the scene, displaying only the straps.

6. With the visible straps selected, activate the Paint Skin Weights Tool. Select the LArmor joint in the Influence section of the tool options, and click the Flood button a couple times to add 100 percent of the joint's influence to the entirety of the selected geometry.

**Figure 4.9** Obvious unwanted deformation directly after binding

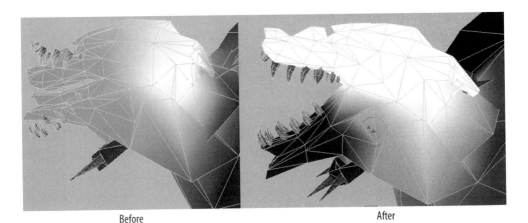

Before                                        After

**Figure 4.10** The influence of the Neck joint before and after editing the skin weights.

7. Now, select the Back2 joint and paint its influence on the two vertices on the ends of the planes closest to the wolf's body. This way, no matter how much we move the armor pieces, the part that is contacting the yoke will remain connected (Figure 4.11).

8. Repeat these steps for the RArmor joint. When finished, move the armor joints back to their original positions.

**Figure 4.11**
The armor pieces bound in such a way as to remain connected to the wolf's armor

### Front Leg Skin Weights

To get started on painting the skin weighting for the front legs, we'll move them and then paint away the irregular deformation we want to get rid of.

1. Select the LFrontFoot handle and move the leg forward. Isolate the WolfBody, hiding the other objects in the scene.

2. With a low brush opacity, paint away any unwanted deformation by adding the influence of other joints (such as the Back2 joint in this case) to take away the influence causing the irregularities (in this case, the LShoulder joint).

3. One thing we want to do is add the influence of the claws to the LFrontToe joint, as shown in Figure 4.12. This way, we can have some good claw extension with the rotation of the LFrontToe joint.

4. Repeat these steps for the other three legs, painting away surface irregularities and adding in the claw influence on each foot's toe joint.

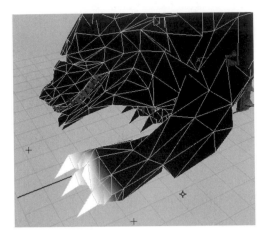

**Figure 4.12**
The LFrontToe joint's influence
on the claw geometry

### Tail and Mane

The remaining surfaces left to weight properly are the tail and the hairy mane. Since
we have only two joints available for the mane, our primary goal is to get just enough
articulation to allow for *some* kind of movement during animation, even if it isn't
extremely realistic or flowing all that much. Having some movement at least will be
much better than none at all.

If the hairy mane remained stiff and unmoving, it would actually be more
noticeable, since our eyes easily recognize when something isn't moving that should be.
Giving the hair a small amount of flowing movement will be enough to trick the eye
into accepting it, therefore making the unrealistic nature of the movement not much of
an issue. Remember, this is a "typical" enemy in the game and not one under nearly as
much scrutiny by the player as the featured characters and creatures!

For the tail, apply the influence along the tail to the tail joints as they are laid
out—the wrapped section near the body weighted to the Tail1 joint, the first two
geometry sections of the bushy part of the tail weighted to Tail2, and the remaining
portion at the tip of the tail weighted to Tail3 (Figure 4.13).

## Tutorial: Run Cycle

With the wolf rigged and weighted, the animation is ready to start. As with animating
anything, it's good to have a clear plan as to what movement you are trying to achieve.
For example, we are going to create a run cycle. If you watch a wolf (or a dog) as it
moves, you can see quite a difference in the animal's feet placement and rhythm of
motion when you compare its walk to a run or even to a trot.

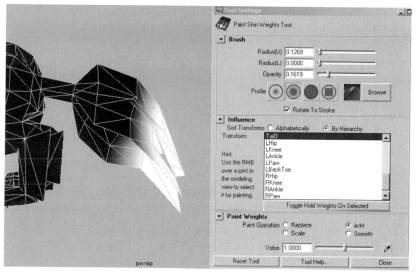

Figure 4.13 The Tail3 joint's influence on the tail geometry

A very good online reference for animal movement is the BBC Motion Gallery. Because of licensing costs, I was unable to get permission to actually show you some of their clips here or on the CD. However, they are easily accessible online at their website: http://www.bbcmotiongallery.com. To find some nice references for this particular project, do a keyword search for "wolf run" or "dog run" and specify the Animals category.

**Note:** To start animating with an already rigged Dire Wolf model, open the DireWolf_RunStart.ma file from the Scenes folder. The values used for positioning in the following tutorials assume this file is being used. Your own scene's positional values may vary.

With our rather limited number of joints in this project, most of our focus will be on the animal's legs and spine, where the dominant movement occurs.

### Spine

The spine of the wolf will be positioned for a mid-run trot, leaning forward.

**1.** Position the Pelvis joint as follows:

TranslateY: 7

TranslateZ: -2

RotateZ: -6

Set a keyframe for all three Translation and Rotation channels at frames 1 and 30.

2. While the Back1 joint doesn't need a rotation change, rotate the Z axis of the Back2 joint 19 degrees and the Z axis of the Neck joint 17 degrees.

3. Keyframe all three rotation channels for all three spine joints (including Back1 even though it had no change applied) at frames 1 and 30.

## Legs

Let's focus on the right legs first. Once they are in motion the way we want them, we can switch to the left side and get them in sequence as well.

1. Position the RFrontFoot as follows:

   TranslateX: 0

   TranslateY: 1.5

   TranslateZ: -2.75

   RotateX: 68

   RotateY: -2

   RotateZ: 4

   Set keyframes for all six channels at frame 1 and frame 30.

2. Adjust the leg's orientation by positioning its RFLegLocator:

   TranslateX: -2

   TranslateY: 6

   TranslateZ: -1

   Set a keyframe for these three channels at frame 1 and frame 30.

**Note:** You may notice that it can be difficult to gain access to the leg locators because of the cramped positioning of all four of them beneath the wolf's body and between the legs. You can make this easier by selecting each locator and adjusting its Local Position channels beneath the SHAPES section of the Channel Box. This moves the locator away from the body but doesn't change how it affects the leg's IK handles.

3. For the RBackFoot, position it as follows:

   TranslateX: -1.25

   TranslateY: 2.5

   TranslateZ: 4.5

   RotateX: 20

   RotateY: 0

   RotateZ: 0

   Set a keyframe for these six channels at frames 1 and 30.

**4.** Position the leg's RBLegLocator:

TranslateX: -2.6

TranslateY: 5

TranslateZ: 0.5

Keyframe these three channels at frame 1 and frame 30.

At this point, we should have a pose much like you see in Figure 4.14. The right front leg is pulled back while the right hind leg is forward, positioned outside the front leg so as not to collide.

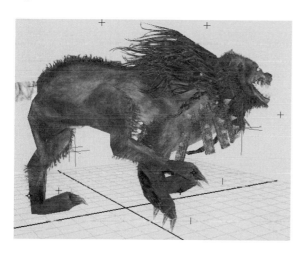

**Figure 4.14**

The initial right side leg positions

Now, we're going to make sure that every element that we have changed along the spine and the right legs has had its keyframes set for both frame 1 and frame 30.

Before we begin, turn on Autokey. This will cause any future changes we make to automatically set keyframes for them.

**1.** Go to frame 15. Position the RFrontFoot as follows:

TranslateX: 0

TranslateY: 3

TranslateZ: 5

RotateX: -8

RotateY: -2

RotateZ: 0

With Autokey turned on, a new keyframe is set at frame 15, applying these changes. However, you'll notice that we left the TranslateX channel unchanged, with a value of 0. Because we didn't make a change to the value, no keyframe was set for that value at frame 15. Therefore, we may want to go ahead and manually set a keyframe for it to make certain that no future changes made will cause this position to also subsequently change. Keep this kind of situation in mind when using Autokey.

2. The RFLegLocator can be moved forward and down to keep the leg's orientation correct:

TranslateX: -2.5

TranslateY: 1

TranslateZ: 4

3. Now, for the RBackFoot, let's move it back to this position:

TranslateX: -0.5

TranslateY: 3

TranslateZ: 3.75

RotateX: 135

RotateY: -5

RotateZ: 5

4. And for the RBLegLocator, move it down and back to this position:

TranslateX: -2

TranslateY: 2.25

TranslateZ: -3

We now have the opposite stride position for the right legs; they are outstretched, pushing and reaching for more forward distance (Figure 4.15).

Next, we'll tackle the wolf's foot strike as it hits the ground.

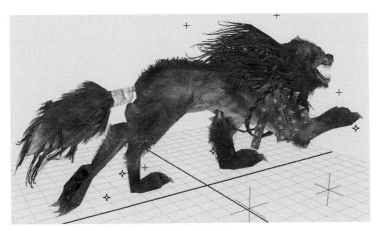

**Figure 4.15** The right legs in stride at frame 15

## Adding Ground Contact

If you play the animation at this point, you can see that we aren't getting a very satisfactory running movement so much as a paddling motion, as if the wolf was swimming. We'll need a couple more keys to put in the effect of ground contact points. Let's start with the right foot.

1.	Go to frame 18. Position the RFrontFoot as follows to create its ground contact:

	TranslateX: 0

	TranslateY: 0.5

	TranslateZ: 3.5

	RotateX: 27

	RotateY: -2

	RotateZ: 0

2.	At frame 6, position the RBackFoot to create its ground contact as follows:

	TranslateX: -0.3

	TranslateY: 1

	TranslateZ: 2

	RotateX: 50

	RotateY: 5

	RotateZ: -5

3.	The RBackFoot doesn't stay in contact with the ground long enough during the full push backward, so at frame 11 we'll create another keyframe, positioning the foot:

	TranslateX: -0.3

	TranslateY: 1

	TranslateZ: -2

	RotateX: 61

	RotateY: 0

	RotateZ: 0

If we play the animation now, we should see a nice run cycle—or at least half of one anyway (Figure 4.16)!

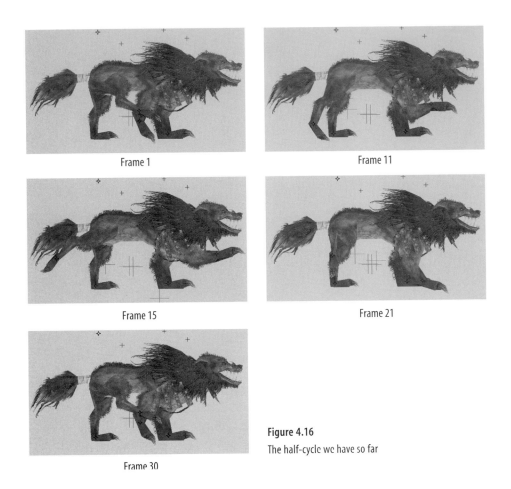

Frame 1

Frame 11

Frame 15

Frame 21

Frame 30

**Figure 4.16**
The half-cycle we have so far

## The Left Side

For the left side legs, we're going to set up a cycle that is essentially identical to the right side's movements. However, we want it to be asymmetrical so that both sides aren't moving exactly in synch. To make this a bit easier, we'll first match the movements of the right side, and then we'll offset the movement to give the entire run cycle enough asymmetry so as to not seem clunky and inorganic.

1. Set the LBackFoot and LFrontFoot to the same values as we did for the right side. The only difference is that our TranslateX value will be the opposite. So where the RBackFoot has a TranslateX value of -1.25, the LBackFoot will use a value of 1.25. Set keyframes for all three Translate and Rotate channels at frames 1 and 30.

2. Position the left leg locators in similar positions as their right-side counterparts, and keyframe their positions at frames 1 and 30.

**3.** We'll do the same at frame 15, mimicking the values we set with the right side for the left feet and the left-side locators.

**4.** Lastly, we'll mimic the ground contact points for the left feet, just as we did with the right side.

**5.** Once the keyframes are set, we can flatten the keyframe tangents at frames 1 and 30, helping smooth the repeating playback of the animation.

### Asymmetrical Movement

Now that the left and right legs are running in synchronized motion, we want to offset one side so that no one will think our Dire Wolf is a robot with stiff, inorganic movements.

**1.** Select the LBackFoot. Open the Graph Editor (Window > Animation Editors > Graph Editor). Here, we see the animation curves of the six keyframed channels of the LBackFoot (Figure 4.17).

**2.** In an empty area of the editor, left-click and drag a marquee selection box around all of the keys displayed in the Graph Editor. Within the Graph Editor menus, choose Edit > Copy.

**3.** Go to frame 30. Within the Graph Editor menus, choose Edit > Paste. The full set of keyframes from frames 1–30 is copied into frames 30–59!

**4.** Go to frame 59 and repeat, using the Edit > Paste command. We now have the run cycle keyframes running three times from frames 1–88.

**5.** Repeat these exact steps for the keyframes for the LFrontFoot, LFLegLocator, and LBLegLocator. When we're finished, we should have the left leg elements' keyframes shown three times in the Graph Editor, as seen in Figure 4.18.

**6.** Select both left feet and both left leg locators. With all four elements selected, left-click in an empty area of the Graph Editor and drag a marquee selection box around all of the animation curves, selecting all of the keyframes.

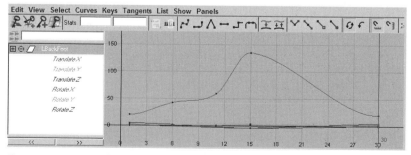

**Figure 4.17** The Graph Editor display for the LBackFoot

**7.** Make sure your Move Tool is active in the toolbar (or press the w hotkey). Hold the Shift key and middle-click and drag to the left in an empty area of the Graph Editor. This moves the *entire* selection of animation curves in a straight line to the left in the timeline.

**8.** Move the curves 28 frames to the left. The animation should play normally since all we did was replace the first 30-frame section with the second 30-frame section. So, we now have our main animation sequence running in frames 1–30 with additional sequences on either side of it in the timeline (Figure 4.19).

Now that we have a continuous sequence both in front of and behind the 30-frame focus of our animation, we can offset the motion as a whole and not worry about the animation's jerking or moving otherwise unnaturally when the 30-frame sequence repeats.

**9.** Select all of the animation curves of the left feet and locators again. Move the entire sequence to the right by five frames.

You should see a very natural, organic asymmetry to the leg movements, with the left feet contacting the ground five frames later than the right (Figure 4.20).

**10.** The last step for animating the feet is to animate the toe joints, keeping the toes from intersecting the ground too greatly. Use what you've learned so far to accomplish this simple procedure.

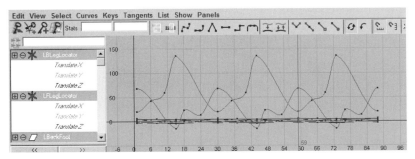

**Figure 4.18** The repeated keyframes for the left leg elements

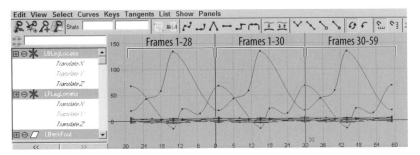

**Figure 4.19** The three keyframe sections placed in the Graph Editor

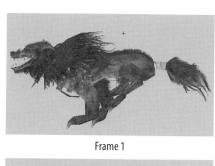
Frame 1

Frame 8

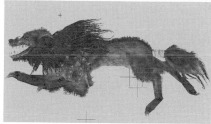
Frame 15

Frame 23

Frame 30

**Figure 4.20**
The finished leg movements of the run cycle

## Finishing Touches

Now that the leg movements are set, and thus the brunt of the animation, we can continue with the rest of the body to finish the run cycle.

1.  Let's get a bit of an exaggerated spine movement in there. At frame 15, make the following spine adjustments:

    **Back1** RotateZ: 20

    **Back2** RotateZ: 44

    **Neck** RotateZ: -30

2.  The tail will have a bit of counterbounce to its movement. At frame 1 (and also frame 30), set keyframes for the following values for the tail joints:

    **Tail1** RotateZ: -26

    **Tail2** RotateZ: 30

    **Tail3** RotateZ: 38

3. At frame 15, set the tail joints as follows:

   **Tail1** RotateZ: 26

   **Tail2** RotateZ: -10

   **Tail3** RotateZ: -20

4. To accentuate the countermovement of the tail, we'll delay the upward and downward rotation by adding extra keyframes at frames 8 and 21:

   | | | | | |
   |---|---|---|---|---|
   | **Tail1** | Frame 8 | Frame 21 | RotateZ: -16 | RotateZ: 25 |
   | **Tail2** | Frame 8 | Frame 21 | RotateZ: 0 | RotateZ: 20 |
   | **Tail3** | Frame 8 | Frame 21 | RotateZ: -1 | RotateZ: 23 |

   You can see the resulting movement in Figure 4.21.

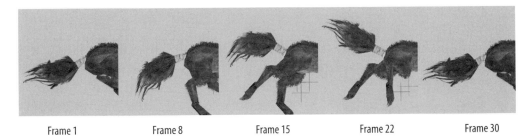

| Frame 1 | Frame 8 | Frame 15 | Frame 22 | Frame 30 |

**Figure 4.21** The tail counterbounce movement

## Secondary Animation

The last elements we have to animate for this run cycle are the secondary animations. This includes the bounce of the armor straps on the front shoulders and of the wolf's hairy mane.

1. The hair's counterbounce will start at frame 1 (and frame 30) at its default position (0, 0, 0), and we'll set keyframes for the rotation channels.

2. At frame 8, rotate the Hair1 joint up 35 degrees in the RotateZ channel.

3. At frame 15, rotate it down to 30 degrees, and at frame 22, bring it down to -6 degrees.

   The hair will bounce slightly as the wolf runs. Try to take what you have learned so far and apply such a bounce to the armor joints. If you'd like to see how mine turned out, take a look at the DireWolf_RunFinish.ma file in the Scenes folder (Figure 4.22).

Frame 1

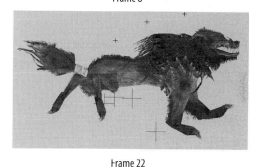

Frame 8

Frame 15

Frame 22

Frame 30

**Figure 4.22**
The final Dire Wolf run cycle

## Artist Profile: Kiel Figgins

**Job Title**  Animator
**Studio**  NCsoft, Austin
**Credits**  *Tabula Rasa, Heaven Vs Hell, Ms. PacMan: Maze Madness 2, GunForge, Leisure Suit Larry's Pocket Party, Azura*
**Personal Site**  http://www.3dfiggins.com

*Continues*

**Q.** Describe your role at your studio.

**A.** I currently work at NCsoft on *Tabula Rasa* as a creature animator and TD (Technical Director). I do animation, setup, exporting, implementation, bookkeeping, and scripting for animation tools. I work alongside three other animators, one more focused on animation, one more on technical aspects, and the last mainly on particles and effects. The four of us all work under the lead animator.

Typically, I am given a variety of tasks on a daily basis, including setting up characters, researching new tech paths, implementing characters into the game, scripting tools, and of course, animating. By working this way, I can take a creature from a model all the way into the game and fix any issues that may arise.

**Q.** What is your favorite style of animation to work with?

**A.** I find that I truly enjoy all facets and types of animation. My particular favorite is exaggerated realism, especially in the form of fast actions and acrobatics. I mainly attribute this to the *Aeon Flux* series. Animating fast action allows you to show so much energy and release the potential in characters. Having a character strike a hard-hitting pose or showing a creature unveil its true form in an eruption of fury really gets the viewer's blood pumping and gets them excited.

**Q.** What is your favorite kind of game?

**A.** Real-time strategy is by far my favorite. Games like *Starcraft*, *Warcraft*, *Command and Conquer*, and the *Dune* series are still on my computer. With the limitless ways to build, command, and ultimately destroy your opponent, they just keep me coming back. Atop that, I truly enjoy micro-managing and seeing how many tasks I can juggle, so building and commanding an army tests that in a great way.

**Q.** Which Maya animation tool, command, or editor could you not live without?

**A.** The Graph Editor, no question. Compared to other 3D packages that have versions of it, Maya has one of the most robust, clean, and functional Graph Editors that I've used. The Graph Editor is essential in all my animations, making it easy to spot loop errors, make tangent corrections, and add subtle nuances to existing curves quickly and accurately.

**Q.** What advice might you have for the up-and-coming animator?

**A.** Define what you enjoy and where you want to be, and it will become so much easier to achieve. If you know the specific company, research them; find out what they are looking for in a demo reel or portfolio. If it's a style, take *Prince of Persia*'s all the way to *Rayman*'s, and start looking up companies that follow that vein. This will give you a wider base of reference to draw from and companies to look into. Once you've established a direction, the process is fairly straightforward:

- Spend every minute of time you can practicing and producing work. But most important is to do it *every single day*, even if it's just for 30 minutes. Doing it daily is better then doing it once a week for a few hours.

- Get a website to show the work you've created, and keep it current. Companies won't just magically call you up and offer you a job. A website will allow you to showcase your work and get your name out there. Atop that, you can e-mail companies a link to your website instead of sending out rather expensive demo reel packages.

- Participate in and post your work on online forums, and keep up on the posts and work of others to see what they are doing and how you can apply that to your own animation. Remember, the people on these forums are your competition but are also a tremendous resource of insight and knowledge. All you have to do is tap into it.

- Revise your work based on the feedback given by the forums. This will not only build your reputation on the forums but will also get you revisiting your own work and bringing it to a higher level.

- Get to know your peers either in school or in the online community. They can show you how to best emphasize your assets and work with you to help create larger, more elaborate projects.

- Compile the very best of your animations, between 10 and 15 clips, or roughly a minute and a half of content, that are suited and aimed at a specific company's style and requirements into a demo reel. Host that on your site, write up a formal cover letter or e-mail, and start down the road to employment. Good luck!

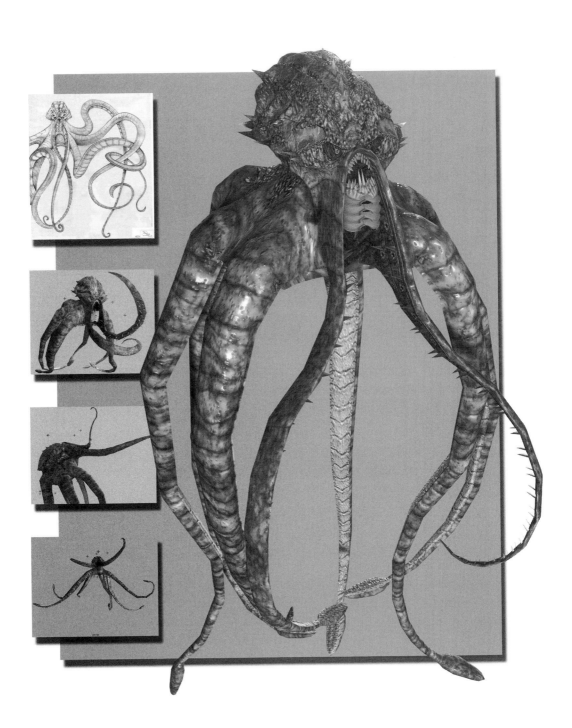

# Project: Giant Kraken

*So far, we've walked through the process of animating the playable character for a game using a biped, Calamity Jane. Then we animated a typical enemy creature, the Dire Wolf, in the form of a quadruped. Next, we'll raise the level of complexity by introducing the boss monster known as the Giant Kraken, an eight-legged, squid-like creature! It serves as a fitting example of what I call a spinal body type, made up of one or more long, sinewy tentacles that we are given the task of making come to life.*

**In this chapter, we'll discuss the following topics:**
Assignment Breakdown
Tutorial: Rigging the Giant Kraken
Tutorial: Idle Cycle
Tutorial: Attack Animation
Tutorial: Death Animation

## Assignment Breakdown

The Giant Kraken is, as its name suggests, a rather large creature, and it will serve the role of a featured "boss" monster. Since this role is similar to Calamity Jane's featured "player" role, we are given a little more freedom with the Kraken to make sure that it is rigged with an adequate level of articulation for quality movement, which is especially important with all the tentacles it has. Even so, we cannot afford to be too haphazard with our skeleton setup and need to keep efficiency well in mind.

### Behind the Giant Kraken

In most games, the player progresses through an environment or a level by fighting enemies, solving puzzles, and traversing obstacles until finally having a confrontation with the featured guardian of the level that the player must defeat before she is able to continue. This guardian is known as the area's "boss monster," and the Giant Kraken, a huge squid-like creature, fits this role nicely!

The model is composed of approximately 11,000 polygons and uses a 1024 × 1024 resolution texture map. In addition to the standard color map, it uses a bump map and a specular map.

A *bump map* is a grayscale image that dictates height information—white areas are high while black areas are low. This information interacts with the lighting of a scene to create the illusion of additional surface detail. A *normal map* is another type of file that makes use of such features.

A *specular map* is an image (it can be either grayscale or color) that dictates *specular* (or highlight) information. The color and intensity of a specular map can make a creature like the Kraken appear wet and slimy when rendered.

Both of these kinds of maps are freely supported within Maya, but it will be up to the game engine your project uses to determine if your game supports such maps. Your art director will make you aware of such freedoms or limitations as dictated by your game engine.

Before we begin the project, take a minute to read about the artist behind the Giant Kraken. His background will give you some insight into the obstacles he faced with the project.

### About the Artist

**Name** David Russ, age 42
**Personal website** http://home.austin.rr.com/misterhombre/
**Describe your role at your current studio.** Senior artist. Mostly responsible for character modeling, texturing, and animation.

**Did you face any significant challenges with the Giant Kraken model?** Keeping within the polycount is always a challenge. The UV mapping on this model was also a bit of a challenge due to the fact that it was one seamless skin, without any "build in" seams like at the edge of clothes or between materials.

**Can you describe your basic workflow?** On this model, I worked from an extruded sphere that I kept refining, adding/deleting/extruding faces until the form filled the drawing, which I loaded into the background plane while working. A few shortcuts, like refining only half the model and then mirroring and modeling only one tentacle and copying it around, saved time.

Concept art by Steve Garcia

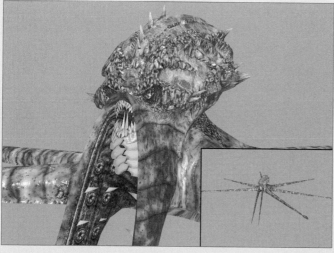

Game art by David Russ

## Tutorial: Rigging the Giant Kraken

To begin, we'll set up our project directory and open the initial file that starts our lesson.

1. 💿 Browse on the CD to Project_Files/Chapter_5/Giant_Kraken. Copy the Giant_Kraken directory to your hard drive. Open the file GiantKraken_Start.ma from the Scenes directory.

   This file contains the modeled and textured geometry for the Giant Kraken monster.

2. We'll start creating the Kraken's skeleton. Let's begin with the legs, since there are so many of them. Go to the Top view, and with the Joint Tool (Skeleton > Joint Tool), lay the first joint at the point where the rear right tentacle joins the main section of the body.

3. Start laying out the joints in a chain, along the center of the tentacle. Position the joints at every second polygonal division in the tentacle, as shown in Figure 5.1.

   We'll use a chain consisting of 12 joints. The 12th joint is placed merely to align the rotation of the previously positioned joint. Once the joint chain is complete, you can delete the 12th joint, leaving the remaining 11.

4. Switch to the Persp view and raise the chain up 5.35 units in the Y direction, positioning it properly within the tentacle geometry. Name these joints **LBackTent1–11** (referring to left back tentacle).

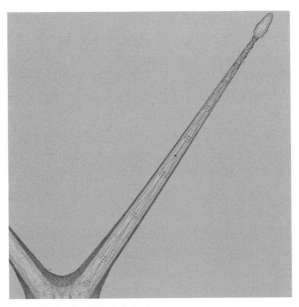

**Figure 5.1** The first joint chain in place

5. Repeat this process for the middle left and front left tentacles, creating 12-joint chains, deleting the 12th, and positioning the remaining 11 joints within the geometry. Name these **LMidTent1–11** and **LFrontTent1–11**, respectively.

   You'll notice that the joints get closer and closer together as they near the tips of the tentacles. This will give us finer control over the more agile ends of the tentacles compared to the thicker area where the tentacles join with the body.

6. In the Side view, we'll start a joint chain for the tentacle on the left side of the Kraken's mouth. These tentacles around the mouth will serve as the main mandibles used for attacking and grasping, so they'll need applicable articulation.

   Starting around the area where the tentacle merges into the body, create a 13 joint chain, again placing a joint at every second polygonal division of the tentacle, as in Figure 5.2. The 13th joint is for orientation purposes and can be deleted after it is placed.

7. In the Persp view, move the joint chain 0.7 units in the X direction, positioning the chain's root joint in the center of the tentacle. Run down the chain, rotating the joints one by one to orient the chain down the center of the tentacle's geometry.

8. Name these joints **LMouthTent1–12**.

   Next, we'll continue the skeleton by creating the joint structure for the Kraken's head and mouth.

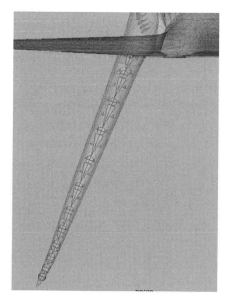

**Figure 5.2**
The mouth's left tentacle joints in place

## Continuing the Skeleton

The head is composed of a few different elements that we'll want to articulate for animation. On each side of the head is a row of gills that will open and close to simulate the underwater creature's breathing. Also, the mouth will open and close.

1. In the Side view, place a five-joint chain that will serve as a sort of spine for the Kraken (Figure 5.3). Name these joints **Root, Neck1, Neck2, Head1,** and **Head2.**

2. Place another joint at the corner of the lower jaw and name it **Mouth.** Parent it to the Neck2 joint.

3. Position a joint in the center of the gills on the left side of the head (Figure 5.4). Rotate it as follows:

   - RotateX: -2
   - RotateY: 20
   - RotateZ: -45

   Name it **LGills** and parent it to the Neck2 joint.

4. Select the first joint of each main tentacle (LBackTent1, LMidTent1, and LFrontTent1) and parent them to the Root joint.

5. Select the LMouthTent1 joint and parent it to the Neck1 joint.

6. Next, we'll mirror the left tentacle joints over for the right side. One by one, select the first joint of each tentacle and use the Skeleton > Mirror Joint command, making sure to do a search and replace to switch the L in the joint names with R in the mirror options (Figure 5.5).

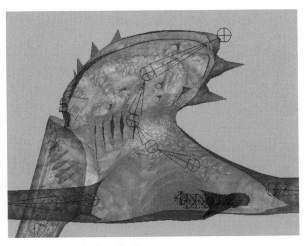

**Figure 5.3** The Kraken's small spine

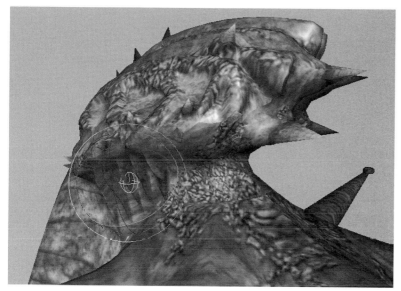

**Figure 5.4** The LGills joint ready to breathe

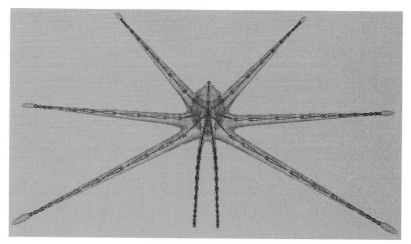

**Figure 5.5** The Kraken skeleton

At this point, we have 98 joints in the skeleton. We can go through and clean this up a bit, removing joints that we don't necessarily have to have. In a real game situation, the player will be facing the Kraken from the front most of the time. Therefore, the middle and rear tentacles will be obscured from view for much of the fight. With this in mind, let's try removing a few joints from those areas to get our joint count lower.

In this case, we'll use the Skeleton > Remove Joint command on the following:

- LBackTent2, 4, 6, 8, and 10
- RBackTent2, 4, 6, 8, and 10
- LMidTent2, 4, 8, and 10
- RMidTent2, 4, 8, and 10

Now we have a progression of articulation ranging from the front tentacles with more freedom of movement to the back tentacles with less (Figure 5.6).

Renumber the joints so that they are in the correct numerical order.

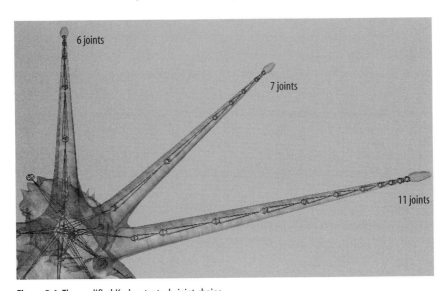

**Figure 5.6** The modified Kraken tentacle joint chains

## Applying Animation Controls

As with all of our projects, we'll add selection handles and selection sets to make element selection for animation faster and easier.

1. Select the following joints: LFrontTent1, LMidTent1, LBackTent1, RFrontTent1, RMidTent1, RBackTent1, LMouthTent1, RMouthTent1, Root, Neck1, Neck2, Mouth, LGills, and finally RGills.

2. With these joints selected, go to Display > Component Display > Selection Handles. The selection handles of the joints will become visible.

3. Click the Select by Component Type button in the status line and enable the Handles selection mask. Now that you're able to select the handles, you can move them away from the model to allow for easier selection (Figure 5.7).

**Figure 5.7**

The Kraken's selection handles displayed in the scene

## Preparing Selection Sets

These tentacles are going to be challenging to animate, especially when we try to recreate the undulating movements such sinewy forms are known to make. Imagine trying to select and rotate each joint in a tentacle one at a time to create a curling motion! Not a favorable scenario. However, there are a few things we can do to make this process easier. Creating selection sets is what we'll explore in this section.

**1.** Select all of the joints of the left front tentacle (LFrontTent1–11).

**2.** Go to Create > Sets > Quick Select Set.

**3.** In the Create Quick Select Set window that opens, type in a name for the selection set, such as **LFrontTentacle**, and click OK.

**4.** Repeat this for the remaining seven tentacles, selecting each of the joints that make up a tentacle and creating a Quick Select Set for them.

**5.** Once you have finished, open the Outliner (Window > Outliner).

The Outliner is simply a list of every element within the scene. You'll see now at the bottom of the list each of our Quick Select Sets. You'll also find them under Edit > Quick Select Sets. Now that these selection sets are within our menu system, we can create shortcuts for them on the shelf in Maya's interface.

**1.** To the left of the shelf in the interface (directly above the viewports) there is a black arrow pointing down. Left-click and hold this arrow to bring up options for the shelf area. Select New Shelf from the available options.

**2.** In the window that appears, name the new shelf **Tentacles**. Click OK.

**3.** A new shelf tab appears, empty and ready to hold new shortcuts. Go to Edit > Quick Select Sets. Hold down Ctrl+Shift and left-click the LFrontTentacle set. It then appears in the shelf as a shortcut.

**4.** Repeat this for all of the tentacle selection sets (Figure 5.8).

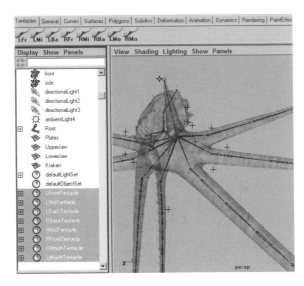

**Figure 5.8**

The tentacle Quick Select Sets in the Outliner and on the shelf

**Note:** When you open my provided files from the CD for this project, this shelf will not be included since it's a modification to Maya's interface and your user preferences. Repeat these four steps to create the shelf and shortcuts when working with the provided files.

You can rearrange the shelf icons by middle-clicking and dragging them to a different location. You can also delete a shelf icon by middle-clicking and dragging it to the trashcan icon on the far right.

### Binding to the Skeleton

Now that our skeleton is completed and ready to be animated, we can bind the Kraken geometry. Not every part of the Kraken will be bound, however. Some elements will not deform, so they will be parented to the joints that best control their movement.

**Note:** To start from an already built skeleton, use the GiantKraken_Skeleton.ma file from the Project_Files/Chapter_5/Giant_Kraken/Scenes directory. The values for positioning in the following tutorials assume this file is being used. Your own scene's positional values may vary.

1. Select the UpperJaw object. Shift+click the Neck2 joint and press the **p** key (or choose Edit > Parent) to parent the object to the joint. These may be easier to select by using the Outliner. However, make sure you Ctrl+click the Neck2 joint instead of using Shift when dealing with the Outliner's listed items.

2.  Do the same with the LowerJaw and Plates objects, parenting them to the Mouth joint.

3.  Select the Kraken object, which makes up the majority of the monster's body. Shift+click the Root joint. Go to Skin > Bind Skin > Smooth Bind > Options.

    In the options, make sure you use the same values that we have been using for our previous projects:

    - Max Influences: 2
    - Dropoff Rate: 8.5

    Click the Bind Skin button to apply the settings.

## Painting the Weights

Because of the long, straight forms that the Kraken's tentacles are made of, you'll find that their vertex weight is usually distributed very nicely without much weight modification. The only area we really need to focus on is the head.

1.  The Mouth joint's only purpose is to control the lower jaw. We don't want any vertex weighting from the head applied to it. With that in mind, select the Kraken mesh and go to Skin > Edit Smooth Skin > Paint Skin Weights Tool > Options.

2.  Select the Mouth joint in the Influence section's list of joints. You can see the joint's influence on the mesh by the gray area that shows up on the geometry. This is the influence we want to get rid of.

3.  Select the Neck2 joint. Lower the Opacity of your brush to around 0.3, and start painting the region over which the Mouth joint had influence. Switch back and forth between the Neck2 joint and the Mouth joint to check your progress. The goal is to completely remove all influence of the Mouth joint.

4.  Next, rotate the Neck2 joint -17 units in the RotateX channel. You'll see that the area around the mouth has a very strong separation of weight from where the influence of the Neck2 joint blends into the influence of the Neck1 joint.

5.  Select the Neck1 joint from the Paint Skin Weights Tool window, and start painting up the folds around the sides of the mouth to smooth the transition (Figure 5.9).

6.  The next bit of weighting we need to worry about is the vertex weighting of the L and RGills joints. Select the LGills joint in the Paint Skin Weights Tool window. You can see from its area of influence that it encompasses much of the side of the head. We want this joint to control only the edges of the gill folds on the left side of the head.

7. With the Opacity of the brush set to 1, paint the edges of the gills on the left side of the head with 100 percent influence for the LGills joint.

8. Select the Neck2 joint in the Paint Skin Weights Tool window, and paint its influence around the left side of the head to replace the influence of the LGills joint over the rest of the head. Your result should look something like Figure 5.10.

9. Repeat for the RGills joint and its influence.

10. Rotate the Neck1 joint 35 degrees in the RotateZ channel. You'll see the body around the base of the tentacles pull away rather rigidly.

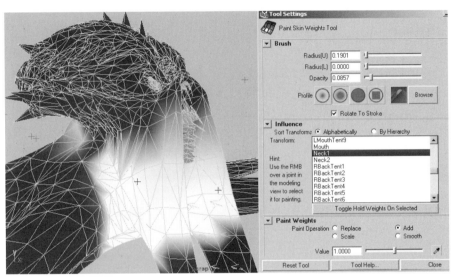

**Figure 5.9** The smooth transition around the mouth

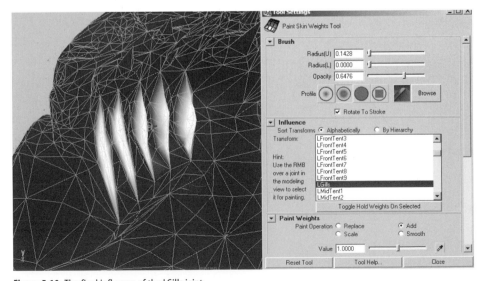

**Figure 5.10** The final influence of the LGills joint

11. Select the Root joint from the Paint Skin Weights Tool window, and begin smoothing out the transition, as shown in Figure 5.11.

12. Lastly, paint 100 percent of each tentacle end joint's influence over the tip of its tentacle.

At this point, the rigging of the Giant Kraken should be complete. Now we'll start animating.

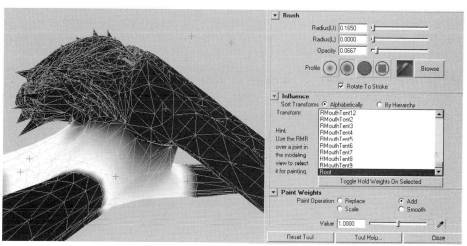

**Figure 5.11** The Root joint's influence on the body

## Tutorial: Idle Cycle

In our previous projects, we've created a walk cycle and a run cycle. The next most prevalent type of animation cycle used in games is called an *idle cycle*, or idle animation. When a character or creature in a game (whether being controlled by a player or not) stops moving, it generally enters some sort of idle state. This is the animation that a character plays while it is literally doing nothing. If it did not have an idle animation, the creature would freeze in place, not moving a pixel, until a different animation is triggered.

In some cases, multiple idle cycles are created for a single character. For example, in Nintendo's *Super Mario 64* for the Nintendo 64, if the player did not touch the controls, the character Mario would stand still, breathing heavily. Every now and then, he might look around. And if the player didn't touch the controls for a minute or so, Mario would look back at the player wondering why he wasn't moving and would eventually lie down and fall asleep. Having multiple idle cycles will help your characters seem more alive by limiting the number of repeating actions they do.

As a default idle cycle for the Giant Kraken, it will simply bob in place, swaying its tentacles through the ocean currents in which it lives.

We'll first want to establish a starting pose for the idle cycle. The easiest way to manipulate the tentacles is to first select a tentacle's Quick Select Set shortcut from the shelf, which selects each joint in a tentacle's chain. Then, rotate the *entire* chain all at once. You'll see that this give you a very satisfactory curling motion of the tentacles.

I also recommend using the Persp/Outliner panel setup. This is easily accessible with the shortcut button on the left side of the UI, beneath the toolbox. It will open the Outliner window as one of your viewport panels. Once you get the entire tentacle curled in the general direction you want, you can then open the tentacle's Quick Select Set section in the Outliner and quickly select a partial section of the tentacle to rotate in a different direction. Let me show you what I mean.

1. Select the LFrontTentacle Quick Select Set, and rotate all of the selected joints -24 degrees in the RotateZ channel.

2. In the Outliner, expand the LFrontTentacle Quick Select Set group by left-clicking the [+] icon next to its name. Then, left-click and drag from LFrontTent5 through 11. This selects these seven joints. Rotate these joints 15 degrees in the RotateZ channel, swinging this part of the tentacle in the opposite direction.

3. And lastly, select the LFrontTent1 joint (easily accessible by the selection handle), and rotate it -55 degrees in the RotateZ channel, swinging the tentacle down a little farther.

You can see how by using the controls we've set up manipulating such a large number of joints at once becomes very quick and easy. Continue to manipulate the other tentacles in this fashion, positioning them in a naturally random way, as in Figure 5.12.

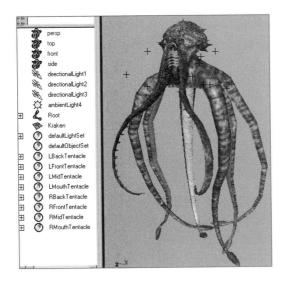

**Figure 5.12**
The initial pose for the idle animation cycle

## Beginning the Animation

The main thing the Kraken will be doing in this animation is an underwater undulating sway of his tentacles with maybe a bob of its head. We'll also include some gill breathing and maybe some kind of small mouth movement. The main goal is to make sure the animation's cycling isn't too deliberate and unnatural looking.

> **Note:** To start from an already rigged skeleton, use the GiantKraken_Rigged.ma file from the Project_Files/Chapter_5/Giant_Kraken/Scenes directory. The values for positioning in the following tutorials assume this file is being used. Your own scene's positional values may vary.

1.  Now that the tentacles are positioned, select each tentacle's Quick Select Set in turn and press Shift+e to set keyframes for all of the tentacle joints' rotation channels at frame 1.

2.  The entire cycle will be approximately three seconds long, so repeat step 1 at frame 90 (30 frames = one second in most cases).

3.  Back at frame 1, select the following joints: Root, LGills, RGills, and Mouth. Press Shift+w to set keyframes for each of these joints' translation channels. Repeat at frame 90.

4.  Lastly, select the Root, Neck1, Neck2, and Head1 joints, and keyframe their rotation channels at frames 1 and 90.

5.  Now that we have our start and end keyframes set, we can start adding the in-between motion. Go to frame 30 and select each tentacle's Quick Select Set and reposition it. Once again, try to position them in naturally random positions, as I have in Figure 5.13.

6.  We'll repeat this one more time at frame 60, creating new rotation keyframes for each tentacle, giving them new positions.

## Smoothing the Cycle's Repeat

As we've done with our other animation cycles, we need to smooth the repeating keyframe values at the beginning and end of the cycle, as well as smooth the animation as a whole.

1.  Open the Graph Editor (Window > Animation Editors > Graph Editor).

2.  Select the LFrontTentacle Quick Select Set. All of the keyframes we set for the animation appear in the Graph Editor. Press the f shortcut key to frame all of the animation curves in our view. Left-click in an empty area of the graph view, and drag to select all of the animation curves.

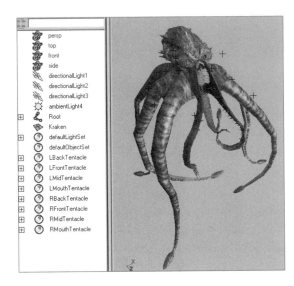

**Figure 5.13**

The tentacle poses at frame 30

3.  With all of the animation curves selected, go to Tangents > Spline. This makes all of the keyframes have spline tangents, which results in very smooth transitions between keyframes.

4.  Left-click and drag a selection around all of the keyframes at frame 1. Hold Shift and drag a selection around all of the keyframes at frame 90, adding them to your selection. With both sets of keyframes selected, go to Tangents > Flat. This will smooth the transition between repeating cycles.

5.  Repeat this process for each tentacle.

## Creating the Head Movement

The head should move very little. We don't want any extreme or obvious movements that detract from the natural look of the animation's repeating. Remember, this animation is simply an idle animation that the creature uses when it's not doing anything and is waiting for the player to interact with it or waiting for its other animations to be triggered.

1.  At frames 30 and 60, give the head a slight rotation using the Root, Neck1, Neck2, and Head1 joints. The direction almost doesn't matter, but make sure it's very small.

    The only thing we're doing here is preventing the body from not moving during its idle animation. Any living creature, even when idle, should have some sort of movement unless it is consciously trying not to move—but then it wouldn't be idle, would it?

2. The gills should be opening and closing throughout the animation. Depending on how fast you want them to move, set keyframes for the gill joints' TranslateZ channel to move the gills back and forth at regular intervals (for example, every 15–20 frames), simulating the opening and closing of the gills.

3. Smooth these joints' repeating values as we did with the tentacles, making them use spline tangents for all of the interior keyframes and flat tangents for the first and last keyframes of the cycle.

4. Lastly, we can give the mouth some movement by opening it slightly at frame 45. We don't want to move the mouth around too much because it would look strange as the animation repeats over and over again.

   At this point, the idle animation is essentially complete. You can see how mine turned out by opening the GiantKraken_Idle.ma file in the Scenes directory.

## Tutorial: Attack Animation

For our attack animation sequence, we'll create a tentacle slash attack across the area in front of the Kraken as if it is striking at the player. The two tentacles around the Kraken's mouth, with their spiked interiors, are its primary weapons. Don't forget that although we'll be indicating forward movement, we won't actually be moving the creature forward. That occurs within the game itself.

1. We want to start with a pose very similar to the first frame pose of the idle animation. You can either re-create the pose or simply use the file from your idle animation (or the one I provide) and delete all of the keyframes except for the ones at frame 1. To save time, don't delete the gill joint movement so you can reuse it for this animation as well.

   If you want to use this pose to start other animations, go ahead and save it as GiantKraken_animStart.ma. I also have provided a GiantKraken_animStart.ma file in the Scenes directory that you can use.

2. For this big tentacle swing, we'll have the Kraken first rear back with his tentacles before coming through with the attack. Go to frame 20. Rotate the Root joint back in the Z direction 25 degrees.

3. We want the Kraken to still be able to see its target, so rotate the Neck1 joint -8 degrees in the Z direction and the Neck2 joint 3 degrees in the X direction to have the head turn down to face the general area where the player would be (Figure 5.14).

4. Next, we'll go in for our first tentacle attack! At frame 45, rotate the Root joint -30 degrees in the Z direction and pull it forward, toward the area where the player would be located.

5. Rotate the RMouthTentacle chain forward, slashing it across the front of the Kraken.

6. Curl the leg tentacles backward, giving them a feeling of forward movement, as seen in Figure 5.15.

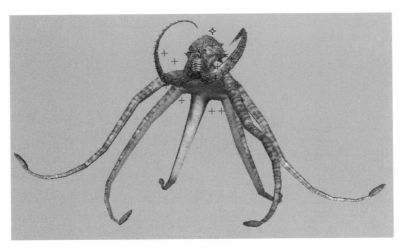

**Figure 5.14** The Kraken ready to strike at frame 20

Frame 45 (Persp)

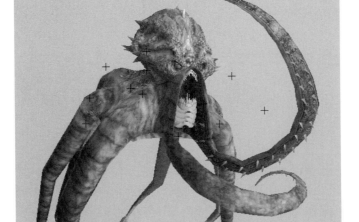

**Figure 5.15** The Kraken's change of position at frame 45 for the tentacle attack

Frame 20                                Frame 45

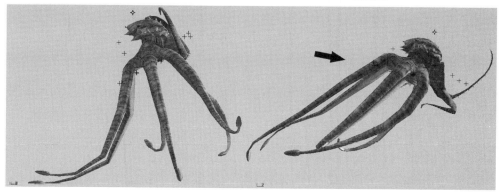

**Figure 5.15** (continued)

**7.** Go to frame 50 and repeat for the LMouthTentacle, curling it forward as it comes in for its own attack swing.

**8.** At frame 55, you can continue the RMouthTentacle's slashing move backward, out of the LMouthTentacle's path.

**9.** In order to accentuate the forward thrust of movement, go back to frame 30 and curl the tentacles up as in Figure 5.16. Now it really looks as if the Kraken is pulling itself through the water as it rockets forward to strike!

**Figure 5.16** Adding anticipation to the Kraken's forward thrust

## Finishing the Sequence

Now that the attack is over, we need to finish the sequence by bringing the Kraken back to a more neutral state, ready for the next animation to be triggered.

1.  Let's go ahead and get the ending pose positioned and then worry about making the Kraken *get* to that pose in between. At frame 80, copy the keyframe values from frame 1 using the methods we discussed earlier:

    • Go to frame 1.

    • Middle-click and drag on the timeline to frame 80, moving time forward without playing the scene.

    • Set applicable keyframes at their current positions.

2.  If we play through the animation here, obviously the Kraken just floats back to its position at frame 80. Go to frame 60 and curl the tentacles forward as if the Kraken's forward momentum has halted. This will help visually sell the fact that the creature has stopped its forward thrust and has finished the movement (Figure 5.17).

3.  We can now add any secondary animation we wish, predominantly with the mouth. For example, when the monster is charging in to attack, perhaps its mouth would be open as if roaring ferociously!

    To see how my attack animation turned out, take a look at the GiantKraken_Attack.ma file in the Scenes directory.

**Figure 5.17**

The Kraken slowing to a stop

# Tutorial: Death Animation

Every character in a game needs, at the bare minimum, three animations (depending on the type of game, of course): walk/run, idle, and death. With just those three actions, a character can seem real. Add in a few attack and reaction animations, and it might even seem to think! But every character or creature in the game needs at least one death animation, ranging from the simple squeak and collapse of a rat to the more elaborate deaths of the player characters themselves.

For the Giant Kraken, our death animation will be rather simple, because of its tentacle-heavy structure.

1.  Open the GiantKraken_animStart.ma file to begin the animation in a neutral pose. You can use the one I provide in the Scenes directory if you'd like.

2.  Right away at frame 10 position the head (using the Root, Neck1, and Neck 2 joints) and mouth tentacles back as if recoiling from a fatal blow (Figure 5.18)! You can also open the mouth wide for the creature's dying roar.

3.  As the Giant Kraken dies, its head will flail around a little before finally drooping down. At frame 20, turn the head in the opposite direction, still recoiled backward.

4.  At frame 40, the last bit of energy left in the creature is being spent, so we'll turn its head forward some.

**Figure 5.18** That's gotta hurt!

**5.** Finally at frame 62, the monster comes to its final rest. Flop the head drastically forward as if bowing down.

**6.** To really accentuate the finality of the death, go back some to frame 50 and rotate the head backward again. If you play the animation now, you can see the head rolling back and forth, flailing for a moment before finally flopping downward, dead as the proverbial doornail (Figure 5.19).

**Figure 5.19**
The head position at the Giant Kraken's dying moment

With the head's movements set in place, we can use them as cues for what the tentacles should be doing. We'll first focus on the tentacles around the mouth.

**1.** Just as we did with the head, we'll make the tentacles flail around in pain and shock at the beginning of the animation until finally coming to their final rest. The mouth tentacles in particular are the Kraken's equivalent "arms" and will react the most violently to the attack.

About every 20 frames from frame 10, curl the mouth tentacles into poses that convey the frantic emotion that the monster is experiencing, for example, as I have shown in Figure 5.20.

**2.** We're going to do the same thing with the rest of the tentacles. However, after the initial recoil movement we make at frame 10, we'll make their additional movements a bit more subdued and not quite as expressive, until finally coming to rest around frame 70.

It's a good rule of thumb to not set keyframes for multiple elements all at the same time. Space the keyframes out a little to get a more natural randomness of movement into the scene.

For example, we may set keyframes at frames 10, 30, 50, and 70 for one or two of the tentacles, but for others we set keyframes at frames 10, 35, 57, 72, and so on.

3.  Set keyframes for each tentacle, finishing up the Giant Kraken's death throes (Figure 5.21).

You can see how mine turned out by opening the GiantKraken_Death.ma file from the Scenes directory.

Frame 30       Frame 50       Frame 70

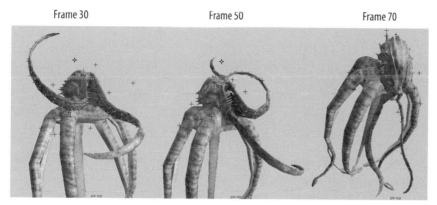

**Figure 5.20** The mouth tentacles' movements in the Kraken's death animation

Frame 10       Frame 30

Frame 50       Frame 75

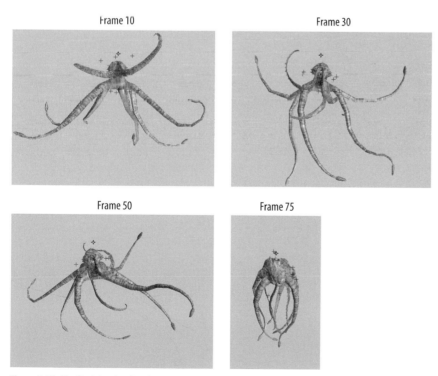

**Figure 5.21** The final death animation sequence

## Artist Profile: Grayson Chalmers

**Job Title** Character lead
**Studio** Midway Studios Austin
**Credits** *Area 51*
**Personal website** http://www.graysonchalmers.com

**Q.** How and why did you get into the game industry?

**A.** I got into the game industry because I grew up loving games. I wanted to help create these worlds that immersed people and entertained. I like the game industry as well because the teams are on the small side compared to movies, and it means you have more influence over how the final product looks. It's fun to have that kind of input; it really makes you proud to see a game you worked on hit the shelves.

As for the how—I got here by just busting my ass working as hard as I could until I got the chance to prove myself in production, at my first job with Warthog Texas. Hard work got me most of the way, but I also believe that you have to constantly compare yourself to what's going on in the 3D world. I was always looking at other artists' websites and forums, checking out their work, always trying to push myself to learn more and improve my craft.

**Q.** Describe your role at your studio.

**A.** Right now I am overseeing everything character related: modeling, texturing, animation, tech, and even cinemas. Most of this I just oversee; the work I actually produce myself is mostly character animation and a bunch of tech R&D work, testing and experimenting with new systems. I'm looking for new and better ways of doing things so that when we hit production, we'll be prepared for whatever we're challenged with.

**Q.** What has been the most inspirational to you in regard to your artwork?

**A.** The main inspiration, and most of the reason why I picked up 3D in the first place, is that I was playing *Warhammer 40k* and I kept visualizing scenarios in my head, and I needed to get them out. But in general, I'm inspired by almost anything. I'm a big fan of dark, eerie photography from guys like Larry Wiese (www.lwiese.com). I also love movies like *Collateral*, *Man on Fire*, and *Blackhawk Down*.

**Q.** What is your favorite style of animation to work with?

**A.** I love physical stuff: characters falling off ledges, tearing open or kicking down doors, jumping up and tackling other characters, and bouncing off every surface. I like big, painful stuff that would probably break bones if you tried to motion-capture it.

**Q.** What is your favorite kind of game?

**A.** I grew up on first-person shooters, and that's what I continue to play. I love them! I'm really happy that most of the developers are still finding new ways to advance this type of game and keep it fun and interesting. I've been playing a lot of *Battlefield 2* lately. I friggin' love that game.

**Q.** Which Maya animation tool, command, or editor could you not live without?

**A.** The Graph Editor and Dope Sheet. I like keeping my keys as few and clean as possible early on so I can retime any part of the animation quickly with the Dope Sheet, and the whole thing can be revised quickly and easily with the Graph Editor [by manipulating] tangents.

**Q.** What advice might you have for the up-and-coming animator?

**A.** *Observe!* Watch the way people and things move. You'll be amazed once you start to look closely. Watch the way people walk, open doors, and react to other people. Watch everything! Also, don't ever get buried in the technical challenges. Remember that it's all about the quality of animation. And lastly, keep your eyes open to what's going on around you in the 3D community. Get inspired by what other people are doing in your industry, and ask yourself if your work holds up to that standard. There is always room to learn more and improve yourself and your animation. Never stop moving forward.

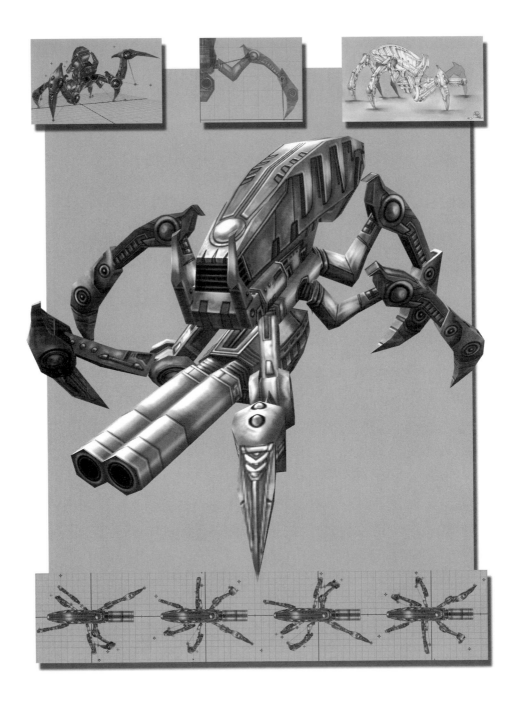

# Project: Storm Tank

*Now that we've faced the challenges of rigging and animating a biped, a quadruped, and a spinal character, we can scale back the number of legs a bit to six. However, in addition to the number of legs involved, we'll add the challenge of bringing to life the movements of an inorganic, mechanical fantasy vehicle along with some additional limitations that certain game types bring into play.*

**In this chapter, we'll cover the following topics:**
Assignment Breakdown
Tutorial: Rigging the Storm Tank
Tutorial: Walk Cycle
Tutorial: Action Sequence

## Assignment Breakdown

The Storm Tank is a mechanical fantasy vehicle, not using any deformation or bending. Because of this, smooth binding is not necessary. Instead, we can simply parent the geometry to the respective joints. Also, because of the nature of the game type that the Storm Tank is designed for, we need to make sure we use as few joints as possible. As described in the following sidebar, this tank is just one part of a large army of units that the player will potentially be using, and with so many animated characters, creatures, and vehicles on the screen at once, the number of joints per character needs to be carefully maintained.

### Behind the Storm Tank

The Storm Tank is designed to be a unit in a Real-Time Strategy game (or RTS). In RTS games, the player manages and controls large armies of characters and/or vehicles. As the game progresses, the player gains access to an increasingly powerful armory, eventually culminating into a single, expensive mega-unit that serves as the army's most powerful weapon. *That* is the Storm Tank!

It consists of approximately 1,100 polygons, which is fairly high for an RTS unit. However, the idea is that the Storm Tank would be so powerful and expensive to make, the player could only have a maximum of 10 or so in his army at any one time, as opposed to the dozens of smaller units he could create. So, because there are never too many on the screen at once, the polycount can be a little higher than the other units.

Right now we're using a 512 × 512 texture for the Storm Tank for printing and presentation purposes. In an actual RTS game, this would be much lower, closer to 128 × 128 or smaller because the camera view would be so far away in order to see the entire army clearly.

Any art limitations and requirements will be made known to you by your art lead in a real project, of course.

Before you get started on your first Storm Tank tutorial, take a minute to read about the artist behind the Storm Tank.

### About the Artist

**Name** Leif Robles, age 24
**Studio** Gearbox Software
**Personal website** http://www.angelfire.com/art2/leif_robles/3d2d/
**Describe your role at your current studio.** I am a high-poly environment modeler, texture artist, and normal mapper.

**Did you face any significant challenges with the Storm Tank model?** The most significant was probably getting the polycount down to the budget given and figuring out what some parts of the tank would look like that were not visible in the concept.

**Can you describe your basic work flow?** It all begins with a concept drawing that I study. Then I make a few simple sketches of the sides and front to give me a better idea of the shape. From there, I begin box modeling. *Box modeling* is a technique in 3D modeling. Using the box modeling method, a modeler starts out with a 3D primitive (typically a cube or cylinder) and extrudes faces from this, resizing them as needed, and connecting the vertices.

With the model finished, I begin UV mapping, using planar projection maps. I then set it all up into one neat and organized UV layout, ready for texturing in Adobe Photoshop.

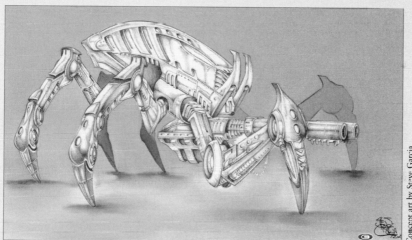

Concept art by Steve Garcia

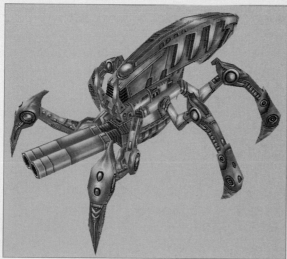

Game art by Leif Robles

## Tutorial: Rigging the Storm Tank

Just as with the previous projects, the first step to rigging the storm tank is to create the model's skeleton and animation controls. Because of the model's inorganic nature, we won't be using typical binding methods. Instead, we'll parent the major moving pieces of the tank to the joints to drive the movement.

**Note:** If parenting geometry to joints is unsupported by your game engine, bind the geometry normally as we have thus far in our projects. Use the Flood command in the Paint Skin Weights Tool options (as described in Chapter 2) to bind an entire object to the joints mentioned later in the lesson *instead* of parenting as described.

1. ⊙ Browse on the CD to Project_Files/Chapter_6/Storm_Tank. Copy the Storm_Tank directory to your hard drive. Open the file StormTank_Start.ma from the Scenes directory.

   This file contains the modeled and textured geometry for the Storm Tank vehicle.

2. In the Top view, with the Joint Tool active (Skeleton > Joint Tool) lay down a four-joint chain through the tank's left middle leg. In the Persp view, fine-tune the placement of the joints at the major points of articulation, as in Figure 6.1.

3. Name these joints **LMidLegBody**, **LMidLegKnee**, **LMidLegFoot**, and **LMidLegEnd**.

4. Select the LMidLegBody joint and duplicate the joint chain. Move and rotate it to align with the left back leg. Name these joints **LBackLegBody**, **LBackLegKnee**, **LBackLegFoot**, and **LBackLegEnd**.

5. Repeat again with the left front leg, repositioning the joints to fit with the major points of articulation of the front leg. Name these joints **LFrontLegBody**, **LFrontLegKnee**, **LFrontLegFoot**, and **LFrontLegEnd** (Figure 6.2).

6. Now, we'll begin creating the skeleton for the central pieces of the tank. We want to have controls for recoil and other bracing effects for the tank's cannon fire animation. With that in mind, in the Side view, place a four-joint chain as shown in Figure 6.3.

7. The fourth joint was placed to align the rotation of the third joint to the direction of the joint chain. Delete the fourth joint, leaving three. Name these joints **Pelvis**, **RecoilShaft**, and **RecoilBrace**.

8. For the cannon, we'll need a two-joint chain, placed in the Side view like in the first image of Figure 6.4. Once the chain is placed, press the Insert key on the keyboard to enter edit pivot mode, which allows you to raise the first joint up to the top of the cannon, where it meets the body, without disturbing the second joint, resulting in the positions you see in the second image.

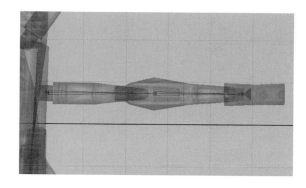

**Figure 6.1**
The middle left leg joints in place
(top view)

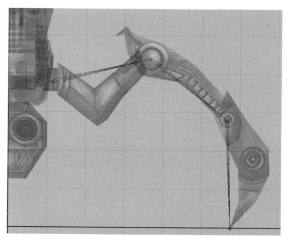

**Figure 6.1**
(side view)

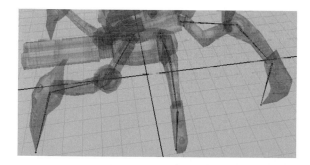

**Figure 6.2**
The front- and back-left
leg joints in place

**Figure 6.3**
The initial central frame joints

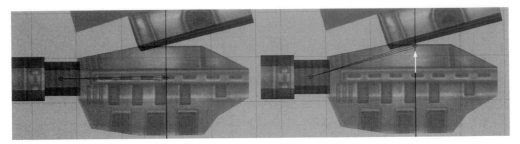

**Figure 6.4** The cannon joints first placed for alignment, then positioned

The reason why we place the chain straight before moving the joint up is to align the joint's rotation with the cannon. Once aligned, we can move it without disrupting that alignment.

**9.** Name these joints **CannonBody** and **CannonBarrel**.

**10.** Parent the following joints to the Pelvis joint: CannonBody, LFrontLegBody, LMidLegBody, and LBackLegBody.

**11.** Now that we have the left legs all rigged and joined into the tank's skeleton, we can mirror them across for the right legs. Select the LFrontLegBody joint. In the **Skeleton > Mirror Joint > Options** window, type **LFrontLeg** in the Search For section and **RFrontLeg** in the Replace With section. Press Apply.

**12.** Repeat for the other two leg joint chains, replacing the first L in their names with an R to designate the right side. Once you've finished doing this, the Storm Tank's skeleton is complete (Figure 6.5)!

Now you're ready for the remaining steps of rigging the storm tank: parenting to the skeleton and creating animation controls.

**Figure 6.5**
The finished Storm Tank skeleton

## Parenting to the Skeleton

Instead of a traditional binding as we've been doing with the organic characters and creatures thus far, this time we will parent entire sections of geometry to the joints to achieve a very inorganic, mechanical look. Parent each child with the indicated parent:

| Child (Geometry) | Parent (Joint) |
| --- | --- |
| Body | Pelvis |
| GunBody | CannonBody |
| GunBarrel | CannonBarrel |
| LBackLegUpper | LBackLegBody |
| LBackBodyJoint | LBackLegBody |
| LMidLegUpper | LMidLegBody |
| LMidBodyJoint | LMidLegBody |
| LFrontLegUpper | LFrontLegBody |
| LFrontBodyJoint | LFrontLegBody |
| LFrontLegKneeTube | LFrontLegKnee |
| LFrontLegKneeJoint | LFrontLegKnee |

Repeat the above for their right leg counterparts where applicable. In addition, parent the remaining unparented body parts to the joints that share their name. For example, the LBackLegKnee object should be parented to the LBackLegKnee joint.

Don't forget to save your file.

## Creating Animation Controls

Just like with our previous projects, we'll add IK handles and selection handles for easy access.

1. With the IK Handle Tool (Skeleton > IK Handle Tool) active (make certain the Sticky option is enabled), left-click the LBackLegBody joint. Then, left-click the LBackLegEnd joint. An IK handle is created between the two joints for the left back leg. Name the IK handle **LBackLegIK**.

2. Repeat with the other five legs, creating IK handles for each and naming them appropriately.

3. Display selection handles for each leg's IK handle, as well as the following joints: Pelvis, RecoilShaft, RecoilBrace, CannonBody, CannonBarrel. We'll also want to display selection handles for each leg's Foot object—the pointed geometry at the end of each leg.

4. Move all of these selection handles around the body for easy access, as shown in Figure 6.6.

Next up, you'll learn about the Storm Tank walk cycle.

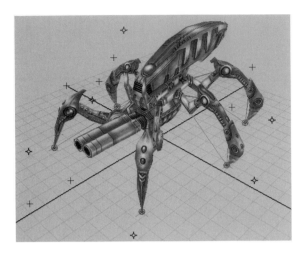

**Figure 6.6**
The Storm Tank's animation
controls in place

## Tutorial: Walk Cycle

With six legs to coordinate, we obviously have some work ahead of us in order to get
the tank walking. Rather than putting it into a pose and working from there, we'll
instead work on the legs in pairs. First, we'll handle the movement of the front legs,
then the rear, and finally the middle.

**Note:** Make sure your scene is set to play at 30 fps. To start with an already rigged Storm Tank, open the
file StormTank_Rigged.ma from the Scenes folder. The values used for positioning in the following
tutorials assume this file is being used. Your own scene's positional values may vary.

1. Select the LFrontLegIK and move it forward, stretching the front leg out as far
   as it will go without bending the joint unnaturally. I took mine about 8.5 units
   in the Z direction.

2. Adjust the IK handle's Twist attribute in the Channel Box to about 10 degrees,
   orienting the leg's knee to point upward.

3. Set keyframes for the IK Handle's Twist and TranslateX, Y, and Z attributes at
   frame 1. This animation will be approximately 45 frames long, so set another
   set of keys for these attributes at frame 46.

4. At frame 23, move the LFrontLegIK backward to 1.1 units in the Z direction.
   Playing the animation now shows the left front leg running along the ground
   back and forth.

5. At frame 38, move the LFrontLegIK up 3.7 units in the Y direction and forward
   a little bit to 7.4 units in the Z direction. Adjust the Twist to 13 degrees.

Now we have a definite reach, grab, and pull motion to the left front leg (Figure 6.7). There are a few other things we can do to accentuate the movement.

**6.**  Select the LFrontLegFoot object (not the joint). Set a keyframe at its default rotation (0, 0, 0) at frames 1, 23, and 46.

**7.**  We're going to accentuate the motion by using the spiked foot on the end of the leg. At frame 32, rotate the LFrontLegFoot object -17 degrees in the Z direction, rotating it downward.

**8.**  At frame 42, rotate the foot 41 degrees in the Z direction, rotating it upward.

For the right side's front leg, we'll be doing the same steps, except when the left front leg is forward, the right front leg is back, and vice versa.

**9.**  With that in mind, move the RFrontLegIK back to 1.1 units in the Z direction at frame 1, setting a keyframe there and also at frame 46.

**10.**  Set the Twist attribute to -17. Set a keyframe for it at frames 1 and 46 as well.

**11.**  At frame 23, when the left leg is back, move the right leg forward 8.5 units in the Z direction.

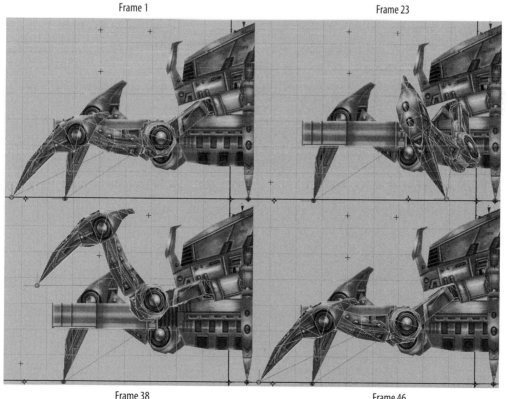

Frame 1        Frame 23

Frame 38        Frame 46

**Figure 6.7** Initial movement of the front left leg

Just as with the left leg, we'll accentuate the right leg's movement by rotating the RFrontLegFoot object.

**12.** At frame 6, rotate the foot down -17 degrees.

**13.** At frame 17, rotate the RFrontLegFoot up 24 degrees (Figure 6.8).

### Setting Back Leg Movement

We have two sets of legs left to animate. Let's skip the middle legs for now and look at the back legs. While the front legs are reaching out to pull the tank forward, the back legs will push against the ground to make forward progress.

### Left Rear

The back legs' positions will be opposite those of the front legs. When the left front leg is stretched forward, we'll have the left back leg pulled inward, and vice versa.

**1.** Move the LBackLegIK forward and to the side with values of -3.3 TranslateZ and 2 TranslateX. Set keyframes at this position for frames 1 and 46.

**2.** Set the Twist attribute of the LBackLegIK to -8. Keyframe this value at frames 1 and 46 as well.

**3.** At frame 23, move the LBackLegIK back -8.5, extending the leg as far as possible without an unnatural bend in the knee. Set the Twist to -6.5, making sure the leg doesn't intersect the body.

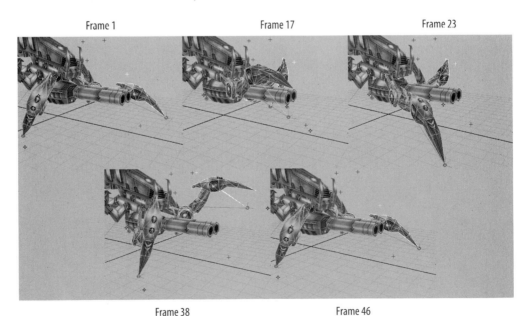

**Figure 6.8** The front legs' movement

4. Go to frame 37. Lift the left back leg up to 3.1 TranslateY and forward -5.1 TranslateZ. Set the twist to -6.1.

5. Let's give the leg's upward movement more of an arc by adding one more keyframe at frame 29. Lift the leg up to 2.5 TranslateY and back slightly to -9 TranslateZ.

We should get an arcing movement as in Figure 6.9.

**Right Rear**

Once again, we'll do the same steps for the right back leg but flip the timing; when the left back leg is tucked in, the right back leg is stretched out, and vice versa.

1. Position the RBackLegIK at -2 TranslateX and -8.5 TranslateZ. Adjust the IK's Twist attribute to 6.5. Set keyframes at this position for these attributes at frames 1 and 46.

2. At frame 23, move the right leg forward to -3.5 TranslateZ and with a 13.5 Twist.

3. Go to frame 14. Lift the right back leg up to 3.1 TranslateY and forward -5 TranslateZ. Set the Twist to -5.

4. Again, for a more arcing movement, we'll add another keyframe at frame 6. Lift the right back leg up to 2.5 TranslateY and back -9 TranslateZ (Figure 6.10).

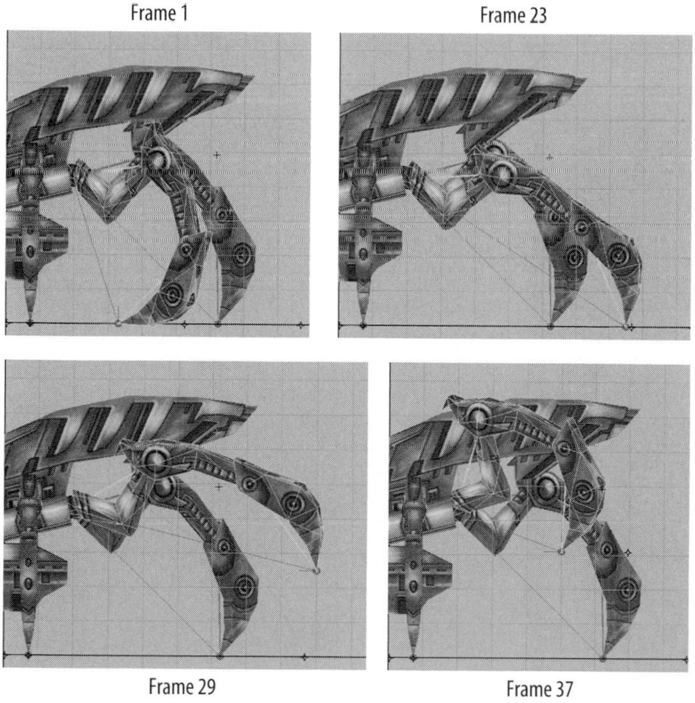

Frame 1    Frame 23

Frame 29    Frame 37

**Figure 6.9** The back left leg movement

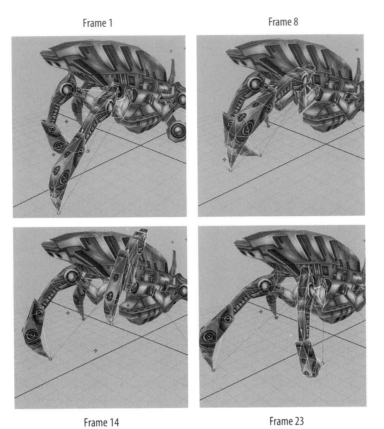

Frame 1        Frame 8

Frame 14        Frame 23

**Figure 6.10** The back right legs' movement

## Creating Middle Leg Movement

Now that we have the front and back legs moving along, we need to animate the middle set of legs. Because the front and back legs are synchronized to both be lifted into the air and touching the ground at the same time, the middle leg will need to counter this, serving as the ground contact while the other two are lifted.

### Middle Left Side

Let's start with the left leg.

1.  At frame 1 (and subsequently frame 46), position the LMidLegIK at 4.5 TranslateX and -5 TranslateZ. Set the Twist attribute to -25, bringing the leg's knee upright.

2.  At frame 23, move the leg forward 0.5 TranslateZ. Set the Twist back to 0. The left middle leg will now slide back and forth between the front and rear legs.

**3.** We want the middle leg to lift while the front and back legs are contacting the ground. So, at frame 14, lift the middle leg upward and position it as follows:

- TranslateX: 5
- TranslateY: 3.1
- TranslateZ: 0
- Twist: -9

Now you can see a definite lift and push movement with the middle leg. You should also notice that the ends of each leg are moving to meet the other as they move along their cyclic paths.

For example, imagine a piece of cloth on the end of the front leg. As the leg moves back, it passes the cloth to the middle leg, which then moves it back and passes it to the back leg, which then kicks it out the back side.

This is exactly how the ground is being "transferred" between the legs as the tank makes its way forward (Figure 6.11).

**4.** At frame 38, set the LMidLegIK's Twist attribute to 5.5 to accentuate the pushing movement by turning the knee to face more of a forward direction.

To further accentuate the movement, we'll animate the LMidLegFoot object to swing outward to "grab" more ground as it pulls forward, just as we did with the front leg's foot.

**5.** Select the LMidLegFoot geometry. Set keyframes at its default rotation (0, 0, 0) at frames 1, 23, and 46.

**6.** At frame 16, rotate the foot outward 36.5 degrees in the RotateZ channel.

**7.** At frame 5, rotate the foot inward -16 degrees in the RotateZ channel.

Frame 1            Frame 14

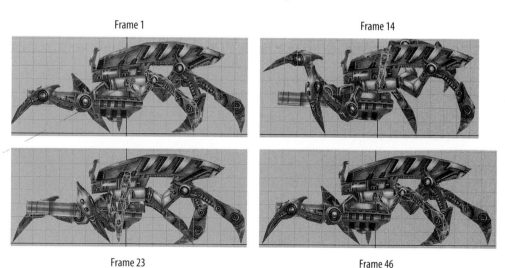

Frame 23            Frame 46

**Figure 6.11** The left middle leg's initial movement

### Middle Right Side

We'll now do the same for the right side's middle leg, making sure it is contacting the ground while the other two right legs are lifted, and vice versa.

**1.** Move the RMidLegIK to the following position:

- TranslateX: -4.5
- TranslateY: 0
- TranslateZ: 0.5
- Twist: 0

Set keyframes with these values at frames 1 and 46.

**2.** At frame 23, move the leg back to -5 TranslateZ and set the Twist to -16 degrees to point the knee forward to accentuate the pulling motion of the leg.

**3.** At frame 37 we'll key the position of the leg at the following:

- TranslateX: -5
- TranslateY: 3.1
- TranslateZ: 0
- Twist: -11

The right leg is now mimicking the movement we set with the left. To accentuate the pulling motion, we'll manipulate the RMidLegFoot object just as we did with the left.

**4.** Select the RMidLegFoot object and set a keyframe at its default rotation (0, 0, 0) at frames 1, 23, and 46.

**5.** At frame 28, rotate the foot object inward -10 degrees in the RotateZ.

**6.** At frame 39, rotate the foot outward 37 degrees in the RotateZ.

The walk cycle is almost complete! We have the legs moving like we want (Figure 6.12). Now we need to animate the body reacting to the movement instead of simply being stationary as it is now.

### Creating Body Movement

The body needs to react to the movement of the legs, rising and falling with the strides.

**1.** At frame 14, position the Torso as follows:

- TranslateX: 0.6
- TranslateY: 6
- TranslateZ: -0.5
- RotateX: -14
- RotateY: 0
- RotateZ: 0

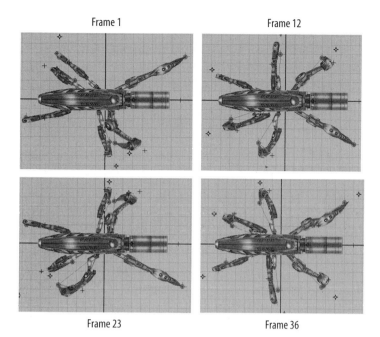

Frame 1          Frame 12

Frame 23          Frame 36

**Figure 6.12** The final leg movement

Set keyframes for the above.

**2.** At frame 36, we'll have the body rotate the other way, as follows:

- TranslateX: -0.6
- TranslateY: 6
- TranslateZ: -0.5
- RotateX: 14

**3.** Now that we have the torso high points, we'll keyframe the low points of the stride. At frames 1, 24, and 46, set all of the Translation and Rotation channels to 0 except TranslateY, which we'll lower to 4.5.

We have the basic torso movement now. However, to add a bit more dynamism to the movement, we can punch up the body's rotation, reacting to the up-and-down motion and delaying the side-to-side motion of the stride.

**4.** At frames 1, 24, and 46, rotate the RotateZ channel to 10.

**5.** At frames 14 and 36, rotate the RotateZ channel to -10.

**6.** For one more tiny adjustment, rotate the RotateX channel to 5 at frames 1 and 46 and rotate it to -5 at frame 24.

You can see how these little rotation adjustments have added a more dynamic motion to the torso as it performs follow-through of the up-and-down and side-to-side movement that we established earlier.

### Establishing Gun Bounce

For a bit of secondary motion, we can give the gun a bit of a counterbounce reaction to the up-and-down movement of the body.

**1.** At frames 1, 24, and 46, rotate the CannonBody joint 5 degrees in the RotateZ channel.

**2.** At frames 12 and 36, rotate it -10 degrees in the RotateZ channel.

With the addition of the secondary motion, the animation is essentially complete (Figure 6.13).

Before we can really wrap up this animation and send it on its way, we just need to smooth the transition at the beginning and end of the cycle. As we have done in our previous projects, select each animated element, select the first and last keyframes in the Graph Editor (Window > Animation Editors > Graph Editor), and flatten the tangents, removing any bumps in the animation's ability to cycle smoothly (Figure 6.14).

To view my finished walk cycle, open the StormTank_WalkFinish.ma file from the Scenes folder in your Storm_Tank directory.

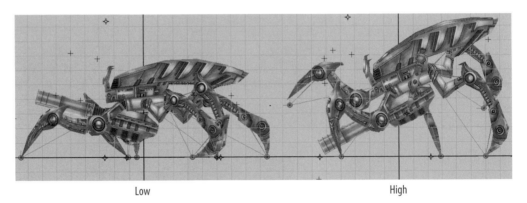

Low                    High

**Figure 6.13** The highs and lows of the walk cycle

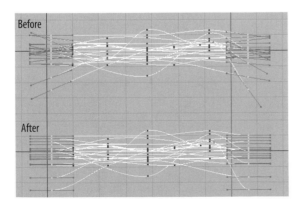

Before

After

**Figure 6.14**
Flattening the tangents of the beginning and end of the animation cycle

## Artist Profile: Adam Houghton

**Job Title**  Animator

**Studio**  Amaze Entertainment

**Credits**  *Sims 2* (DS and GBA), *Robots* (DS and GBA)

**Personal website**  http://www.myartiscool.com

**Q.**  How and why did you get into the game industry?

**A.**  I always had an interest in art and computers, so it was a very natural progression. I started out doing graphic design while in college and after a couple years decided to focus my education on video games. I was in a rather broad Digital Media program, but with the indulgence of my instructors, I was able to base many of my projects on building an art portfolio for games. After graduation I packed up and moved to Seattle. I knew that I had a much better chance of getting my foot in the door if I lived in the area where I wanted to find work. I spent some time filling out my portfolio and then hit the pavement. I asked anybody I could find in the industry to take a look at my work and review my portfolio. Eventually I lucked out and asked the right person for advice. It turned out his studio was in need of junior artists and I was in!

**Q.**  Describe your role at your studio.

**A.**  The division of the company I work in specializes in handheld games, in particular the Nintendo GBA and DS. Handheld development differs from console or PC in that we have shorter project cycles, smaller teams, and a lot of technical challenges. That being the case, we tend to wear a lot of hats. On any given day you can find me modeling, texturing, animating, or troubleshooting problems with artists and programmers. I was once told that the core of what we do as artists is problem solving, and I wholeheartedly believe that today.

**Q.**  What has been the most inspirational to you in regard to your artwork?

**A.**  I've always been inspired by the Renaissance old masters. Their dedication to their craft was a lifelong endeavor. I am still amazed by the golden age of Disney. I find it so incredible that they produced work that still holds up and even puts to shame much of what is produced today. Most of all, I am continually impressed and inspired by the artistic community that I interact with online and the people with whom I've had the good fortune to work.

**Q.**  What is your favorite style of animation to work with?

**A.**  On *Sims 2* I had the chance to work on two styles of animation that I really enjoy, albeit for different reasons. The goofy comedic style of some of the characters came very naturally. I'm a complete clown, so getting to animate someone peeing their pants or an alien with a Napoleon complex was awesome. Other times we needed simple naturalistic animation like a character showering or washing its hands. Studying and breaking down everyday actions and then portraying them in an entertaining and believable way can be extremely difficult. However, you learn so much about the world around you in the process that makes it totally worth the extra effort!

**Q.**   What is your favorite kind of game?

**A.**   Seeing as I'm a really busy guy, a game has to really grab me to justify spending time on it. I like games that deliver a complete package, inventive and polished visuals that serve great game play. *Shadow of the Colossus* is a great example of that. There are also a lot of fun and innovative smaller-scope games coming out right now that utilize the novel features of the DS such as wireless network play, the real-time clock, and the touch screen.

**Q.**   Which Maya animation tool, command, or editor could you not live without?

**A.**   Maya's Graph Editor is my very best friend. I like to take a minimal approach to keyframing. The fewer keys I have, the cleaner my animation will be in the event that I have to revise or copy it. The Graph Editor allows me to keep it simple and organized and to use well-tweaked curves rather than additional keyframes.

**Q.**   What advice might you have for the up-and-coming animator?

**A.**   Pay attention to the fundamentals of animation as well as your knowledge of anatomy. Those are the foundation upon which your animation career will be built. Make sure that you are well versed in all sorts of animation styles. It may look like all a game animator does is run, shoot, and death animations. However, that is rarely the case. Your reel should include challenging animations. How does a sad character open a refrigerator door and remove a jar of mayonnaise? How does that differ from a depressed character opening a cabinet and removing a ketchup bottle? How can you show those feelings without using facial expressions? How does a brave character fight? How does that differ from a character who is scared silly but fighting anyway?

Also, take every opportunity to learn from those around you. If you see someone's work that impresses you, ask them all the questions they'll allow. Never let competition or ego get in the way of a chance to learn.

A degree means absolutely nothing if you don't have the skills to back it up. Your education is your own responsibility, so go the extra mile whenever possible. Gauge your skill by looking at the best of the best, as those will be the people you'll be competing with for jobs!

There is a natural inclination to specialize, but being a good all-around artist makes it *much* easier to find work. Having a broad skill set also gives you insight into how your work fits into the big picture. You'll be best off if you are adept at everything: drawing, modeling, texturing, rigging, and animation.

Once you are working, you are going to make mistakes. Everyone does. When it happens, fix it efficiently and learn from the error. Giving excuses or trying to shift blame just makes you look bad. What will make you look good is the speedy way you fix it and move on.

The industry is a close-knit family, and your reputation will follow you wherever you go, for bad or for good. So do your best to build bridges, not burn them.

Be flexible. If a new tool or technique comes along that you can incorporate into your workflow, take the time to learn and use it!

But most of all, remember to have fun!

## Tutorial: Action Sequence

For our second animation sequence, we'll create a cannon-fire action sequence. Now we could do a simple action, firing the cannon from its current position and doing all of the secondary actions and so on, but let's make things a little more interesting. Let's say that the tank's weapon is actually a long-range artillery cannon and has to get into a firing position before actually letting loose with the shooting.

So, with that direction in mind, we need to get the cannon on top of the tank and brace it to the ground, ready to fire!

**Note:** To start with a clean version of the Storm Tank, use the StormTank_Rigged.ma file from the Scenes folder.

1. First, we need to keyframe the position of each leg so that they remain in contact with the ground as we manipulate the tank's body. Select each IK handle and keyframe their Translation channels at frame 1.

2. Next, let's go ahead and track the movement we want the cannon to travel. Set a keyframe at the CannonBody joint's original position at frame 1.

3. At frame 25, move the CannonBody as follows:
   - TranslateX: -6.9
   - TranslateY: 0.3
   - RotateZ: -50

   This brings the cannon back to the rear of the body (Figure 6.15).

4. Go to frame 40 and flip the cannon up on to the top of the body with the following values:
   - TranslateX: -7
   - TranslateY: 0.8
   - RotateZ: -170

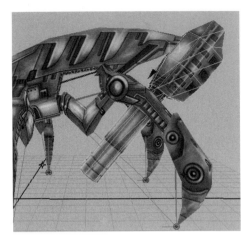

**Figure 6.15**
The cannon moving to the
back of the body

5. At frame 78, move the cannon forward with the following values:

   • TranslateX: 1.5

   • TranslateY: 1.3

   • RotateZ: -210

6. The cannon will hit our recoil bracket and bounce back slightly to its final resting spot at frame 85 with the following values:

   • TranslateX: 1

   • TranslateY: 1.4

   • RotateZ: -207

7. The cannon dips too far down on its way to its final resting spot, intersecting the body geometry, so at frame 70, raise the cannon as follows:

   • TranslateX: -2.1

   • TranslateY: 2

   • RotateZ: -194

8. I also want the cannon to slow down a bit before making its way to the end of its path, so at frame 55, let's do that with the following:

   • TranslateX: -5.5

   • TranslateY: 1.5

   • RotateZ: -170

   To fulfill the action sequence, we need to create body movement and recoil brace animation, and then we need to ensure that the sequence continues. So, that's what we'll do in these next sections.

## Creating Body Movement

Now that the cannon's path is known, we can animate the body parts to accommodate this movement. To do that, we'll use six keyframes, set as follows:

Frame 1

- TranslateX: 0
- TranslateY: 4.2
- TranslateZ: 0
- RotateX: 0
- RotateY: 0
- RotateZ: 28.5

Frame 30

- TranslateY: 4.3
- TranslateZ: -1.5
- RotateY: 2.5
- RotateZ: -23

Frame 45

- TranslateY: 4
- TranslateZ: 0.5
- RotateY: 2.5
- RotateZ: 21

Frame 60

- TranslateY: 5.2
- TranslateZ: 1.3
- RotateY: 2.8
- RotateZ: -16

Frame 75

- TranslateY: 4
- TranslateZ: 2
- RotateY: 3
- RotateZ: -8

Frame 85

- TranslateY: 4
- TranslateZ: 2
- RotateY: 2
- RotateZ: 6.5

You should see now why we made some of the movements of the cannon as we did. The additional movement of the body worked to really help sell the believability and weight of getting something with the cannon's mass up on top of the tank chassis and into the locked firing position.

### Making Recoil Brace Animation

Before this aspect of the preshooting sequence is complete, we have one more bit to animate: the recoil brace. We animated the cannon's reaction to the brace but haven't animated the brace for it to react to!

1. Select the RecoilShaft joint and set a keyframe at its original position at frame 55.

2. At frame 80, rotate the RecoilShaft up 13 degrees in the RotateZ channel.

3. Select the RecoilBrace joint and set a keyframe at its original position at frame 75.

4. At frame 80, move the RecoilBrace joint back 3 units in the TranslateX.

5. At frame 85, move the RecoilBrace joint forward 2.5 units in the TranslateX.

Now, with the recoil brace's movement in place, the cannon's bounce at the end of its animation makes visual sense (Figure 6.16).

### Continuing the Sequence

The next part of the sequence is for the tank to dig in its front legs to brace itself for its cannon's powerful blast!

1. Select the LFrontLegIK handle and set a new keyframe at its original position for frame 85.

2. At frame 95, lift the leg 3 units in the Y direction. Then, at frame 100, bring the leg down through the ground plane -1.5 units in the Y direction.

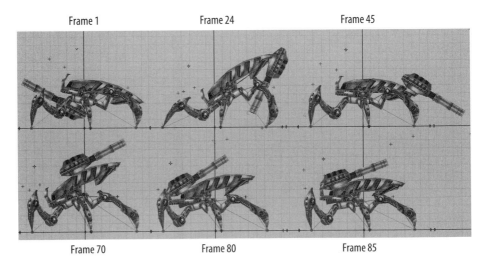

Frame 1    Frame 24    Frame 45

Frame 70    Frame 80    Frame 85

**Figure 6.16** The animation sequence so far, frames 1–85

**3.** We'll do the same with the RFrontLegIK handle, starting at frame 100. Set a keyframe at its original position.

**4.** At frame 110, move the right leg up 3 units in the Y direction. Then, at frame 115, lower the leg through the ground plane -1.5 units in the Y direction.

We've now animated the tank drilling its front legs into the ground. Just as we did with the walk cycle, we'll rotate the foot objects to accentuate the "grabbing" motion.

**5.** Select the LFrontLegFoot object and set a key at its original position at frame 85.

**6.** At frame 95, rotate it up 67 degrees in the RotateZ direction.

**7.** At frame 100, rotate it back down to 0.

**8.** Repeat for the RFrontLegFoot object for frames 100, 110, and 115.

### Creating Additional Body Movement

We can't move the legs like this without having the body react in *some* way, can we?

**1.** At frame 85, make sure you have a keyframe set for all three Translation channels and all three Rotation channels where they are for the Pelvis joint. This way, we won't mess up any of our previous set keys when we start adding new ones further down the timeline.

**2.** At frame 95, we'll rotate the Pelvis as follows:

- RotateX: 14.5
- RotateY: -5
- RotateZ: 37

You can see now that the body is reacting believably to the lifting of the leg (Figure 6.17). Go ahead and set a keyframe for the current Translation channel values.

**3.** At frame 110, we'll do the same thing in the opposite direction:

- RotateX: -14.5
- RotateY: 5
- RotateZ: 37

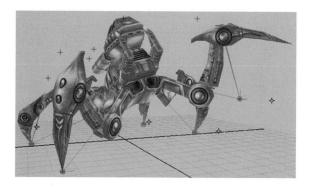

**Figure 6.17**
The body rotating upward
with the lifting of the leg

**Set keyframes for the current Translation channel values here as well.**

4.  Now, at frame 100, we'll lower the body and rotate it toward the downward motion of the driving left leg (Figure 6.18).

    - RotateX: -17
    - RotateY: 3
    - RotateZ: -3

5.  Again, we'll mirror this at frame 115 when the right leg is being driven down into the ground.

    - RotateX: 17
    - RotateY: -3
    - RotateZ: -3

6.  At frame 140, we can have the body stabilize itself, setting all the rotation channels to 0. Move the body to the following:

    - TranslateY: 4
    - TranslateZ: -0.3

### 3... 2... 1... FIRE!

We're now ready to fire the cannon! At frame 140, make sure the Translation and Rotation channels of the CannonBody, CannonBarrel, RecoilShaft, RecoilBrace, and Pelvis joints are all set at their ready positions.

1.  Boom! At frame 143, we'll move all our pieces to indicate a large, kicking recoil like we see in Figure 6.19.

    Here are the values I used to get this pose:

    Pelvis

    - TranslateZ: 2.3
    - RotateZ: -32

    CannonBody

    - TranslateX: 2.4
    - RotateZ: -226

    CannonBarrel

    - TranslateX: 1.6

    RecoilShaft

    - RotateZ: 2.5

    RecoilBrace

    - TranslateX: 3

# Game Animation

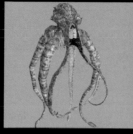

## in Color

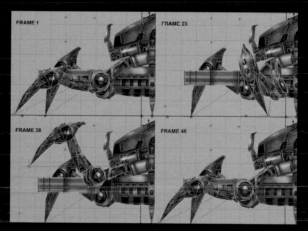

This full-color section showcases work from this book's projects as well as additional game work from talented artists and animators all over the world. With Maya's increasing influence in the video game-creation industry and the growing power of today's gaming machines, the content of your games is limited only by your imagination!

The basic composition of all game art starts with creating the geometry, followed by creating textures, adding the rigging, and finally producing the animation. Calamity Jane comprises approximately 9,000 tris. She was created by Michael McKinley.

www.mtmckinley.net

For most game art, opacity-mapped planes of geometry are used to simulate hair and fur. The Dire Wolf consists of approximately 2,000 tris. This creature was created by Gary Bergeron.

www.garybergeron.com

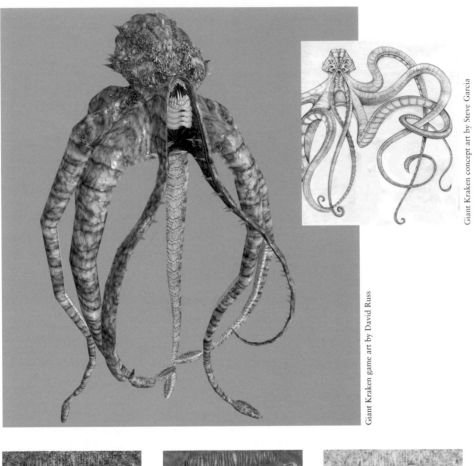

Giant Kraken game art by David Russ

Giant Kraken concept art by Steve Garcia

To convey additional surface detail, you can use a bump map and specular map with the color map. The Giant Kraken contains approximately 10,000 tris. David Russ created this creature for the book.

http://home.austin.rr.com/misterhombre

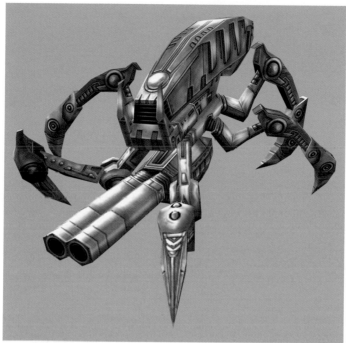

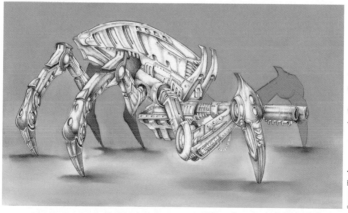

Having a small amount of geometry shouldn't limit your ability to create very interesting
and entertaining animations! The Storm Tank is composed of approximately 1,100 tris.
The talented Leif Robles created this piece .

www.angelfire.com/art2/leif_robles/3d2d

Tarsier game art by Paul Greveson

Tarsier concept art by L. D. Austin

Planning ahead with a concept image is the right way to start any project. Tarsier is by Paul Greveson , with the concept art by L. D. Austin. This piece contains 4,000 tris and uses two 512 × 512 and one 256 × 256 resolution texture.

www.greveson.co.uk

www.1daustinart.com

Cutesy Characters by Sam Chester

Game art can span any and all artistic styles, from realistic to cartoon-like, as in the above example. These Cutesy Characters are by Sam Chester . The little guy consists of 1,682 tris with one 512 × 512 texture. The slug creature contains 1,226 polys and also uses a 512 × 512 texture.

www.fatcapdesigns.com

December Sendai by Jared Lewis

The December Sendai project is by Jared Lewisand is composed of 4,881 tris. It uses two 512 × 512 textures and makes use of specular and opacity maps.

Have fun creating your own game characters!

www.jaredlewis.com

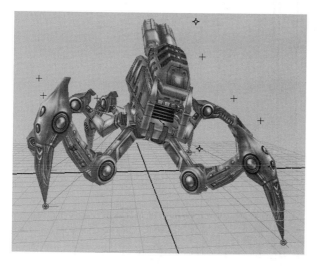

**Figure 6.18**
The body rotating downward with the drilling of the leg

Frame 140                    Frame 143

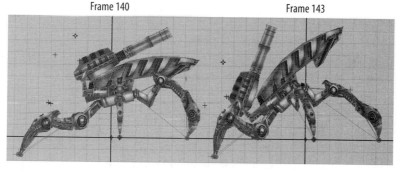

**Figure 6.19** The recoil reaction to the cannon blast!

2.  At frame 160, reset all of the above to their prefiring position except the Pelvis joint.

3.  For the Pelvis, we'll move forward to frame 165 and rotate it forward a bit more to accentuate the amount of energy that has just gone through it:

    •   TranslateY: 3.5

    •   TranslateZ: -0.5

    •   RotateZ: 37

4.  Go to frame 140, middle-click and drag to frame 180, and set the keyframes at their positions to copy the values from 140 to 180, getting the tank in position and ready to fire again, effectively completing the animation!

    You can see how mine turned out by opening the StormTank_ShootFinish.ma file in the Scenes folder.

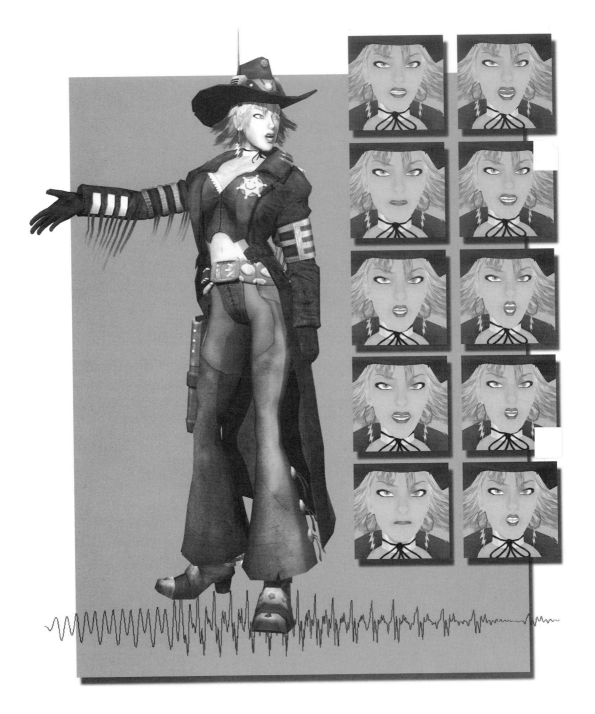

# Lip-Synching

*These days, the majority of character-based video games have full-fledged, professionally written stories that are just as complex and intricate as any Hollywood film. They include intrigue, comedy, action, and suspense, all working together to convey the drama and provide a setting for the game, making the user's experience as immersive as possible. The advent of compact discs in the '90s made available immense storage space compared to the previous video game consoles that used cartridges. The new areas of storytelling allowed a full musical score as well as professionally acted dialogue. In this chapter, we'll explore the animation principles behind lip-synching to audio as well as the concept of acting and how it relates to animation.*

**7**

**In this chapter, we'll discuss the following topics:**

Acting in Video Games

Using Audio in Maya

Tutorial: Lip-Synching

Tutorial: Conversation Animation

## Acting in Video Games

Acting is a big part of animation. Whether you are animating an attack sequence, a walk cycle, or a death scene, they all make use of acting. Take a walk cycle, for example. What we did with Calamity Jane back in Chapter 3 was a fairly standard, straightforward walk cycle. But what if she were injured? Her walk cycle would change, right? Maybe she'd hold her side, drag her right leg, and slump her shoulders. These developments would suddenly alter our outlook on Jane's mood and situation.

In no other scenario is acting more important than with dialogue. When audio first made the leap to the video game market, it had a bit of a rocky start. One of the first games to make heavy use of spoken dialogue to convey a story was Capcom's *Resident Evil*. 3D games were still relatively new with the release of the Sony Playstation, and the power of the machine allowed the characters little in the way of articulation. They had no moving mouths, eyes, and so on. The only way to tell which stiffly animated character was speaking was to see which character was waving his arms around or bobbing her head while the audio played!

Today, with video games becoming much more sophisticated, it's not unusual for big-name Hollywood actors to be cast as the voice talent of big-budget game titles. Each title in Rockstar Games' *Grand Theft Auto* series has been more star studded than the last, with voice credits reading like the invitation list to a red-carpet event. Video games with movie tie-ins also generally have the actual actors from the films in speaking roles for the games, such as in Electronic Arts' *Lord of the Rings* games.

The technology behind these games has become equally impressive. The digital characters now have much more articulate faces, allowing for more expressive acting. With the promise of even more power in the next generation of video games, the ability to effectively convey recorded dialogue in a game is becoming increasingly important.

## Using Audio in Maya

Maya allows you to import audio files into your scenes. The audio file formats Maya supports are .wav, .aif, and .aiff. There are a couple of ways of importing an audio file into a scene. First, you can simply choose File > Import and then browse to the audio file you want and click Import. You can also drag and drop a supported audio file into your Maya scene. You should see the audio file appear in your timeline, indicated by the wavelength pattern of a sound file as in Figure 7.1.

You can also import multiple audio files into a scene. To select the sound you want to play, right-click the timeline, choose the Sound menu item, and then choose the desired audio file from the list. You can also turn the audio off here.

To delete an audio file from your scene, go to Edit > Delete by Type > Sounds and choose the file to delete. You can also select Edit > Delete All by Type > Sounds to remove all audio files from the scene at once.

To position an audio file in your scene's timeline, you can use the Trax Editor (Window > Animation Editors > Trax Editor). When your scene contains an audio track, the Trax Editor will look something like Figure 7.2. To move the block that represents the audio file, simply drag it to a new frame within the Trax Editor window.

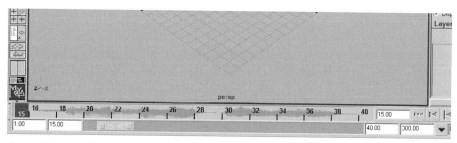

**Figure 7.1** A .wav file visible within Maya's timeline

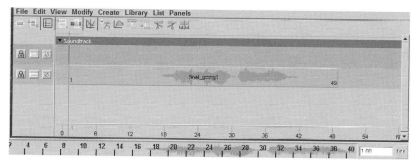

**Figure 7.2** An audio file visible within the Trax Editor

## Tutorial: Lip-Synching

Browse on the enclosed CD to Project_Files/Chapter_7/Lip_Synch. Copy the Lip_Synch directory to your hard drive. Open the file Jane_LipSynch_Start.ma from the Scenes directory.

This file contains the modeled, textured, and rigged geometry for the Calamity Jane character model we used in Chapter 3, and it already includes the basic blend shapes we'll be starting with in this lesson.

In this tutorial, you'll learn how to use phoneme shapes for lip-synching.

## Phoneme Shapes

The act of matching a character's mouth movements to dialogue recordings is known as *lip-synching*. As we mentioned in Chapter 2, key mouth shapes that are used to create the majority of phonetic vowel and consonant sounds are called *phoneme* shapes. You can create individual blend shapes for each of these sounds, but many are possible simply by using combinations of the shapes I've provided.

To make forming the following phoneme shapes easier, we'll use Set Driven Key.

1. Create a locator and place it near Jane's head (Create > Locator). Name the locator **Phoneme_Controls**.

2. With the locator selected, go to Window > General Editors > Channel Control. Here you can see all of the keyable channels of the locator (Figure 7.3). Select them all from the left column and press the Move>> button to move all of the channels to the Nonkeyable Hidden column. This removes all of the locator's keyable channels from the Channel box, giving us a clean slate to add our own attributes.

3. With the locator still selected, choose Modify > Add Attribute. In the Add Attribute window, make the following changes:

   - Attribute Name: A_I
   - Minimum: 0
   - Maximum: 1
   - Default: 0

4. Click OK. A new attribute will appear in the Channel Box called A_I. This attribute's value, by default, will be set to 0 and will only go as high as a value of 1. This will serve as our first Set Driven Key control.

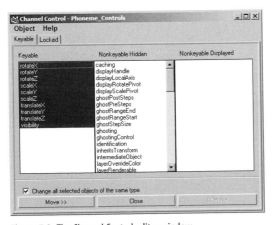

**Figure 7.3** The Channel Control editor window

5.  Deselect everything and open the Set Driven Key (SDK) window (Animate > Set Driven Key > Set > Options).

6.  Select the Phoneme_Controls locator, and click the Load Driver button in the SDK window, loading the A_I attribute into the top column.

7.  In the Blend Shape editor, press the Select button next to the Head_Blends collection of sliders, and click the Load Driven button in the SDK window, loading all of the blend shape sliders into the lower column.

8.  Select the A_I attribute as the Driver and all of the blend shape attributes that involve animating the mouth (in my case, MouthOpen, Smile, Grrr, Frown, O, M, and Eh) as the Driven. With everything at the default 0 value, press the Key button in the SDK window.

9.  Raise the A_I attribute of the Phoneme_Controls locator to a value of 1.

    Now, we'll form the Phoneme shapes, which include Phoneme A I.

## Phoneme A I

For Phoneme A I, example sounds are as in the words *apple*, *daddy*, *plate*, and *cat*.

1.  To accomplish this mouth shape with my provided blend shape controls, use the following combination of blend shapes in the Blend Shape Editor (Window > Animation Editors > Blend Shape):

    *   MouthOpen: 0.5
    *   Smile: 0.4
    *   Grrr: 0.3
    *   Eh: 0.5

2.  With this facial expression set up (Figure 7.4), again press the Key button in the SDK window. If done correctly, raising the A_I attribute will form the A I phoneme mouth shape we're wanting by automatically adjusting the blend shape slider combinations we set.

    We'll repeat these steps for each phoneme shape we want to create. First create a new attribute for the Phoneme_Controls locator. Select it as the Driver in the SDK window and the applicable mouth blend shapes in the Driven section. Set a key with both the locator control attributes and all of the blend shapes set to 0. Raise the locator control to 1, make the change to the face, and set the second key in the SDK window to finish setting up the control. The rest of the phoneme shapes are listed below with their applicable blend shape values.

### Phoneme E

Example sounds for Phoneme E are as in the words *sheep*, *leaf*, *eat*, and *egg*.

To accomplish this mouth shape (Figure 7.5) with my provided blend shape controls, use the following combination of blend shapes in the Blend Shape Editor:

- MouthOpen: 0.3
- Smile: 0.5
- Grrr: 0.7

**Figure 7.4** The A I phoneme shape for Jane

**Figure 7.5** Jane's E phoneme shape

### Phoneme O

Example sounds for Phoneme O are as in the words *lock*, *dog*, *pot*, and *cough*.

To accomplish the Phoneme O mouth shape (Figure 7.6) with my provided blend shape controls, use the following combination of blend shapes in the Blend Shape Editor:

- MouthOpen: 0.7
- Smile: 0.3
- O: 0.9

### Phoneme U

For the Phoneme U mouth shape, example sounds can be found in the words *you*, *under*, *clump*, and *pleasure*.

To accomplish this mouth shape (Figure 7.7) with my provided blend shape controls, use the following combination of blend shapes in the Blend Shape Editor:

- Smile: 0.2
- O: 0.6
- Eh: 0.7

**Figure 7.6** Jane's O phoneme shape

**Figure 7.7** Jane's U phoneme shape

## Phoneme Ch

While called Phoneme Ch, this mouth formation can actually be used for a large number of sounds. Example sounds are as in the words *cou__ch__*, *__z__oo*, *__sh__epherd*, *__d__ead*, and *__d__o__dge__*.

To accomplish this mouth shape (Figure 7.8) with my provided blend shape controls, use the following combination of blend shapes in the Blend Shape Editor:

- MouthOpen: 0.2
- Smile: 0.2
- Grrr: 0.2
- O: 0.8

**Figure 7.8**
Jane's Ch phoneme shape

### Phoneme S

While called Phoneme S, this mouth formation can actually be used for a large number of sounds. Example sounds are as in the words *sla̲n̲g̲*, *s̲i̲t*, *weddin̲g̲*, *eas̲y̲*, and *dig̲*.

To accomplish this mouth shape (Figure 7.9) with my provided blend shape controls, use the following combination of blend shapes in the Blend Shape Editor:

- Smile: 0.2
- Grrr: 0.6
- O: 0.1
- Eh: 0.2

### Phoneme F V

Example sounds for Phoneme F V are found in the words *f̲avorite*, *v̲olume*, *f̲ierce*, and *v̲ery*.

To accomplish this mouth shape (Figure 7.10) with my provided blend shape controls, use the following combination of blend shapes in the Blend Shape Editor:

- Smile: 0.1
- M: 1.0
- Eh: 0.25

### Phoneme Th

With the Phoneme Th mouth shape, example sounds can be found in the words *t̲h̲e*, *t̲h̲umb*, *t̲h̲icket*, and *t̲h̲ey*.

**Figure 7.9** Jane's S phoneme shape

**Figure 7.10** Jane's F V phoneme shape

This particular phoneme shape requires a bit of tongue action to properly convey. Since the tongue's movements are very dependent on the mouth movements that precede and follow the "th" sound, we won't include the tongue in the Set Driven Key controls, but we will animate it separately as we come to it, using the situation in question as our guide for how it should move. To accomplish this mouth shape otherwise (Figure 7.11) with my provided blend shape controls, use the following combination of blend shapes in the Blend Shape Editor:

- MouthOpen: 0.3
- Smile: 0.2
- O: 0.6
- Eh: 0.2

## Phoneme L

Example sounds for the Phoneme L include the sounds in the words _elevator_, _lady_, _low_, and _lavish_.

This particular phoneme shape also requires a bit of tongue action to properly convey. As with the Th phoneme shape, we'll not include the tongue's movements in the Set Driven Key and will instead animate it as the situation calls for it. To accomplish this mouth shape otherwise (Figure 7.12) with my provided blend shape controls, use the following combination of blend shapes in the Blend Shape Editor:

- MouthOpen: 0.4
- Smile: 0.3
- Grr: 0.25
- O: 0.25

**Figure 7.11** Jane's Th phoneme shape, minus the tongue

**Figure 7.12** Jane's L phoneme shape, minus the tongue

**Phoneme M B P**

Example sounds for the Phoneme M B P are found in the words _m_other, _b_oy, _p_op, and _m_ayday.

To accomplish this mouth shape (Figure 7.13) with my provided blend shape controls, use the following combination of blend shapes in the Blend Shape Editor:

- MouthOpen: -0.1

- M: 1.0

You'll notice here that we used a negative value for the MouthOpen blend shape. You can set blend shapes beyond their default 0–1 set of values by typing the value you want directly into the input box next to the slider in the Blend Shape Editor. It uses the movement that we established in the blend shape, averages it, and compounds that movement further in a positive or negative direction to achieve accurate results. You'll want to use this sparingly and not go too far with negative values or values higher than 1, because the results can become pretty comical and unnatural! In a cartoon-style character, however, such values can be very useful to create the over-the-top stretchy, elastic animation that such styles usually call for.

Now that we have the phoneme shape controls in place, we can begin the animation!

**Figure 7.13**
Jane's M B P phoneme shape

## Matching the Mouth

When animating a character's mouth to dialogue, one thing to keep in mind is not to react to each and every syllable of the recorded phrase. I remember the first time I did a lip-synching animation a number of years ago: I would carefully scrub through the audio and close my character's mouth after each phoneme shape. When it played, it looked nearly right, but something was off about it.

If you watch a person talk, she won't enunciate every sound of every word. She'll smooth her mouth formations together; possibly never completely closing her mouth except for the necessary consonants (the M B P phoneme, for example) and "ums" and other pauses she might have. In my first lip-synch, while the mouth did match the audio, the character's mouth seemed to be moving too frantically as its lips rushed to close after each sound.

So keep that in mind when animating to dialogue. Repeat the lines into a mirror and pay attention to how your own mouth moves. If your character's mouth just seems to be flapping uncontrollably, yet is following the audio exactly, try not being so precise with it and allow some smoother transitions between phoneme shapes for a more natural result. You can even try dropping some phoneme shapes completely, even though the audio may seem like it calls for them.

Never let technical details get in the way of a good performance!

## Setting Up the Audio for a Scene

We'll begin synching audio to mouth movements by importing our audio into the scene.

193

> **Note:** To start animating with a phoneme control locator already set up with Set Driven Key, open the Jane_LipSynch_Controls.ma file from the Scenes folder. The values for positioning and animating in the following tutorials assume this file is being used. Your own scene's values may vary.

1.  Choose File > Import. Browse to the CD's Audio folder and choose the final_horse2.wav file.

2. If the audio doesn't immediately appear in your timeline, right-click the timeline, and from the opening marking menu, make sure Sound is not turned off and is pointing to the final_horse2 file.

3. We'll also want to make sure that our scene is set to 30 frames per second (fps) by going to Window > Settings/Preferences > Preferences. In the Preferences window that opens, click the Settings item in the column on the left, and set the Time to NTSC (30 fps).

   Click on the Timeline item in the left column, and make sure that Playback speed is set to Real-time (30 fps).

   With the Preferences window still open, press the Play button to hear what the audio sounds like. If you'd like, you can change the playback speed to make the sound play slightly faster or slower, changing the pitch. To do this, choose Other for the Playback speed. The numerical input box on the right will become available. Type in the fps at which you'd like the scene to play. Entering numbers lower than 30 will make the scene play slower and will deepen the pitch of the audio. Entering numbers higher than 30 will make the scene play faster and will raise the pitch of the audio. For this tutorial, we'll simply keep it at 30 fps. For most situations in a real studio, the audio's pitch and length have already been edited before the animator receives it.

4. Click Save in the Preferences window when finished.

Let's also change our playback range of frames to be only those that take place with audio. As mentioned earlier in the chapter, you can move the audio forward in time, but I do like to have a little padding before the audio in case I want to animate any anticipation to the character speaking. If you don't use these padding frames, most game engines will allow you to export only the necessary frames rather than include the silent section.

5. Change the Playback Start Time to frame 23 and the Playback End Time to frame 95, centering the audio within the visible timeline.

### Focusing on Dialog

The audio file I have chosen to focus on is a line of dialogue that reads:

*"Now where...did I park my horse?"*

Our first task is to simply animate the mouth to this line using the blend shapes and SDK controls. We are concentrating on the mouth only and not animating the eyes, neck, or other body parts just yet. Because the line of dialogue is never going to change (at least, ideally), having the mouth first match what the line is saying is our top priority. From there, we can play with the model's performance of the line all we want.

It's important to get very familiar not only with what the line is saying but *how* it's being said. Is the character sad? Angry? Or just annoyed? Also notice the emphasis and lengthening of the word *where* and the pause that follows it. The word *now* also has a slight lengthening to it:

*"Noow wheeeerrre...did I park my horse?"*

One way to interpret this is that the character is actually looking around for her four-legged ride during the first two words, the act of which is slightly distracting as she begins talking to herself in a mildly bemused tone. Perhaps she gives up looking and centers her focus as she finishes the rest of the sentence in a normal speaking cadence. We'll need to convey all of these things in our animation. Of course, you'd receive direction as to what the character is actually doing and feeling in any assigned situation.

But in any case, let's begin by matching the mouth to the audio. One thing that you might find useful is thinking of the phrase as it *sounds* and not necessarily how it's spelled:

*"Noow weh-aaaair...dehd aye pahrrk mai horss?"*

You might find it easier to match phoneme shapes to this line of thought rather than simply reading the printed script. The first word we come to is *now*. We'll bypass forming an *n* phoneme shape (using the Ch phoneme in combination with the tongue) and go straight to the *ow* part of the word. This is because the lengthened part of the word has the most emphasis, and holding any time for the *n* could seem a bit forced in relation to the audio we are hearing.

1.  At frame 23, at the beginning of our visible timeline, keyframe the O attribute of the Phoneme_Controls locator at a value of 0. You might find it easier to turn on Autokey at this point.

2.  At frame 30, at the peak of the *ow* section of the audio, raise the O phoneme to 0.7.

    We don't have to use the maximum values all the time. This way, if we ever want to really accentuate something, we'll have a higher value we can reach to give such emotional highs a unique emphasis.

3.  At frame 36, *now* is ending and *where* is starting. Lower the O phoneme to 0.2 and keyframe the E phoneme with a value of 0, getting ready to start using it.

    We didn't lower the O phoneme all the way to 0. If you repeat the phrase "now where..." to yourself out loud, you should notice that, when speaking normally, your mouth doesn't close completely between the two words. It actually takes a bit of effort to do so! We'll simulate the mouth remaining open here in our scene as well.

4.  At frame 39, the *wh* is about to merge into the over-lengthening of the *ere* part of the word. Raise the O phoneme back up to 0.6. Also increase the E phoneme to 0.4.

    Including the E phoneme widens the mouth and shows more teeth, helping to accentuate the *weh* sound at the beginning of the word *where*.

5.  While still at frame 39, keyframe the A_I phoneme with a value of 0, as it is about to come into play.

6.  At frame 42, we are within the elongated *ere* section of the word. Because this part of the word has such an emphasis applied to it, we'll have an equally strong emphasis on the A_I phoneme, increasing its value to 0.7 and lowering the E phoneme to 0. We'll also lower the O phoneme to 0.3 to allow the A_I phoneme to widen the mouth a bit.

7. Also at frame 42, we'll keyframe the Ch phoneme at a value of 0, before it adds its influence to Jane's face in the following sound.

8. At frame 48, Jane's voice has entered a strong hold on an *r* sound. We'll lower the A_I phoneme considerably to a value of 0 while raising the Ch phoneme to 0.5. The O phoneme can be lowered a tad to 0.2 as well.

9. At frame 51, the *r* is trailing off but still very audible. We'll keyframe the O phoneme again at 0.2 to maintain its influence, but we'll lower the Ch phoneme to 0.3.

10. To end the word, we'll come to a nearly closed mouth, as there's a small pause before Jane continues the rest of her sentence. So, at frame 55, lower all of the phonemes to 0 except Ch, which will stay at 0.1, keeping the mouth just barely open.

"Now where…" has been animated (Figure 7.14)! Scrub through the timeline, looking at our progress, and play the animation in real time to see what you think. One thing I noticed was we could use the smallest bit of separation between the words *now* and *where*. Let's add a slight pause by doing the following:

1. Back at frame 35, keyframe the O phoneme again at its value of 0.2.

2. Move the O phoneme's keyframe at frame 36 forward one frame to frame 37 in the Graph Editor.

N        OW        WEH

A        AIR        …

**Figure 7.14** NOW WEH A AIR …

This adjustment helps give the transition between words a bit more power. Also notice how using a combination of phoneme shapes blending to and from each other for the *whe* part of the word *where* gave us a nice result with Jane's visible enunciation of the sound.

We can now continue with the rest of the phrase "did I park my horse?" These words are spoken with a more natural cadence. Once again, repeat the phrase to yourself, being conscious of how your mouth *wants* to move as you say it. These words fly through pretty quickly, so we'll also be changing phonemes in quick succession!

1. At frame 53, before the word *did* begins, we'll place a keyframe for the S phoneme with a value of 0.

2. As we go through the *deh* sound of the word *did* at frame 57, raise the S phoneme to 0.7 and lower the Ch to 0.

   If you speak the phrase "did I" to yourself, you may notice that the second *d* sound of the word *did* tends to get blended over as your mouth goes into the heavy *aye* sound of the *I* pronoun. With that in mind, we'll go back a few frames to begin the transition to the *I* and allow that phoneme to have a strong blend with our current sounds.

3. Go back to frame 55 and keyframe the A_I phoneme at 0, getting ready for it to take over Jane's mouth formation as she says *I*.

4. At frame 61, raise the A_I phoneme to 0.9 and lower the S phoneme to 0.

   By allowing the A_I phoneme six frames to blend through the *did* part of the phrase, it flows together much better.

   The next word is *park*. The *puh* (or in this case, more like *pah*) sound requires the lips to press together with a slight moment of air building up behind them. Releasing this puff of compressed air produces the sound. This will actually be the first time that the mouth has closed completely since the sentence began!

5. At frame 64, before the *puh* sound starts, keyframe the M_B_P phoneme at a value of 0.

6. At frame 66, raise the M_B_P phoneme all the way to 1.0 and lower the A_I phoneme to 0. We'll also want to keyframe the O phoneme at 0 at this point as well.

7. As we enter the *ah* part of *park* at frame 68, we'll lower the M_B_P phoneme back to 0 and raise the O phoneme to 0.7.

8. At this same frame, we'll want to keyframe the Ch phoneme at 0 as well, as it is about to enter the scene to help with the *r* sound.

9. At frame 70, we'll increase the Ch phoneme to 0.7 and lower the O to about 0.1. As you can see, we're going back and forth very quickly with lots of different phoneme shapes to achieve the results we're looking for!

Because the *ar* sound ends rather abruptly with a *k* sound at the end of the word *park*, we'll suddenly drop the values after just one frame.

10. So, at frame 71, we'll lower the Ch phoneme to 0.5 and take the O phoneme down to 0.

    In less than 20 frames, we've spoken three words (Figure 7.15)! People can definitely speak very quickly while still being perfectly clear in their meanings and enunciation. Play through the animation and see if any moments could use some fine-tuning. I found a couple.

11. Around the word *did* we could put a bit more emphasis on certain syllables. Back at frame 55, where we keyed the A_I phoneme at 0, let's also lower the S phoneme to 0.1.

12. At frame 58, we can lower the S to 0.2. This word won't "float" through so much now and will have the emphasis needed to help convey the strong consonant sounds.

We have two words to go in the phrase "my horse." Just like with the *pah* sound in *park*, we'll close the mouth to press the lips together to form the *m* sound in *my*.

1. Still at frame 71, keyframe the M_B_P phoneme at 0 before that shape occurs.

2. Raise the M_B_P phoneme to 1.0 at frame 74 as the word *my* begins. For the following *aye* sound, we'll want to use the A_I phoneme. So, go ahead and keyframe it at 0 here.

...D     EHD     AYE

P     AH     RRK...

**Figure 7.15** ...D EHD AYE P AH RRK...

3. For frame 76, lower the M_B_P phoneme to 0 and increase the A_I to 0.8.

4. To begin the word *horse*, we'll go to frame 80 and keyframe the O phoneme with a value of 0. Lower the A_I phoneme to 0.3. We don't need a big indication of the *h* sound; just enough of an opening to believe the sound could happen before we blend into the emphasized *or* sound of the word.

5. At frame 83, raise the O phoneme to 0.6 and lower the A_I phoneme completely to 0. To prepare for the forthcoming *r* sound, keyframe the Ch phoneme here at 0.

6. For frame 85, increase the Ch phoneme to 0.9 and lower the O phoneme to 0. We're switching phonemes again, so keyframe the S phoneme here with a value of 0.

7. For the strong *ss* sound in the word *horse*, go to frame 87 and raise the S phoneme to 0.8 while lowering the Ch phoneme to 0.

8. We've made it to the end of the phrase! You can have the S phoneme blend to Jane's rest state by going to frame 93 and lowering all active phonemes to 0.

Play back the entire sequence and look for any areas that could use some tweaking. I went back and added an additional keyframe for the two M_B_P phonemes so that they stay at a full 1.0 value for two frames rather than just one to help them read a little better. But overall, the lip-synch is complete (Figure 7.16).

You can see how mine turned out by opening the Jane_LipSynch_Finish.ma file from the Scenes directory. Now that Jane's mouth is moving, we can work on the rest of her!

...M          AI          HO

RS          SS

**Figure 7.16**
...M AI HO RS SS

## Tutorial: Conversation Animation

With the lip-synch complete, we can work on animating the rest of Jane's body to follow along with what she's saying. Her statement is referring to her misplacement of her horse, so let's have our animation start off with her looking around for it as she begins to mutter to herself. We'll get the head movement blocked in and then work our way down the body.

**Note:** To start with Jane's lip-synch animation already in place, open the Jane_LipSynch_Finish.ma file from the Scenes folder. The values for positioning and animating in the following tutorials assume this file is being used. Your own scene's values may vary.

1.  Change the Animation Start Time to frame 1, giving us the first 23 frames of the animation before Jane begins speaking.

2.  Select the Head joint, and key its rotation channels (Shift+E) at frame 1 with their default values of 0.

3.  We'll have her start looking around before she actually starts speaking. At frame 5, turn her head to her right by rotating the Head joint about -40 degrees in the RotateX channel. We want her to be looking in that direction for a few frames before she starts to turn to look in the opposite direction, so set another key at frame 17 at -50 degrees. We'll use a different value so that her head doesn't freeze in place for 12 frames and will instead seem like there is still some life in it.

4.  Rotate the head in the opposite direction at frame 32, about 45 degrees.

5.  Again, we want her to look that way for a half-second or so, so keyframe the head again at frame 45 at about 60 degrees.

6.  She's about given up looking at this point (maybe she's been looking for a while now), so at frame 63 or so, you can bring the head back to facing the front.

    Let's fine-tune the head motion before we continue. As mentioned back in Chapter 2, all organic movement is done within an arc, even something as simple as turning one's head. Therefore, let's carry that through this animation.

7.  At around frame 23, in the middle of Jane's head turn from the right to the left, lower her head by rotating the Head joint's RotateZ handle down about -7.5 degrees.

8.  We can do the same at frame 55 as she turns her head toward the front by lowering it slightly, about -4 degrees.

9. Let's give the word *where* a bit of an emphasis with her head movement. At frame 36, right before the word, rotate her head back a bit around 8 degrees.

10. Then, at frame 41, lower her head about -6 degrees, giving her head a bit of a swift forward bob as she puts emphasis on the word *where* in her statement.

With the head's basic movement ready, we can now go about animating the other elements of the head, namely the eyes and brows, to react to these movements and the spoken line.

## Creating Eye Movement

If you really pay attention to a person's eyes as she is looking around, you'll notice that the eyes will move around very quickly, focusing on different things as they scan the surroundings. When people blink, their eyes tend to rotate upward slightly to meet the eyelid's downward motion and drop back down as the eyelid reopens.

Blinking is something you want to be careful about. If you use it too much, the character seems to be having eye problems! Too little and she may seem very robotic. In the 2001 film *AI* for example, child star Haley Joel Osment plays a very realistic robotic boy. While a very good actor, extraordinary in fact for his age, there's something else about him and his performance that really makes him seem eerily mechanical. In the entire film, he never blinks! So, achieving an acceptable frequency for blinks and knowing when they are appropriate can be very important in making the difference between a digital puppet and a "real" breathing character on the screen! The trick is to make the occurrence of a blink in your scene completely unnoticeable. If it calls very much attention to itself, in general, it's incorrect.

In this sequence we'll include three blinks. It's actually very obvious where they should go. If you were to look from one side of the scene to the other as Jane is doing, your eyes would be generally forced to blink. This is due to your eyes having to change focus. In fact, any time you are focused on one thing in particular and turn your head to look at something else, you invariably blink!

1. At frame 3, as Jane is making her first head turn, open the Blend Shape Editor and press the Key button next to the Blink blend shape slider with its value set at 0.

2. Blinks are obviously very quick actions, lasting only a few frames. Move to frame 5, and raise the Blink slider to 1.0.

3. At frame 9, lower it back to 0, finishing the blink.

You may notice, although it's very subtle, that closing the eyes for a blink took only two frames, while opening them back up again took four. Yes, it's *very* subtle, but this is based on the slight effort it takes to raise the eyelid compared to letting it drop. Also, by making the time it takes to close and open the eyes slightly different, we avoid a mechanical "shutter" effect and make things look a bit more natural and organic (Figure 7.17).

Frame 22      Frame 24      Frame 28

**Figure 7.17** Blinking during the turn

4. We'll repeat these steps at frames 22 and 53, setting keyframes for the blink with a value of 0.

5. After two frames (frames 24 and 55), raise it to 1.0.

6. Lower the value back to 0 after four frames more (frames 28 and 59).

We'll next animate the eye movement. These movements should be very subtle. We also don't want the eyes to just float around. They should focus on a target for a couple of frames before changing focus to another target in their field of view. This will require two keyframes to hold their position for several frames before moving on to their next position.

1. At frames 1 and 8, keyframe the rotations of the REye and LEye for their starting positions.

2. Go to frame 11, rotate both eyes just slightly, so that Jane seems to have focused on something in the distance (someone's horse perhaps?).

3. At frame 14, set another keyframe at this same position. This way, the eyes stay focused for four frames.

4. Go to frame 17, and rotate the eyes slightly to another point where Jane focuses on another target, looking for her missing horse. At frame 19, key the rotations again with the same value.

5. If the animation curves of the eye rotation are causing the eyes to flow through their values rather than holding them for the number of frames that we're looking for, select the curves in the Graph Editor (Window > Animation Editors > Graph Editor), and make them use clamped tangents (Tangents > Clamped in the Graph Editor menus).

   As described in Chapter 2, clamped tangents ensure that two adjacent keyframes of the same or similar values do not use a smooth interpolation that will skew their positions.

6. Between frames 38 and 52, repeat these steps, setting a keyframe for the eyes' rotation for two frames that are between three and five frames apart. You should be able to do this about three times within that timeframe.

7. Copy the eyes' original positions at frame 55. As explained previously in the book, the easiest way to do this is to go to frame 1 and middle-click and drag to frame 55 on the timeline, going forward in frames without playing the animation. At frame 55, and with the scene's position still at frame 1, keyframe the eye's positions.

## Adding the Details

At this point, the head's animation is basically complete. We can add a few details, though. For instance, we can make better use of Jane's eyebrows, perhaps raise them when she emphasizes the word *where*. We can also put in a bit of secondary animation by jiggling the earring joints.

1. At frame 34, keyframe the Surprise blend shape at a value of 0.

2. Raise the Surprise blend shape slider to 1.0 at frame 41, when Jane is saying *where*. Set a key again at frame 43 with the same value, causing the raised brow to hold for a couple of frames.

3. Lower it back to 0 at frame 47.

For the earrings, the main idea is for them to react to Jane's turning her head back and forth. We want them to have momentum, like pendulums, so that when Jane's head pauses, they continue to swing in the turned direction for a moment before swinging back again.

1. At frame 1, set keyframes for both the LEarring_Joint and the REarring_Joint's starting rotations.

2. Jane immediately begins turning her head to her right, so at frame 6, rotate the earrings to point toward Jane's left as if they were left behind and need to catch up.

3. At frame 12, Jane's head has paused, so rotate the earrings toward the right, having their momentum follow through with the turning movement.

4. The earrings shouldn't just float there, even though Jane's head is not turning back right away. At frame 21, have the earrings rotate back in the opposite direction, obeying the pull of gravity.

5. As Jane's head turns again, rotate the earrings again to be "left behind" during the movement at frame 27.

6. At frame 37, have the earrings catch up with this new turn by rotating them to the left, in the direction of Jane's movement.

7. This is where Jane bobs her head to accentuate the word *where* in her speech. So, in reaction to that, we can have the earrings start to rotate a little wildly here. At frame 43, rotate the earrings back in the opposite direction a little farther than normal.

8. Make the earrings rock back and forth relatively quickly at frames 47 and 51, but have each rock be a little less powerful than the last because the earrings will start to lose the momentum that they gained when Jane bobbed her head.

9. With the last turn of Jane's head, have the earrings be "left behind" again at frame 59.

10. With the head coming to settle at this point, keyframe the earrings back to their starting values at frame 67. The head's animation is finally complete (Figure 7.18)!

You can take a look at my finished head animation by opening the Jane_Animation_Head.ma file from the Scenes folder.

## Animating the Body

Now that the facial expressions and head movement are laid out, the hard part of the conversation is over. We can next start focusing on the body movement. How should Jane be moving during this encounter? I picture her as simply looking in both directions for her parked horse, perhaps shifting her body weight from one leg to the other as she

**Figure 7.18** "I don't think that's my horse...."

makes her brief search. Finally giving up, she might place one hand on her hip in resignation, maybe flipping her opposite hand in a slightly helpless gesture.

**1.** First, let's get Jane into a good starting pose. I've put her into a fairly relaxed stance, as you can see in Figure 7.19. When you get her into a pose you like, set keyframes for her skeleton to hold that position at frame 1.

Notice that I have Jane's weight resting mostly on her right leg and her pelvis rotated so that it's angled upward on the right side. I also have her spine flexing to have her stand upright to compensate for the pelvis' position. I did this by moving the Pelvis joint to the side and rotating it and the spine joints to achieve the desired pose. Let's continue by animating the pelvis and spine's movement during the sequence. Then we'll go back for the arms, hands, and secondary movement.

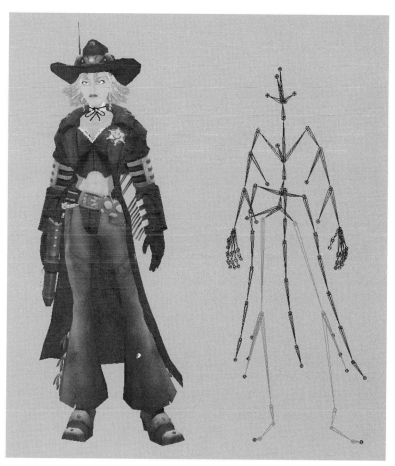

**Figure 7.19** Jane's starting pose for the conversation animation

2.    At the beginning of the sequence, Jane looks to her right. Let's have her spine rotate some to accentuate this turning movement. At frame 20, rotate the Pelvis slightly toward Jane's right. Work up the spine, rotating the BackWaist, Back-Low, and BackMid joints toward the right as well.

3.    We don't want the chain of joints going up Jane's back to all rotate at the same time, however. The animation will have a bit more of a "live" feel to it if each joint works its way into position as the movement travels up the spine. With this in mind, select the BackWaist joint. In the Graph Editor, move the keyframe we set at frame 20 to frame 22 by selecting it in the editor's Graph view and, with the Move Tool active, holding the Shift key and middle-clicking and dragging to the right. Holding Shift will keep the keyframe level.

4.    Repeat this with the BackLow joint, moving its keyframe to frame 24, and finally with BackMid, moving its keyframe to frame 26. The turning motion will seem subtly more alive with this sequential movement as opposed to the mechanical result that moving them all at once would have.

5.    For Jane's turn to her left, let's have the pelvis shift its weight to her left leg. Go to frame 36 and move the pelvis to the opposite side, over her left leg. Rotate it to be tilted in the opposite direction, pointing upward on her left side. Since Jane is turning, we can also rotate her pelvis to the left to help with the turning movement.

6.    Rotating Jane's pelvis in this way obviously shifts her torso to a weird angle. At this same frame, rotate the spine joints we have been using to reposition her torso into a natural standing position. We'll also want to rotate the torso to Jane's left to accentuate the turning movement.

7.    Just as we did with the previous turning movement, stagger the keys we set at frame 36 so that each joint finishes its turn a few frames after the previous one. So BackWaist's key gets moved forward a bit to about frame 42, BackLow's to frame 44, and BackMid's to frame 47.

8.    We can add a little detail to the shifting of weight from the right leg to the left leg by raising the Pelvis joint as it travels from one side to the other. At frame 30, raise the Pelvis joint just enough so the knees don't suddenly get locked straight up. We can also rotate it a little to allow the pelvis to "lead" the animation, with the rest of Jane's torso following slightly behind (Figure 7.20).

9.    At frame 60, Jane has turned back toward the front, so rotate the Pelvis joint back to facing more to the front as well. Just as before, rotate the spine joints to face more to the front, but stagger their keys so that they don't all turn at the same moment but follow the pelvis' lead.

Let's continue the animation by next focusing on the arm movement.

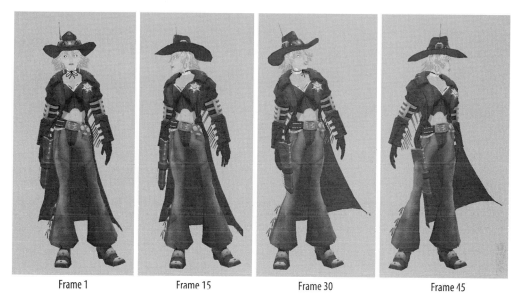

| Frame 1 | Frame 15 | Frame 30 | Frame 45 |

**Figure 7.20** The pelvis and spine turning with Jane's movements

## Arming the Animation

For the arm movement, we'll have the right hand make a defeated gesture around Jane's emphasis of the word *where*. Then toward the end of the sequence the left hand will settle on Jane's hip as she looks forward.

1. Set rotation keys for the RClavicle, RShoulder, RElbow, and RWrist joints at frame 1 for the starting pose.

2. Set these keys again at frame 23.

   For Jane's defeated gesture, we'll raise the arm up and project it forward slightly, with the fingers outstretched in a sort of "why me?" moment before dropping the arm back to Jane's side.

3. At frame 32, raise the arm up, pointing out and to Jane's right toward the direction she had just faced.

4. Straighten the arm outward, as if Jane is giving a slight shove forward at frame 40.

5. At frame 48, lower the arm and have it finally come to rest at Jane's side at frame 56.

   This is probably easier to picture by taking a look at the movement depicted in Figure 7.21. Also take a look at the hand movement. We'll discuss that next!

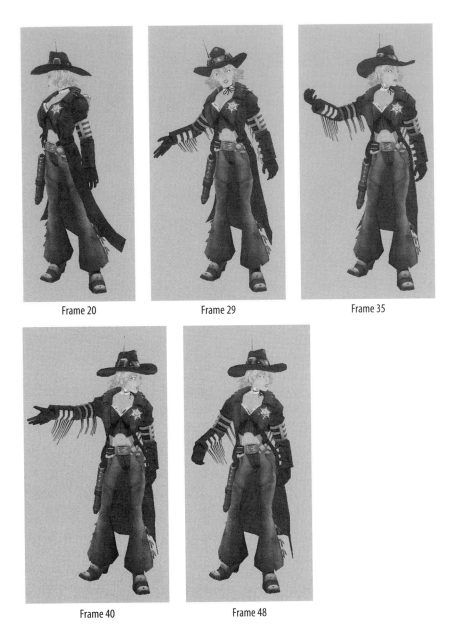

Frame 20          Frame 29          Frame 35

Frame 40          Frame 48

**Figure 7.21:** The right arm's movement

We want the hand to make heavy use of follow-through. As the arm rises through frame 29, the hand should droop downward until the arm reaches the apex of its height at frame 35, at which point the hand catches up with the arm's upward momentum, flipping upward. In our case, the hand's palm is facing upward so it doesn't droop downward during the upward motion as much as it would if the hand were facing downward instead.

Also take a look at the fingers. As the arm is rising, the fingers bend backward slightly, accentuating the upward momentum. As the hand flips upward at the top of the movement, the fingers can also contract. This contraction will also add contrast to the outstretched movement in frame 40, where we'll also spread the fingers out to give the motion more power.

Let's start the movement of the left arm. It will rise up and then settle on Jane's left hip.

1. At frames 1 and 45, keyframe the LClavicle, LShoulder, LElbow, and LWrist joints at their starting positions.

2. At frame 61, raise the left arm with the LElbow bent downward, forming an "L" shape with the arm.

3. At frame 69, rotate the arm joints to rest the left hand on Jane's left hip.

Once again, this is easier to see than to describe. Look at Figure 7.22 and take note of the hand and finger positions as well.

Frame 45      Frame 61      Frame 69

**Figure 7.22:** The left arm's movement

## Adding Secondary Animation

At this point, all of the major animation is complete. The only parts left are the obvious secondary animation elements such as the coat, the leather bits under the arms, and the holster.

1.  As we did with the Kraken's tentacles, the easiest way to manage the coat joints is to select them all and rotate them all at once. This is probably easiest to do in the Outliner (Window > Outliner). Select all of the coat joints and keyframe their initial starting rotation values at frame 1.

**Note:** To quickly locate an object within a cluttered Outliner when you have lots of objects and you want to avoid scrolling and searching, select it in your scene, and within the Outliner window, press the f hotkey to focus on it within the list. Also don't forget that you can hold Shift when you expand a skeleton hierarchy or group within the Outliner to expand it in its entirety rather than one element at a time.

2.  At frame 20, adjust the coat joint rotations to prevent the coat joints from intersecting the character's geometry.

3.  At frame 33, as Jane shifts her weight to her left leg, rotate the coat joints to be pointed subtly toward Jane's right as if being left behind by the motion.

4.  At frame 49, the coat can swing back to Jane's left, its follow-through catching up with the movement.

5.  As the animation ends, you can have the coat joints settle to a stop, following gravity's pull downward.

For the arm's leather fringes, the main thing we want to do is keep them following gravity as well as the momentum of the arm that they are attached to by setting keys for their joints' translation and rotation channels. The process is similar for the holster. We'll simply keyframe its rotations to prevent it from intersecting Jane's leg.

Play through the animation and see if you notice any other areas that might benefit from adjustments or additions. One thing I did was to add a slight turn to the right foot during Jane's emphasis of the word *where*.

1.  Select the RFoot group, and keyframe its rotation channels at frame 31. Keyframe the RKnee_Locator's position here as well.

2.  Rotate it to about -30 degrees, having it turn toward Jane's right at frame 42. Move the RKnee_Locator toward the right side as well to keep the knee's direction oriented with the foot in a natural position.

3.  At frame 36, halfway through the foot's turn, raise the toe, rotating the RFoot group upward about -7 degrees so that the foot isn't dragging itself across the ground to make this slight adjustment.

Once all of your secondary animation is completed, the conversation animation is finished (Figure 7.23)! You can see how mine turned out by opening the Jane_Animation_Finish.ma file from the Scenes directory.

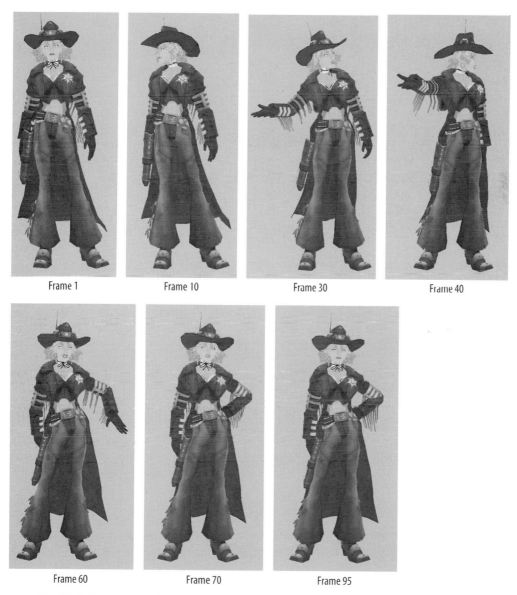

Frame 1      Frame 10      Frame 30      Frame 40

Frame 60      Frame 70      Frame 95

**Figure 7.23:** The final conversation animation!

# Other Animation Projects

*The goal of this book is to give you a representative piece of nearly every character archetype so that when you are given an animation task in your future game job, you should always be able to pull from these lessons general guidelines for nearly any task. So far, we've done a biped (two-legged humanoid), a quadruped (four-legged creature), a spinal body type (multitentacled creature), and an inorganic vehicle. There are just a few other fairly frequently seen animated forms that I think you need to learn to complete your catalog of animation knowledge: wings, blobby structures, and a standard vehicle suspension.*

**In this chapter, we'll discuss the following topics:**
Assignments Breakdown
Tutorial: Taking Flight
Tutorial: Oozing Blob
Tutorial: Getting Ready to Drive
Final Thoughts

## Assignments Breakdown

There are three projects in this chapter, each encompassing animation tasks that are not as common as the previous projects in this book, but common enough to make them just as important to learn.

With the success of fantasy games in today's market, many more games are adding fantastical elements to their themes. Two very popular forms of this fantastical element are winged creatures and unstable elements, such as fire, water, or, as in our lesson, slime or ooze.

In contrast to fantasy, racing games are still very popular, and nearly all games with urban settings will need to make use of vehicles. Creating an easy system for controlling the wheels will make animating them that much easier.

### Behind "Taking Flight," "Oozing Blob," and "Getting Ready to Drive"

Here's some background information on our three projects:

The first project is "Taking Flight." The provided file is an example wingspan for which we will animate a flying cycle with flapping and folding movements. Obviously, birds are the first creatures with such physical structures to come to mind, but more fantastical creatures like dragons or fairies would also utilize the same basic principles. The model contains approximately 200 polys and makes use of a 512 × 512 texture. Depending on the size of the winged creature in question, this texture resolution could be much smaller. A normal bird in the background, for example, could be as small as 32 × 32.

The next project is "Oozing Blob," and it provides a small blobby slime monster for us to play with. The idea is to animate something that lacks a rigid physical form. While a slime monster is a little extreme, these same concepts can come into play when dealing with special effects for liquids and flowing substances. For our little slime guy, we'll go over a "walk" cycle for him as well as a little attack he might do. This model contains approximately 1,100 polys and also uses a 512 × 512 texture.

And finally, we'll go over a simple four-wheeled vehicle suspension in "Getting Ready to Drive." In the vast majority of games dealing with vehicles, the undercarriage of a car is seldom shown, and if it is, it is rarely technically accurate. So, we won't worry too terribly much about technical accuracy. As artists and entertainers, our primary focus, in any project, lies in two questions: "Does it look good?" and "Is it fun?" For this project, we'll mainly talk about how using Set Driven Key can help make such precise, rigid movements much easier to manage. The model I've provided isn't a true representative game model. In an actual vehicle modeled for a game, you'd obviously have the completed frame, and the texture would also include those details. For this project, though, it's good to have a clear view of the elements you will be working with. You can then use this information to animate completed vehicles.

Before we begin the chapter, take a minute to read about the artist behind the project files. His background will give you some insight into the obstacles he faced with the models.

## About the Artist

**Name**  Evan Calderaro, age 27
**Studio**  KingsIsle Entertainment
**Personal website**  www.evanimation.com

**Describe your role at your current studio.**  Character rigger/animator. I receive various characters and creatures from our modelers and create individual custom rigs (because of their diversity), create keyframed animation sequences, and manage exports for our game engine.

**Did you face any significant challenges with the models?**  Well, it's always a challenge to create smooth, flowing, organic characters, such as the slime creature, on a restricted polygon budget. My technique for modeling him was to just model the shapes I wanted and then collapse vertices in as many places as I could while still keeping the silhouettes and edge loops intact until I achieved my goal poly count of around 1,100 tris.

**Can you describe your basic workflow?**  Ideally, I begin with concept sketches all around: a basic layout of the character design for modeling and texturing and also quick action sketches for animation concepts. I like to know what motions a character may go through during animation before modeling. That way, for example, if I know a character will be driving a racecar 90 percent of the time, I can save polys in the legs and utilize them in the face and upper body for more detail and articulation where it is needed. Next, I bring the character concept into my 3D application for reference and build on top of it. Afterward, I concentrate on unwrapping the [UVs of the] mesh neatly, as a good unwrap makes a huge difference in the ease of texture painting (which is done in Adobe Photoshop). Rigging is handled with bones, IK solvers, and spline controls. Then I'll run around my desk like a goof, acting out my animations, to get a feel for what I'm creating!

Game art by Evan Calderaro

## Tutorial: Taking Flight

For "Taking Flight," we have a basic wing model. It consists of approximately 200 triangle polygons. Our first task is to rig it with a basic skeleton.

1.  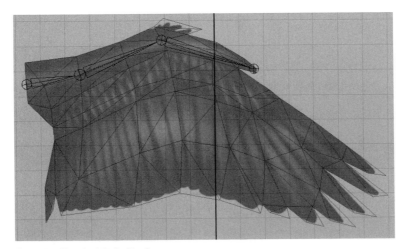 Browse on the CD to Project_Files/Chapter_8/Wings. Copy the Wings directory to your hard drive. Open the file Wings_Start.ma from the Scenes directory. This file contains the modeled and textured geometry for the wing model.

2.  In the Front view with the Joint Tool (Skeleton > Joint Tool) active, place a chain of four joints along the wing's upper ridge, as pictured in Figure 8.1, starting with the point where the wing would contact the creature. Be mindful that the joints need to be placed at points of deformation. This means placing the joints along an edge within the geometry and not between two edges.

3.  Name them **WingBase, Spine1, Spine2,** and **Spine3,** respectively.

4.  With the Joint Tool active, left-click the Spine1 joint. This makes it the active joint. Any additional joints you place will be joined to the Spine1 joint.

    Place two joints down the line of the edge where you placed the Spine1 joint—one about halfway, the other at the bottom.

5.  Repeat this for the other two spine joints. Your result should be similar to Figure 8.2.

6.  Name these joints **Rib1A, Rib1B, Rib2A, Rib2B, Rib3A,** and **Rib3B.**

7.  Select the Wing mesh. Shift+click the WingBase joint, and choose Skin > Bind Skin > Smooth Bind. This binds the mesh to the skeleton.

For the wing animation, we'll create a simple wing-flapping animation cycle. This would be used for flying creatures the same way a run or walk cycle would be used for those that are landlocked.

**Figure 8.1** The wing's "spine" in place

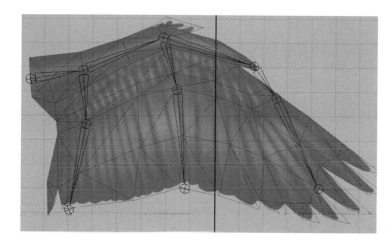

**Figure 8.2**
The ribs of the wing positioned in the geometry

**Note:** To start animating with an already rigged Wing model, open the Wing_Rigged.ma file from the Scenes folder. The values for positioning in the following tutorials assume this file is being used. Your own scene's positional values may vary.

1. At frame 1, make the following rotation adjustments:

   **WingBase**

   RotateX: 85

   RotateY: 0

   RotateZ: 10

   **Spine1**

   RotateX: 11

   RotateY: 22

   RotateZ: 2

   **Spine2**

   RotateX: -10

   RotateY: 22

   RotateZ: 3

   **Spine3**

   RotateX: 0

   RotateY: 15

   RotateZ: -19

   The resulting position is with the wing up as if on the back of a bird in flight (Figure 8.3). Set keyframes for each joint's rotation (Shift+e).

2. Go to frame 30 and set these keyframes again.

3. At frame 15, rotate the wing downward to the opposite position, as in Figure 8.4.

   If we play our animation now, we'll get a simple flapping motion, but it's not very realistic. Its movement lacks life and just seems very mechanical and stiff right now. Let's make a few adjustments.

4. Go to frame 8. With the initial three keys, the wing is positioned in a downward movement, blending from frame 1 to frame 15. However, let's delay that blend a bit. Change frame 8's position as shown in Figure 8.5, with a more upward position.

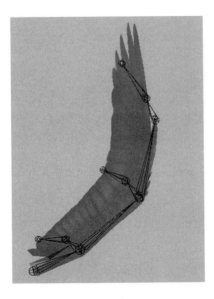

**Figure 8.3**
The wing's first and last frame pose

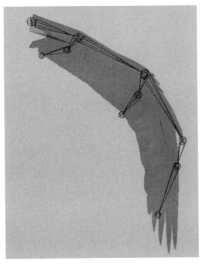

**Figure 8.4**
The mid-animation pose of the wing in its downward position

Frame 8

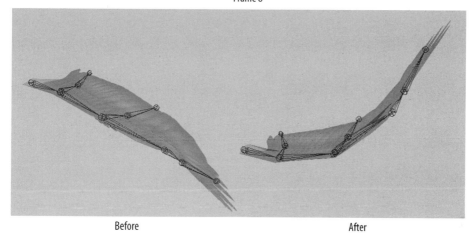

Before                                                    After

**Figure 8.5** The change to frame 8's position

5. We'll do the same thing at frame 23. Its current blending position from frame 15 to frame 30 is rather straight. Let's bend it downward as in Figure 8.6.

   If we play the animation now, we'll see a much more flowing motion to the bird's flapping since the bending of the wing is delayed, demonstrating air resistance and weight.

6. We'll repeat the above steps with the Rib1A, Rib2A, and Rib3A joints. They'll be raised slightly at frame 8 and lowered at frame 23.

7. Lastly, we'll smooth the animation's transition in the Graph Editor. Select all of the animating joints (all except the Rib B joints).

   Open the Graph Editor (Window > Animation Editors > Graph Editor). All of the selected joints' animation curves are displayed in the Graph view. Press the **f** key to frame all of them in view.

8. Left-click in an empty space in the Graph view and drag a selection around all of the curves (make sure you select all of the curves and not just a few of the keyframes on the curves).

   Choose Tangents > Spline to make the movement flow smoothly from one keyframe to another.

9. Drag a selection around the keyframes at frame 1. Hold down Shift and drag another selection around the keyframes at frame 30. Go to Tangents > Flat. This will smooth the transition between the start and end of the animation to avoid any jerking or jumping when the cycle repeats.

   With that, the flapping animation is complete! You can see how mine turned out by opening the Wings_Flapping.ma file in the Scenes directory (Figure 8.7).

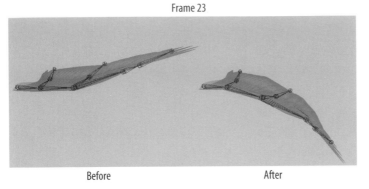

Frame 23

Before                    After

**Figure 8.6** The change to frame 23's position

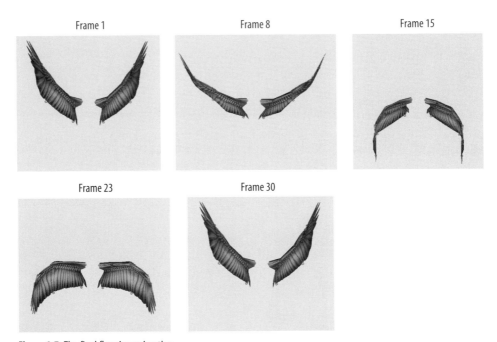

Frame 1          Frame 8          Frame 15

Frame 23          Frame 30

**Figure 8.7** The final flapping animation

## Tutorial: Oozing Blob

For our next project in this chapter, we'll create an array of joints within the provided slime monster to simulate a surface with a gel-like consistency as it moves.

1.    💿 Browse on the CD to Project_Files/Chapter_8/Blob. Copy the Blob directory to your hard drive. Open the file Blob_Start.ma from the Scenes directory.

   This file contains the modeled and textured geometry for the slime monster.

**2.** We'll begin by creating a skeleton for the creature. Because of its slimy consistency, it actually is a benefit to place your joints haphazardly. That is, they don't necessarily need to be placed regularly or neatly in the body.

There will be, however, an underlying skeleton that serves a purpose. The first image of Figure 8.8 shows these joints: a Root joint placed in the lower center of the body with two joints extending upward for the head movement. Name these joints **Neck1** and **Neck2**.

**3.** In addition, there are four joints extending outward to control the tentacle like weapon the slime monster uses. I named these joints **Arm1–4**.

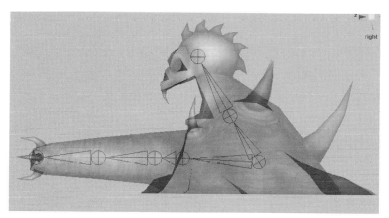

**Figure 8.8** The slime monster's skeleton layout

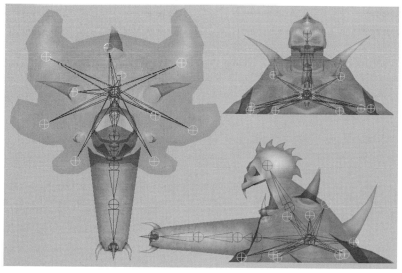

**Figure 8.8** (continued)

4.   The second image of Figure 8.8 shows the additional joints that I added to this skeleton. These joints control the gelatin-like movements of the creature's body. Name these as you see fit, using their locations, for example, **LShoulder**, even though there are no shoulders, technically.

5.   Once these joints are complete, select the SlimeMonster body. Shift+click the Root joint to add it to the selection. Choose Skin > Bind Skin > Smooth Bind to bind the geometry to the skeleton.

6.   Because of the amorphous shape of our creature, the skin weighting is usually okay right at the start, with a few minor adjustments. The first adjustment we will make to the skin weights is for the "skull" head and the spikes. These parts are probably the most rigid of the body.

Paint 100 percent of the head's weight to the Neck2 joint using the Paint Skin Weights Tool found under Skin > Edit Smooth Skin > Paint Skin Weights Tool > Options.

7.   The spikes should never be torn in half because of their skin weights being distributed among multiple joints. Go through the joint list in the Paint Tool's options, and look at the weight distribution around the body. Fix any conflicts found for any of the spikes.

Such conflicts in other parts of the body are actually okay, because of the gooey nature of the creature.

With the weights adjusted, our simple skeleton array is complete and ready for animation.

## Oozing Down the Street

For our first slime monster animation, we'll do a simple "walk" cycle. It's not so much of a walk cycle as it is a "slide" cycle. Our goal is to have him slosh his way forward and to make certain we sell the fact that he's made of ooze!

**Note:** To start animating with an already rigged slime monster model, open the Blob_Skeleton.ma file from the Scenes folder. The values for positioning in the following tutorials assume this file is being used. Your own scene's positional values may vary.

1.   First of all, let's retract the monster's "arm." Grab the Arm joints and pull them in, retracting the arm as in Figure 8.9. We'll use the arm more in the next animation.

2.   Select the Root joint, and set keyframes for its current translation channels for frames 1 and 30.

**Figure 8.9**
The slime "arm" retracted

3. At frame 15, move the Root joint forward in the Z direction about two units.

4. Select all of the joints along the ground. In my provided file, these are Tail joints (LF_Tail, LM_Tail, etc.). It may make it easier to create a Quick Select Set with these as we did for the Kraken's tentacles in Chapter 5.

   Keyframe these joints' translation positions at frames 1 and 30.

5. At frame 12, move the Tail joints backward about two units, simulating a drag effect on the lower thresholds of the monster's body as it's moving forward.

6. At frame 23 or so, move the Tail joints forward, stretching them out in front of the monster to create the effect of reaching out to grab more traction during movement.

7. If we play the animation now, the drag and reach of the Tail joints would seem to work okay, but they look a little unnatural. What we can do to alleviate this is to spread out their keyframes. Instead of having all of their keys at 12 and 23, individually move some of them forward or backward (move them to frame 10 and 26, for example).

   Once you do this for all of the joints so that few of them share the same keyframes, the blob flows much more naturally and its movement is not too mechanical.

8. We can play with the other joints to give a blobby feel to the movement, such as having the head bobble and reach forward as the creature moves forward.

9. At this point, the walk is essentially done! All we have left to do is smooth out the transition in the Graph Editor when the cycle repeats, as we did with our previous projects.

   You can see my resulting movement by opening the Blob_Walk.ma file from the Scenes directory (Figure 8.10).

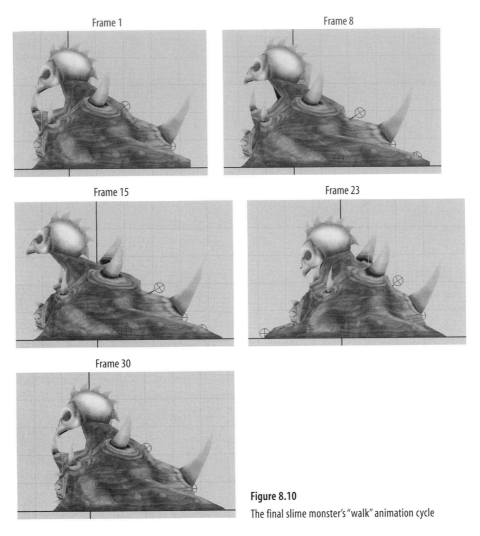

**Figure 8.10**
The final slime monster's "walk" animation cycle

## Getting Mean

Now, let's do a simple little attack animation, making good use of the blobby "arm" in front of the body. Start with your final rigged model or use the provided Blob_ Skeleton.ma file from the Scenes directory.

1.  To begin, retract the arm as we did with the walk cycle. Keyframe its retracted positions and rotations at frame 1.

2.  At frame 8, extend the arm, curling it to the right, using the same method as we used for the Kraken's tentacles from Chapter 5—selecting the Arm1, Arm2, and Arm3 joints and rotating them together.

3. At frame 13, swing the arm in the opposite direction, as if it's slashing at the player.

4. Go to frame 20, and reel the arm back in as in frame 1.

That's the extent of the attack. Now we need to make the body match the arm's movements.

5. Select the Root joint, and keyframe its translation and rotation positions at frame 1.

6. At frame 8, rotate the Root joint backward 19 degrees in the RotateZ channel, and lift the body upward and back. The entire body is rearing up for the attack!

7. At frame 15, rotate the Root joint forward -25 degrees in the RotateZ channel, and bring the body back down and move it forward. This is the moment of impact.

8. Back at frame 20, copy the keyframes from frame 1, putting the body back into its original position (Figure 8.11).

Next, we'll animate the rest of the joints to keep the body in contact with the ground and help show the creature's sliminess as it moves.

Frame 1          Frame 8          Frame 15          Frame 20

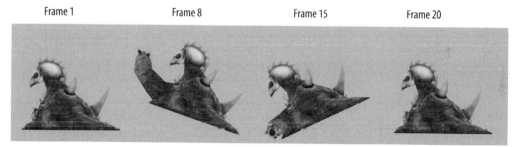

**Figure 8.11** The Root joint movement during the attack

## Stretching Out

As we go about pulling the slime monster's folds down about him to keep him in contact with the ground, you'll notice a lot of stretching. In a typical situation, this would be a bad thing, but because of the nature of the creature in question, having the joints stretch and pull at the body goes along with the whole idea of a slime monster and is acceptable.

1. Select all of the joints touching the ground (my Tail joints), and keyframe their translation and rotation positions at frame 1.

2. Go to frame 8, pull the joints downward, rotating them if necessary to keep the creature's lower edge in contact with the ground. The stretching also helps convey the amount of effort the creature is putting into the attack.

3. We'll do the same at frame 15, pulling and stretching the Tail joints around to help maintain contact with the ground. If some parts of the body don't want to stay in touch with the ground, it's okay, as it still helps convey the elasticity of the slime monster's composition.

4. Finally, at frame 20, we'll copy the joint's frame 1 positions to put the creature back into its default pose (Figure 8.12).

The last step is to set up the secondary animation for the head and neck as well as the other body joints. Use what you've learned so far from this book to give this movement your own interpretation. You can see how mine turned out by opening the Blob_Attack.ma file from the Scenes directory (Figure 8.13).

## Tutorial: Getting Ready to Drive

This next section isn't a lesson in animation so much as a lesson in animation setup. The goal is to create a system using Set Driven Key (described back in Chapter 2) to make controlling the wheel suspension system as easy as possible for future animations.

1. 💿 Browse on the CD to Project_Files/Chapter_8/Suspension. Copy the Suspension directory to your hard drive. Open the file Suspension_Start.ma from the Scenes directory.

This file contains the modeled and textured geometry for the simplified vehicle suspension system.

Frame 1        Frame 8        Frame 15        Frame 20

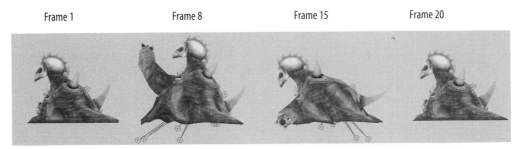

**Figure 8.12** Keeping the slime monster grounded

**Figure 8.13** The final slime monster attack animation

**2.** Select the LF_Wheel (the left front wheel). Its initial pivot is placed at its inner center point. This allows you to rotate the wheel with a simple turn of the vehicle.

When the wheel travels over uneven terrain, however, it needs to be able to rise and fall, making use of the suspension system. Therefore, we essentially need two pivots. In order to accomplish this, we'll Group (Ctrl+g or Edit > Group) the wheel to itself, creating a new node with its own pivot point. Name this group **LFWheel_Raise**.

**3.** By default, new group's pivot points are at the origin (0, 0, 0 coordinates in XYZ space). First, we'll center the pivot of the new group by choosing Modify > Center Pivot.

**4.** Next, press the Insert key on your keyboard to enter edit pivot mode. Move the pivot across the support bar to the far right end, as pictured in Figure 8.14. Press Insert again to exit edit pivot mode.

**5.** Repeat this step for the three remaining wheels, naming their groups to correspond to their positions in the car's structure.

**6.** The support bar between the front wheels also needs to have multiple pivots. At first, its pivot is simply centered. In times when both front wheels rise at the same time (going up an incline, for example), we can simply raise the front support bar to correspond.

When the wheels are bumping up and down at different intervals, however, we'll need different pivot points from which to animate. Select the Front_Support, and group it to itself. Center the new group's pivot, and place it on the far left end of the support bar. Name this group **RFWheelSupport_Raise**.

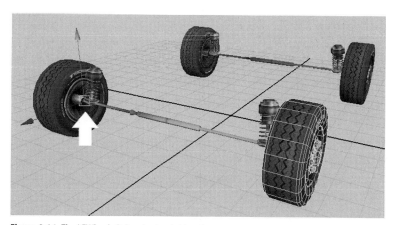

**Figure 8.14** The LFWheel_Raise pivot point location

**7.** With the group still selected, group it to itself again. Place this pivot point at the opposite end of the support bar. Name this group **LFWheelSupport_Raise**.

Now, when either front wheel jumps upward when it hits a rock or drops into a pothole, the support bar can angle upward or downward to maintain the vehicle's structure.

**8.** Repeat this for the Back_Support.

**9.** To make things easier to select later on, display the selection handles for the Wheel_Raise groups (Display > Component Display > Selection Handles).

Don't forget when you position the selection handles that they need to be next to the wheel they affect to avoid confusion. For example, the RFWheel_Raise selection handle should be next to the RF_Wheel, even though its pivot is closer to the LF_Wheel.

Now that we have the main groups we need, we can start to put together the Set Driven Key system we'll use to make all the different parts work together.

 **Note:** To start with an already grouped suspension model, open the Suspension_Setup.ma file from the Scenes folder. The values for positioning in the following steps assume this file is being used. Your own scene's positional values may vary.

**1.** Deselect everything. Go to Animate > Set Driven Key > Set > Options. This opens the Set Driven Key (SDK) window, where we'll establish the relationships of our system.

**2.** Select the LFWheel_Raise group, and press the Load Driver button in the SDK window.

**3.** Select the LFWheelSupport_Raise group (select the Front_Support object and press the Up arrow key on your keyboard twice), and press the Load Driven button in the SDK window.

**4.** In the Driver's list of channels, highlight the RotateZ channel. Do the same in the Driven's list. Press the Key button.

**5.** Select the LFWheel_Raise group and rotate it 5 degrees in the RotateZ direction. Select the LFWheelSupport_Raise group and do the same, rotating it 5 degrees in the RotateZ direction. Press the Key button.

**6.** Do the opposite now, rotating the LFWheel_Raise group -5 degrees in the RotateZ direction, following suit with the LFWheelSupport_Raise group and pressing the Key button again.

If you now rotate the LFWheel_Raise group between 5 and -5 degrees in the RotateZ direction, the support bar will automatically stay connected to it!

7. Repeat these steps for the remaining three wheels, making sure the Driver and Driven group prefixes correspond (the *LB*Wheel_Raise group drives the *LB*WheelSupport_Raise group, for instance).

Notice that with this set up correctly, you can have the left front wheel rise up and the right front wheel drop down, and the support bar will maintain its connection to both of them (Figure 8.15)!

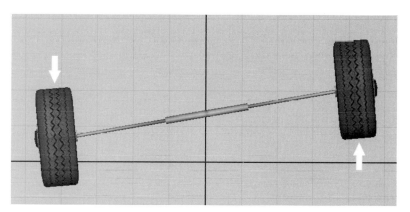

**Figure 8.15** The front support maintaining the structure

The next phase of the setup will be to get the shock absorbers working, having their springs contract and expand as wheels bounce along the road.

1. Make the LFWheel_Raise group the Driver in the Set Driven Key window. Select the LF_SusBrace object and make it the Driven.

2. For the Driver's attribute, select the RotateZ channel again. For the Driven's attribute, select all three rotate and translate channels. Press the Key button at the default position.

3. Rotate the Wheel group up 5 degrees. Reposition the LF_SusBrace object to maintain its position on the support bar as the wheel rises up. You'll also want to rotate it to keep it aiming toward the LF_SusPiston object (we'll rotate the piston later to have it aim correctly as well).

   With the LF_SusBrace object in a satisfactory position, press the Key button.

4. We'll do the same with the wheel group rotated downward -5 degrees. Reposition the brace and press the Key button.

**5.** We'll repeat these steps for both the LF_SusPiston and the LF_SusSpring. The LF_SusPiston attributes we'll be driving are the three rotation channels. At the important wheel group rotations of 5, 0, and -5 degrees, rotate the piston to always aim toward the brace object we positioned first.

For the Spring object, we'll be manipulating the three rotation channels as well as the ScaleY channel. At the key rotation positions, scale the spring up or down to maintain its connection between the piston and the brace, pressing the Key button at the same three positions.

When this is done correctly, you should get the result shown in Figure 8.16.

**6.** Repeat this process for the remaining three wheels.

At this point, the setup is complete. With this system attached to the bottom of a vehicle, you'd easily be able to drive it over rocky, uneven terrain and not blow a gasket trying to keep the wheels from falling all over the place! To see how mine turned out, take a look at the Suspension_Finish.ma file in the Scenes directory.

5 degrees        0 degrees        -5 degrees

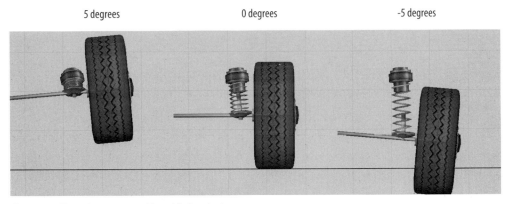

**Figure 8.16** The spring system working with the wheel

## Final Thoughts

And suddenly we're at the end. Animation is such a broad field that it's always difficult to narrow down such a subject into a structured lesson. However, I feel that once you are able to master the provided projects within this book, you can master very nearly any animation project that can possibly be given to you!

For instance, do you have to animate the mythical snake-headed Medusa? Simply combine the principles of the Calamity Jane biped skeleton from Chapter 3 with the spinal animation methods of the Giant Kraken from Chapter 5 for the snakes. Rigging the half-eagle, half-lion gryphon? Add the wing principles mentioned in this chapter to those of the Dire Wolf in Chapter 4's quadruped setup. A scorpion? The six-legged movement of Chapter 6's Storm Tank combined with the Kraken's spinal formations for the scorpion's stinger should do the trick. And the list goes on and on!

I definitely hope you have enjoyed the lessons in this book and have learned how to rig and animate in the process. I look forward to working with you in the field and playing your games!

## Artist Profile: Steve Garcia

**Job Title** Concept artist and animation supervisor
**Studio** Feverpitch Studios, Junction Point Studios
**Credits** The Iron Giant (film), The Simpsons (TV), X-Men Evolution (TV), Hit & Myth, Johnny Whatever, Conquest 2: Vyrium Uprising, Shadow of the Ring
**Personal website** http://www.crunchamunch.com

**Q.** How and why did you get into the game industry?

**A.** Well, I was becoming more and more discontent with the [feature] animation industry. After The Iron Giant it seemed as if the studios all wanted to go back to making the same old type of movie. A pal of mine at Disney Interactive told me that a lot of comic book illustrators and animators were gravitating toward game development. So since my art history is pretty much illustration and animation, I figured it might be a perfect fit. I found a great studio with the best bunch of guys, at what was then known as Feverpitch Studios, under Eric Peterson four years ago, and the rest is history.

**Q.** Describe your role at your studio.

**A.** My role has been primarily as a concept artist, in charge of creating character and environment designs for games. But because of my 12-year history in the feature animation industry, I've been called upon to do storyboarding for in-game cinematics and to also oversee their animation.

**Q.** What is your favorite kind of game?

**A.** Well, maybe it's the art guy in me, or maybe I'm just a codger, but I like the games in which I can just sit and wander around and look at things—I love those. Just admire the beauty of the created worlds. World of Warcraft is gorgeous! Games like that I just love—where it is almost a "sidebar" event when a monster jumps out at you. See? I told you… codger be I!

**Q.** What animation trick of the trade could you not live without?

**A.** Could I not live without? Hmm… Well I'll tell you instead what I could stand to see less of. Maybe a little less MOCAP [motion capture]. With so many beginning animators these days, there is the tendency to want to see everything fast! Instant results! And with technology these days, you can. Although, that does not mean that you get better animation. Which is possibly the reason why I see so much stiff and lifeless animation in games. Because of the over usage of MOCAP and because there doesn't seem to be enough practice of the basic fundamentals of animation.

*Continues*

The point of animation is not just to move something or someone around but to inject it/them with life. And therefore the best way to do that is to think "bigger than life." Which is why I could do with less MOCAP. You are pretty much bound to the confines of reality—to whatever movements you're getting, from whatever subject is tied to the MOCAP. And in animation, "realism" (Rotoscope [creating animations by "tracing" video reference] or motion capture), oftentimes feels static or stiff and lifeless.

For instance, the difference between [the films] The Incredibles and something like The Polar Express is that The Incredibles uses traditional animation principles, which make the characters believable, enjoyable, and filled with life that jumps off the screen at you, while the latter feels stiff and almost leaves you with an uncomfortable feeling—for the sake of capturing realism. So again, I could do with less MOCAP and with more knowledge and usage of basic animation fundamentals. Don't throw MOCAP out entirely, just know when to use it and when not to. Hopefully that made sense! Ha!

**Q.** What advice might you have for the up-and-coming animator?

**A.** Well, along with what I've already stated, I guess I would tell him to keep up his traditional skills. Don't ever stop drawing. You don't always have a mouse and screen in front of you! You can (and should) always have pencil and sketchpad in front of you. Take it everywhere you go—for quick sketches and notes.

Also, look at everything! From the way a tree moves in the wind, the way a baby stumbles and falls, the way a girl twirls her hair, to the way someone picks his nose. Animation is also about personality in movement. Not just movement.

Watch movies—not just watch them, study them. The best ones to watch are old movies. Yes, the old black-and-white ones! The worst ones are the new movies. Why? Because the old ones are acted by people coming from a theater or vaudeville background so the movements are broader... more interesting... it's life exaggerated! The new ones are dealing with more close-up acting. And there really isn't a whole lot going on and they're more dialogue driven. And for animation that's... well... boring.

Feed off of the energy of your co-workers. Their passion about what they do is like a hundred cups of coffee to me! Should be to you as well.

And finally, never, never, never stop learning! If you feel you've learned everything that there is to learn about animation, then you've become better than the old Disney animators, because not a one of them ever thought that they had it all learned. You can learn from everyone and everything—from your art director to your programmers to the guywho picks up your garbage at night. Become a "people watcher" (but in a harmless and uncreepy sort of way) and constantly watch. And take that sketchpad and make scribble sketches of the things you observe. Fill it with scribbles. And don't be afraid of criticism of your animation or drawings. Don't let your ego get in the way of you learning.

Your goal should never be solely "to be an animator." I have often said (to many of my animation colleagues' chagrin) that there are far too many animators in the world and not enough artists. You can't be a great animator without being first a good artist. So strive to be the best artist you can be.

# Glossary

**animation** The state of being alive; the illusion of life in media such as video games

**animation curve** A representation of the interpolation between keyframes in the Graph Editor

**animation cycle** An animation that is designed to seamlessly cycle or repeat

**anticipation** Secondary animation that leads up to a primary animation

**arc** The type of path all organic motion should take to avoid rigidness and linearity

**articulation** The degree of freedom of movement a model or part of a model is capable of

**blend shapes** Also known as **morph targets**; a type of vertex animation that blends the position of one mesh's vertices to that of another mesh's vertices

**bump map** A grayscale texture that provides the illusion of surface depth using light information. White areas are raised, while black areas are lowered.

**centaur** An archetypal character setup that involves a biped torso blended into a quadruped body.

**character set** Used in the Trax Editor for grouping animation controls together under one node

**clamped tangent** A type of key tangent that makes use of linear tangent interpolation for adjacent keyframes that have little change in value and spline tangent interpolation for

those that have a more significant change in value

**clip** Used in the Trax Editor as a single selection node for an animation sequence

**clusters** Control handles that allow you to manipulate points (vertices, CVs, etc.) either individually or in groups

**control vertices (CVs)** Control points for NURBS surfaces and curves

**ease-in** An accelerating secondary animation leading up to a primary animation

**ease-out** A decelerating secondary animation following a primary animation

**emphasis** Using exaggeration and dynamism to make certain that every action is easily understood and readable to the audience

**fixed tangents** Allows a keyframe's values to be edited without changing the key's tangents

**flat tangents** Setting the in tangent and out tangent of a keyframe to have a horizontal flow, resulting in no change in value for a brief number of frames

**follow-through** Secondary animation following a primary animation

**forward kinematics (FK)** A method of manipulating joints in order down the skeleton's hierarchy

**Freeze Transformations** A command that makes all transformation information of an object, including the position values of vertices, go to zero without actually changing the shape

**geometry** The surface of a 3D model; what a model is made of

**idle cycle** A repeatable animation conveying an animated model in an idle state and not performing any specific actions

**in tangent** The flow of interpolation into a keyframe on an animation curve

**in-betweening** Also known as **tweening**; the method in traditional 2D animation that involves a team of animators filling in the frames that take place between the keyframes of an animation

**interpolation** The blending between keyframes in 3D animation

**inverse kinematics (IK)** A method of manipulating joints in order up the skeleton's hierarchy

**joints** Individual elements that make up a skeleton and allow for the deformation of geometry in animation

**key tangents** Control handles that manipulate the interpolation into and out of a keyframe on an animation curve in the Graph Editor

**keyframe animation** The standard method of animating using keyframes

**keyframes** A moment in time when the shape and position of an animating object is set; a major pose in an animation

**linear tangents** A type of key tangent that results in a direct animation curve from one keyframe's value to another with no delineation of that value's change

**mits** Also known as **mittens**; the articulation method in which the four fingers of the hand are not rigged individually but all together using a single joint chain; can also refer to the method of modeling a hand, creating a

clump of geometry that represents the four fingers

**non-weighted tangents** Key tangents are set to this by default; provides simplified handles for manipulating the angle of key tangents

**out tangent** The flow of interpolation out of a keyframe on an animation curve

**overlapping action** A type of secondary animation where an animating element's reaction to a primary animation is delayed

**pacing** An aspect of timing involving the delivery or beat of an animation's playback that produces a satisfactory reaction from the audience

**phoneme shapes** Mouth shapes used to form audible vowel and consonant sounds for accurate lip synching

**plateau tangents** A type of key tangent that ensures the flow of an animation curve does not supersede a keyframe's set value

**poly count** The number of triangle faces budgeted to a model

**pose-to-pose animation** An animation technique that involves setting up the key poses at important moments interspersed throughout the scene

**rest** A moment of pause in an animation to help with readability, convey emotion, etc.

**rigging** The act of binding geometry to a skeleton and creating animation controls

**root joint** The top joint in a skeleton's hierarchy; usually the Pelvis in a character skeleton

**scrub** Manually moving through an animation using the Time Slider

**secondary motion** Animation that is a result of

or leading up to a primary motion

**selection sets** An alternative to character sets; the grouping of elements under one node for easier selection

**Set Driven Key** An animation method that involves setting up relationships between the attributes of two or more objects

**settle** Used in conjunction with **rest**; animating a movement coming to a pause

**skeleton** A hierarchy of joints that is used to deform geometry to create movement

**smooth binding** A method of binding geometry to a skeleton that allows for smooth deformation

**spans** Divisions in a surface or curve

**specular** The specularity, or shininess, of a surface

**specular map** A texture map that controls the intensity and color of specularity on a model

**spinal** A creature or object that makes use of flowing tendrils, such as an octopus' tentacles

**spline IK** A method of inverse kinematics that uses a curve to control the movement of joints

**spline tangents** A type of key tangent that creates a smooth flow between keyframes

**sprites** Small planes that are affected by dynamic forces such as gravity, wind, or turbulence; used in nearly all video game particle effects

**squash and stretch** A method of demonstrating flexibility or stiffness in animation

**stepped next tangents** A type of key tangent that immediately following a keyframe will

change to the next keyframe's value

**stepped tangents** A type of key tangent that will change to a keyframe's value only upon reaching it in time, with no change in value until then

**straight ahead animation** An animation technique that involves animating a character from beginning to end with little to no use of key poses as a guideline; the opposite of **pose-to-pose animation**

**tangent weight** The amount of influence a key tangent has on an animation curve

**textures** Image files that create the surface details of a model

**timing** The overall identifier of a subject's speed and weight, as well as how long a particular action or sequence of actions should last

**tris** Triangle faces of geometry

**vertex animation** The method of animating the position of a surfaces vertices without the use of a skeleton

**vertex weight** The amount of influence a joint has on a bound vertex

**weighted tangents** Key tangents that represent the amount of influence they have on the animation curve by indicating it in the length of the tangent

# Index